ON THE DAILY WORK OF PSYCHODYNAMIC PSYCHOTHERAPY

ON THE DAILY WORK OF PSYCHODYNAMIC PSYCHOTHERAPY

Ian Miller and Alistair D. Sweet

Routledge
Taylor & Francis Group
LONDON AND NEW YORK

First published 2018
by Routledge
2 Park Square, Milton Park, Abingdon, Oxon OX14 4RN

and by Routledge
711 Third Avenue, New York, NY 10017

Routledge is an imprint of the Taylor & Francis Group, an informa business

British Library Cataloguing-in-Publication Data
A catalogue record for this book is available from the British Library

Library of Congress Cataloging-in-Publication Data
A catalog record has been requested for this book

ISBN: 978-1-78220-564-7 (pbk)

Typeset in Palatino LT Std
by Medlar Publishing Solutions Pvt Ltd, India

CONTENTS

ABOUT THE AUTHORS

Ian Miller is a clinical psychologist and psychoanalyst, practising and writing in Dublin, Ireland. He is the author of *Defining Psychoanalysis: Achieving a Vernacular Expression* (Karnac, 2016); *On Minding and Being Minded: Experiencing Bion and Beckett* (Karnac, 2015); and, with Kay Souter, *Beckett and Bion: The (Im)Patient Voice in Psychotherapy and Literature* (Karnac, 2013).

Alistair D. Sweet is director and senior psychotherapist with Meriden Psychotherapy, based in Belfast, United Kingdom. He is also an honorary lecturer and training supervisor in clinical psychology, Queen's University, Belfast. Before entering full-time private practice, he held posts as both senior psychotherapist and head of clinical services with the Northern Ireland Community Addiction Service. His research work on the addictions, disturbances of attachment, and earliest object relations has appeared internationally in a range of peer reviewed journals.

INTRODUCTION

Our book is about recognitions in the daily work of psychotherapy. How and what the therapist recognises. What the patient recognises (beginning with her first utterances to the therapist) and is able, through therapy, to shape to her own lights, in her recognitions.

We could not have begun to think the things we arrive at were it not for others, stretching backward to antiquity; but more recently, within the last century or so, to the very human insights into the human condition generated by psychoanalytic clinicians.

Fundamentally, our book is a description of applied psychology, remembering Freud's observation that the only "pure" psychology is in the meeting between two individuals.

It is also in the elaboration of therapeutic action, what Freud once termed its "active step". And we see that all of our contacts with our patients may be folded into the discernible realm of our activities, passive or overt. It is up to us to observe these and their effects on the other.

Recognitions, or what experienced adventurers call "landmarks" (Macfarlane, 2015) are at the centre of our work. Our chapters range across a realm of landmarks beginning with the domain of serious psychopathology, as understood from within the Kleinian development of psychoanalytic practice. From here, we look at the ways we anchor psychological experience from its bodily representation to a preverbal sense of vivid immediacy to verbalisation. Next, we discuss what is really at the centre of this work: the actions involving the therapist's intuitive receptivity, expression to the patient, and the patient's acceptance or rejection of this now one-person clarification, originally within and now returning to the two-person field of therapeutic interaction.

Our recognitions of these actions cause us to see something else: how the elements of psychoanalytic thinking, its "vernacular" (Miller, 2016a), may similarly be seen as a parallel process at the conceptual level of ideas within and about psychoanalysis. We call this recognition **d** and offer some examples.

Following these recognitions we began to observe, through readings at different historical moments within the voluminous literature documenting psychoanalytic development that expressed differently in different historical moments, clinicians of different theoretical orientation have recognised similar clinical forms in a manner we take to reflect the evolving patterns of our applied social science discipline. However different our starting points, our dedication to the essential daily work of psychotherapy leads us, if open-minded, to similar clinical situations.

Using these tools, we illustrate our concepts. And these occupy us through the conclusion of the book. Among our illustrations in thinking are: our location in literary expression of the same formal process we discern in clinical contact; our own personal wrestling with complicated, if vague, conflict, presenting originally as a knotted and unnamable "wicked problem"—and through adherence to the intuitive process of d emergences over time, our arrival at significant understandings; and multiple readings of foundational psychoanalytic texts in illustration of our present thinking.

Psychotherapy is complicated work, though its occasional arrivals at relief may seem simple. Similarly, *On the Daily Work of Psychotherapy* is a simple statement. We hope that the journey through the landmarks we discern provides the reader with a worthwhile clinical tool.

CHAPTER ONE

Forms within the clinical setting

Psychotherapists come to recognise clinical forms initially through education and training; and then, through what emerges during years of work with patients, "through uncharted swamps" of clinical practice beyond the boundaries of classical neurotic symptoms (Green, 1975, p. 4).

While much is conveyed explicitly, much emerges cumulatively between the gaps of formal, procedural knowledge. Although such tacit learning is a commonly acquired form of professional practice (G. Klein, 2009), its elevation within the psychotherapist's consciousness places a formidable demand upon self-awareness in learning psychotherapy. In addition to self-inquiry, the therapist must be dedicated to making explicit what is, in its clinical nature, transitory and often subtly fused together with other aspects of the patient-therapist interaction.

Not only does the therapist strive to aid the patient in becoming conscious of unrecognised and dissociated experience, but must also aid herself in discerning what has been unrecognised previously within daily clinical process. Necessarily, considerations of time are central to psychotherapy as are the events that emerge within and between therapeutic co-participants under time's umbrella. Both within and across sessions, this includes the generation of thinking, causality, and accountability grounded in personal agency; and extends to the patient's capacity for experiential enjoyment as well as the temporal integration of present, past, and future within memory, reliving, fantasy, and dreaming.

The originally implicit, transitional forms of clinical presentation become built up, case by case, through the particularities of the clinical situations faced by each clinician. However individually unique within the pairings of therapist and patient, such recognitions are subordinated to what Wilhelm Reich in his training lectures in Vienna and Berlin called a "supreme principle" wherein

> the analyst must endeavor to wrest the special technique of the case and the individual situation from each individual case and from each individual situation without, while so doing, losing the general continuity in the development of the analytic process. (1972, p. 7)

Freud originally observed clinical phenomena in sequential or serial order with the series of symptoms, dreams, and transference as a prime example. Yet, as Foucault (1989) observes, large gaps exist between elements in each series; and because these are unmarked, they contribute to what is unknown. The unknowns generated in the transitory process of achieving knowledge amplify what already exists outside our awareness: the detritus remaining after the conceptual splittings noted by Freud within the therapeutic process itself, as fused wholes are fragmented by analysis into the partial objects of inquiry (1910a). Both these formally recognised elements of our conceptual series and the implicit, if unrecognised, elements emergent in procedural process form the groundwork of clinical psychotherapy.

Historical understanding of the emergent form of clinical method is to "seek out the avenues which lead from purely empirical practice, pass through theory, and terminate in a theoretically well-grounded practice" (Reich, 1972, p. 3).

Our own point of departure is the recognition by W. R. Bion, of a clinical algorithm, PS ↔ D PS (n+1) ↔ D (n+1) (♀♂), based in the clinical recognitions of Melanie Klein.

The value of this formalised, mathematical abstraction, winking backward across time to the mathematical forms of philosophical derivation depicted by Descartes (1637) and Spinoza (1677), entirely fits the form of the Freudian series: empirical practice data> theoretical recognition> practical utility. Bion's algorithm begins as an abstraction from empirically demonstrated recognitions within practice, those behaviours termed "objective" by Winnicott (1949) in their consensual agreement by multiple observers. Next, the algorithm points to a generalised pathway alerting clinicians to clinical emergence from the persecutory, split, and incommunicable private registrations of inchoate experience along a road of therapeutic transit from rupture to repair, in search and research. Its elements, passive and active, operative across time's horizon, describe movements between paranoid, schizoid, and depressive aspects of personal experience. This pathway is close to the usually partial and unsatisfactory conciliation with reality, enacted clinically within the spatial-temporal events of relating between patient and therapist.

Following Bion's own understanding, such theoretical registration by the therapist becomes communicable to the patient, languaged again in the particulars of his own experience (Bion, 1992; Miller, 2015).

To appreciate the force of particular experience underlying Bion's universalised abstraction, it is helpful to return to the descriptive domain of words. Joan Riviere's depiction of internal life, from infancy onwards, elaborates the sense of persecution, unpleasure, and entrapment of the paranoid/schizoid position. Writing in 1936 she describes an inner world characterised by

> Loose motions, flatus and urine are all felt to be burning, corroding, and poisoning agents. Not only the excretory but all other physical functions are pressed into the service of the need for aggressive (sadistic) discharge in phantasy. Limbs shall trample, kick, and hit; lips, finger and hands shall suck, twist, pinch; teeth shall bite, gnaw, mangle and cut; mouth shall devour, swallow and "kill" (annihilate); eyes kill by a look, pierce and penetrate; breath and mouth hurt by noise, as the child's own sensitive ears have experienced. (p. 402)

Here, the persecution, beginning with the body's persecution of itself, under warlike conditions of annihilation and helpless isolation, embroider what is reduced simply to P/S in its Kleinian notation. Conceptually, it is as if the Bionian algorithm at any moment in therapeutic time (n) were to be met by the patient's articulation that, "I feel as if something is killing me," accented by a furtive gesture, a glance at the therapist as if to indicate that whether by persecutory intrusions of his presence and verbal participation, or through the glance of his eye, something within the here and now of therapeutic time feels destructive to the patient. It is within this verbalised and gestural return by the patient to elaboration of the therapist's articulation of his intuitive abstraction, that the motion of psychotherapy is propelled forward (Bion, 1962a).

The general movement implied by the clinical activity represented by Bion's algorithm is between particular experience, persecutory, fragmented, and felt by the patient to be beyond understanding or remediation, and the therapist's generalised recognition at a more universal level, though discernible through the particularities of the therapist's personality, internal world, and training in clinical practice. Reciprocally, the therapist's attempt to clothe response in the language of the patient's complaint, in the form "what you call X, I call Y", bridges the inter-human distance between them (Buber, 1951, 1957a), allowing communication of a universalised understanding, which then undergoes elaboration, whether in acceptance or in rejection, by the patient. Within the complications of thinking and human action necessitated in clinical use of Bion's algorithm, we discern in clinical action a descendant of the Kantian imperative by which particularised forms of individual experience are located in more universal, generalised patterns, an essence underlying common characteristics (Freud, 1912–13, p. xv).

We take this shift, from the particularity of "thick" experience towards its refinement in generalised abstraction, as analogous to Freud's artistic metaphor of psychoanalytic similarity to sculpture rather than to painting in that interpretation shears bulk from the patient's particularity of expression, revealing its hidden lineaments (1905a). And through the actions of the therapist's immersion in listening and affective resonance with the projective world of the patient through introjective experience, he comes to articulate that Bergsonian dimension of analytic action contributed to psychoanalysis through Bion's reading of Poincarré (Bion, 1992). Bion's clinical contribution to psychoanalysis is that the clinician's intuitive discernment of the universalised "significant fact", expressed within the shape of the patient's particulars of presentation, is the interpretive vehicle for the patient's resultant use of therapeutic communication.

With the articulation of such changing generalisations to the patient, the elements of thinking are freed to be used productively as resources in creation or destruction, following the pattern of Bion's algorithm, from time (n) to time (n+1). In Chapters 4 and 7, we detail the motion within clinical psychoanalysis of these continuous arrivals at consensual moments of interpersonal communication.

Bion's algorithmic abstraction emerges from clinical experience; but equally, in Bion's own writing, the shaping of thought communicated in the form of the psychoanalytic essay is oriented to sculpting how psychoanalytic practitioners think. Writing of the essay form in *Attention and Interpretation*, Bion directly addresses the necessity of particular experience, the experience of clinical practice, in illuminating through inchoate, non-languaged experience, the linguistic imperative necessitated by the essay. He says

> Any psycho-analyst who is *practicing* can grasp my meaning because he, unlike those who only read or hear *about* psychoanalysis, has the opportunity to experience himself what I in this book can only represent by words and verbal formulations designed for a different task. (1970, p. 1; emphasis in original)

From its origins in case studies (see Chapters 9 and 10), psychoanalysis has disclosed both the highlighted and unnoted particulars of therapeutic activity; but, in parallel with the critical essay as a model of psychoanalytic thinking. The vernacular expressions of psychoanalytic elements, the dominant arrivals within the operational thinking of psychoanalysis at any particular time, have been surrounded by the essay as their vehicles of arrival, a transitional form of argument, itself communicating the form of clinical practice as thinking. We observe that two domains emerge from the essay, which has meant a "trying on" since its demonstrations by Montaigne, Rousseau, and Kant, in providing an exploratory form common to the development of Enlightenment thought (Bakewell, 2011; Goetschel, 1994). The first domain is conceptual. The essay is designed to convey specific points to the reader, both in process and in conclusion. The second domain is experientially evocative, with the essay resonating in the reader's experience as illustrated above by Bion's explicit statement, or by the reader's considered resonance with Riviere's depiction of internal life, or indeed, by the reader's confrontations with any and every affecting presentation in psychoanalytic thinking—as in the contemporary "best seller" list of the Psychoanalytic Electronic Publishing (PEP) archives (Miller, 2016a).

Like therapeutic interpretation from within the Bion algorithm, the essay's formal presentation of ideas attempts articulation of new arrangements of thinking through the emotional evocations of language and the juxtaposition of thought's elements. William Grossman (1992) argues that "On Aphasia" together with Freud's technical papers reflect such demonstrations, applicable to discerning Freud's therapeutic model of inquiry. Bion's own recognition of the essay's function in conveying the form of clinical thinking is demonstrated within his own late-life shift in literary presentational forms. We trace this change in written form between his descriptive 1957 paper "Differentiation of the Psychotic from the Non-Psychotic Personalities" and the deeply experiential form of his 1959 paper, "Attacks on Linking". Bion's shift in the presentational form of his writing discloses a demonstration of therapeutic understanding in keeping with the emergence of what has become in our own time, the contemporary psychoanalytic vernacular expression (Miller, 2016a).

The essay's form of argument is disruptive and provocative. The writer leads the reader along a path of argument, clarifying points of arrival from one moment in time to another. Thinking about the literary form of the essay from our experiential perspectives within clinical process, detailed in Chapter 4, we have come to think of such points of arrival as momentary statements of an "emboldened d" (**d**) that form successive building blocks, like courses of brickwork, towards the construction of the essay's conclusion. In the rhythm of an essay's elaboration, **d** elements are transformed through transition from one articulation of thought to another. Referring back to Bion's algorithm in its clinical parallel to the essay, the **d** element at time (n) is discernably different from the new form of the **d** element at time (n+1); and the **d** element which forms in the reader's understanding at the essay's conclusion is different still.

Yet, as a by-product of how we read and how we remember, not only does the essay generate a line of argument advancing the writer's viewpoint, but also contributes resources for the reader's future use, in the form of multiple **d** elements. The generation of such forms within the significant essay papers studied by psychoanalysts has provided the conceptual units, the saturated and unsaturated "beta elements" by which clinicians construct their personalised matrices of thinking within expressions of contemporary clinical practice (Miller, 2016a).

A partial reading of an early Freud essay provides an illustrative example; and with it, Freud's forceful arrivals at the essay's multiple points of emphasis underscore the author's intentionality in evoking a resonance within the reader through this form of communication. Freud demonstrates how the essay itself becomes the evocative object for the reader's thinking. His "Psychical (or Mental) Treatment" (1890a), written during the same period as *Studies on Hysteria*, begins with the premise that the activity which we will come to recognise as psychodynamic psychotherapy operates through the influence of mind upon mind. That is, Freud insists, rather than being a treatment of "the pathological phenomena of mental life", psychical treatment denotes "treatment taking its start in the mind, treatment (whether of mental or physical disorders) by measures which operate in the first instance and immediately upon the human mind" (p. 283).

The contemporary therapist-reader is struck immediately by the lack of directionality in this statement. The therapist as much as the patient is affected by the mental activity of the other; and so, long before our contemporary articulation of the relationship between one-person and two-person psychologies (Mitchell & Aron, 1999; Rickman, 1951), Freud acknowledges the inter-human process of the bipersonal therapeutic field.

Freud achieves this statement of emboldened d (perhaps the first **d** element in psychoanalysis) through a disruption of the reader's expectations. Expecting that psychical treatment will be a treatment focused on psychopathology, Freud up-ends expectations. While psychopathology may ultimately be implicated, what Freud is driving towards are the unrecognised dynamics of psychological communication between individuals.

With the residue of this **d** element still resonant in the reader's thinking, Freud expands his considerations to contemplate the Cartesian split between mind and body; and specifically, turns towards the positivist form of medical practice of his present day Vienna. Here, Freud's essay is deeply attuned to his own historical moment and to the medical politics of treating the hysteric. His field of action will be exactly that landscape where consideration of such psychological communication has been barred, within the Viennese practice of medicine. Deftly, Freud comments upon the relatively new evidence-based discoveries of science at the level of micro-organismic identification, which had allowed medical science both independent social status and its professionalised distancing from philosophy. And then in a rhetorical flourish, he illustrates what will later be termed a "defence" mechanism in psychoanalytic thinking in his observation that historically, "... physicians came to restrict their interest to the physical side of things and were glad to leave the mental field to be dealt with by the philosophers whom they despised" (1890a, p. 284).

Within this narrative aside, the contemporary reader may locate a later psychodynamic **d** element, here observed by Freud in the development of the late nineteenth-century Viennese medical field. This is his preconceptual statement of defensive operations, bounded within a particular professional field and driven by its anxieties about the scope of its omniscient knowledge, of institutional definition by splitting and projection.

Yet, facing into this split, Freud reminds his medically informed audience of the reciprocal intertwining within medical practice of body and mind. Moving from consideration of symptomatic plasticity, as well as the magical valence of words, Freud presents his reader in rapid order with multiple and disparate considerations including a carnival seer who reads facial expressions, the behaviour of children, consideration of religious martyrs, and the tenacity of wounded soldiers engaged in combat.

For a moment, the reader is confused; and realises that the author has engineered a continuum of thinking which ranges from the plausible to the implausible. In so doing, Freud again disrupts, forcing thought and with it, the reader's registration of affective arousal. The reader becomes aware of felt annoyance in the destabilisation of the lulling word and argument into frenetic thinking and uncertainty. And it is within this deft disruption of the reader's previous state of imagined stability and clarity, that Freud's essay accomplishes an aesthetic brilliance mirrored by clinical process. Much of clinical practice unfolds in a swamp of uncertainty, of thick language and association, affectively fused and difficult to clarify. Here, the Freudian essay touches the clinical experience, exactly that experience signalled by Bion when he gestures towards the *practising* therapist, indicating in his own essay the difference between the level of what can be verbally stated in language and what is intuitively sensed, if inchoate, and must be tolerated in its containment by the therapist.

Still within the domain of language, Freud shifts gears from a flattened and linear intellectual argument, engaging the reader's emotional arousal in confusion and discomfort. It is as if he transforms the two-dimensional essay form into three-dimensionality. Because in following his argument, not only has the reader begun to consider points of arrival or the explicit **d** elements that Freud seeks to convey, but has also begun to register emotional destabilisation.

Looking backward, the reader observes how Freud accomplishes this; but its recognition comes only as a result of an après-coup, by application of thinking itself generated only as a function of the historical development from emboldened d at time (n) to emboldened d at time (n+1), in the development of psychoanalysis itself! For it is Bion, in his 1962 paper on the dynamics of thinking, who best comments on what Freud has done to the reader at this moment in his 1890 essay. Freud has piled idea upon idea, forcing the reader's thinking from its sheer agglomeration into a felt collapse of its loosely piled thoughts. Of this, Bion writes that thinking itself, the yield of the psychoanalytic essay, is "forced on the psyche by the pressure of thoughts" (1962a, p. 306). And in linking thinking with clinical practice, within the form of the psychoanalytic essay demonstrated here by Freud, Bion's thinking registers in the clinician's mind as another **d**, illuminating the process by which Freud, seventy-two years earlier, has engaged his future reader!

Deftly, in the next paragraphs, with consideration of an articulated **d**-level concept called "expectation", Freud rescues the reader by naming in a different context the very expectation that has been derailed. In effect, Freud has taken the thick expression of particularity which has disrupted the reader's thinking (and which has been induced within the reader by Freud as writer, much as the therapist supplies a sometimes disruptive interpretation to the patient), and again "interpreted" it through his supply of the concept "expectation". For in the anxious collapse within the reader's thinking, it is exactly the expectation of the reader's dependence upon the writer in assuring the essay's continuity which has become disrupted.

The effect of the essay as demonstrating the psychoanalytic process of thinking remains hidden in plain sight. What Freud demonstrates through essay form is the polysemic nature of expression, operating at multiple levels of experienced meaning. Not only does Freud now produce a new field of d elements for consideration—as in examples of patients' expected hopes or fears in affecting health, grounded empirically in differing epidemiological outcomes for individuals exposed to plague—but he has also demonstrated the influence of his thinking upon the mind of the attentive reader, attempting to follow his argument. He has accomplished a disruption, felt viscerally and then relieved, as his argument "interprets", through the word "expectation", exactly that which had been disrupted in the reader through Freud's fragmented and fragmenting considerations of: side-show entertainer; children; religious martyr; and wounded soldier: objects of thought difficult to group under one conceptual heading.

It is as if in his essay, Freud accomplishes procedurally within the task of understanding an essayist's argument, what Bion makes explicit seventy years later: that the inchoate, unrecognised dimension of influence, mind to mind, is as significant within psychoanalysis as the markers we use linguistically "by words and verbal formulations designed for a different task"—the fleeting clinical emergence of d, and the conceptual emergence of more enduring **d**, within the clinical essay. Once articulated either in clinical or literary form, these become recognisable under deconstructed conditions; and unsaturated, become permeable to reinvigoration under new and particularised uses. Such recognitions become the clinical forms which we fashion into self-constructed landmarks, clinically directed matrices of mind, brought by the clinician to the setting of the consultation room and progressively elaborated through clinical experience towards new horizons of therapist thought and expression. The essay form therefore allows modification, extension, as well as heretical shifts within formally presented descriptions of psychoanalysis (Bergmann, 1999), underscoring fascinated and disenchanted communities' recognition of what is fundamental within psychoanalysis at any given time in its historical development (Govrin, 2016).

Returning to the Bion algorithm, the psychoanalytic essay also provides linguistic description of shifts from within the individual clinician's particularised—so, persecutory, split, and private forms of knowing, towards conciliatory arrivals with the larger psychoanalytic field; and in the same movement, illustrates clinicians' discretely particular reckonings with psychoanalysis, themselves to be subjected to a universalising, generalist movement as an element or form useful within the wider clinical field of application. The psychoanalytic essay, while paralleling through the actions of writer-reader the dynamics of doer-done to also observed within clinical practice (Benjamin, 2004), achieves a particularity radically different from the abstracted universalism of the Bion algorithm. The essay "clothes" in its discernments through provocation of the norms it seeks to disrupt, the process by which thinking arrives at its more generalised transitory expressions of **d**.

As we now write and comment upon different aspects of therapeutic thinking: on pathological forms; on symbolisation; on the form of clinical thinking and writing; on trauma; on historical essays; on sequences of clinical presentation; on frustrations and contradictions attendant upon the real-time pressures of our own clinical practices, our thoughts range over a landscape already long discerned within clinical thinking. These include what over forty years ago, André Green recognised as the multi-levelled aspects of the "present situation within psychoanalysis", both then and in our own times, including three domains of contradiction: 1) between the practice of psychoanalytic therapy and its receptivity by the social environment, its practice setting; 2) between social reality and the training models (and the institutions in which they are embedded) by which therapists learn the dynamic topography of psychotherapy; and 3) within the theory and practice of psychoanalytic thought itself (Green, 1975).

Even by the time of Green's writing, psychoanalysis itself had been generative in contributing to a proliferation of psychotherapeutic practice forms, with its own most time-intensive "classical" form occupying one end of a vast therapeutic continuum (Miller, 2016a). As authors, our work in psychodynamic psychotherapy, over a joint accumulation of roughly sixty years in clinical practice, has brought us face-to-face with the multiple contradictions spelled out by Green: of psychodynamic practice in the contemporary social environment; of psychodynamic practice whether in its openness or closed-ness to change and evolution and its forms of local training and practice; and with the theory and practice of psychodynamic therapy itself in the everyday work of therapy.

For us, such considerations are simultaneous, interactive, and continuous. Our thinking, as authors along multiple lines, has emerged together within a rough timescale of two years, though with much longer roots in thoughts' percolations. Our reflections are upon the everyday work of psychotherapy; yet by necessity, the essays we have crafted attempt to articulate that which is always, in the end, elusive: the inchoate experience of practising therapists.

What differs uniquely in the therapeutic from the essay form is its immediacy of feeling in the binding of time and setting, its here-and-now as the defining characteristics of evocation through its central "object" of inquiry, the patient. Yet in its small and large resonances, all that is carried forward, partial and whole, meets intuition's capability within the therapist, at least momentarily, before falling backward into the associative fusions of the patient, which follow the articulation and agreement upon d in the clinical situation and **d** in the development, history, and understanding of clinical psychodynamic practice.

CHAPTER TWO

Psychopathology and d elements: fusion and de-fusion within the psychotherapeutic encounter

As we observed in the previous chapter's introduction of forms presented within the clinical setting, the therapist is repeatedly faced with the difficult task of negotiating what are often transitory and subtly fused aspects of the patient-therapist interaction. These involve an ongoing dyadic relationship in which (1) the therapist attempts to discern within herself a complex array of thoughts, affects, and fantasies/phantasies generated in the presence of the patient, while (2) approaching and attempting to understand the patient's similar complexities. These become the recurring basis for (3) the therapist's situating dyadic experience with the patient in the context of the therapeutic relationship. As we later explore in relation to d elements in the clinical setting (Chapter 5), such dimensions of fusion and de-fusion in the encounter between patient and therapist may be met combatively through the patient's pathological dominance of persecutory action or against the patient's tentative and precarious equilibrium of personality, tenaciously defended before the interpretation and working through of fusional states give way to the more obvious emergence of d elements in de-fusion.

In what follows, we outline key aspects of the conceptual models that have shaped our thinking on psychopathology and its manifestations;

and we develop those clinical forms that we have previously outlined as automata states, mimetic fusing, and the twin concepts of both intrapsychic black holes and white holes (Miller & Sweet, 2017; Sweet 2010, 2011, 2012, 2013; Sweet & Miller, 2016). First, we offer some thoughts on the developmental trajectory of the individual, from a Kleinian psychoanalytic perspective.

The developing child's growing ability to tolerate radically different impulses and emotions on the spectrum of love and hate as these are directed towards his objects, led Klein (1935) to her description of what became known as the depressive position (D). The concept, theoretically and clinically, has become the cornerstone of psychoanalytic understanding and practice within the Kleinian tradition. Far from remaining conceptually or clinically static, the concept of the depressive position offers fertile ground within which a disparate range of clinical ideas has taken root.

Our own particular reading, which stresses discrete d movements within the global dynamics of the depressive position proper, owes much to those writers and thinkers who have enhanced and expanded our understanding. Here we offer a brief synopsis of earlier developments in relation to the depressive position, before outlining our understanding of complex psychopathology in the daily work of psychotherapy and our approach to its treatment.

It is a tribute to the rich and polyvalent nature of the depressive position envisaged by Melanie Klein, that the concept has given rise to many further theoretical and clinical innovations. Klein's recognition of a significant transition in child development, involving threats to the emergent self, is central to depressive functioning. This shift concerns the qualitative nature of anxiety; and it features movement between a predominance of paranoid anxiety through its transmutation into anxiety that evidences a depressive valence.

In contrast to paranoid anxiety, which according to Klein is redolent with fears of destruction emanating from outside, depressive anxiety is marked by the emergence of anxieties concerning the fate of objects, both external and internal to the psyche. Such dynamics are posited to evolve due to the phantasied destruction that the child fears to have occurred, as a function of his own oral aggression. As a result, the child, tentatively, begins to experience a sense of his world as barren, arid, and empty in which he is alone, terrified, and vulnerable. Klein then offers a conceptual theoretical leap, suggesting that in the face of such a situation the child attempts to do the only thing possible in order to redress the extreme damage that it is felt to have caused: the child attempts to repair the damage he feels himself to have inflicted upon his objects.

This reparation, Klein contends, is evidence of the child's phantasied omniscience and omnipotence in the service of his love for his objects. She goes further in a later work (1957), and suggests that reparation of the damaged object is a genuine expression of love and regret for the damage so inflicted, and that this is intimately related to the emergence of a deep sense of gratitude for the goodness and love which the child has received from the primary caregiver.

Assimilation and further developments in thinking about Klein's construct of the depressive position gained considerable momentum during the 1950s and 1960s. Broadly considered, these developments reflected the curiosity of a range of Kleinian analysts who were interested in such areas as: the evolution of the creative impulse and impediments to its fuller development (Jaques, 1965; Segal, 1957); the origins of thinking and clinical work with psychotic patients (Bion, 1959, 1962a, 1962b, 1963; Money-Kyrle, 1965, 1968; Rosenfeld, 1965; Segal, 1957); and the thorny topic of narcissism, with particular reference to borderline personalities (Rosenfeld, 1964). In the three decades that followed, 1970–2000, attention focused further on the internal structures and experiential worlds of such patients.

A group of contemporary Kleinian thinkers, influenced by Bion, Rosenfeld, and Segal, illuminate our understanding of defensive pathological organisations of the personality in relation to the depressive position (O'Shaughnessy, 1981; Rosenfeld, 1971; Steiner, 1993). Britton (1998) developed ideas of both stasis and movement in relation to the depressive position. He has shown how the apparent static fixity of the depressive position may indicate a rigidity of mind, likely to be operating defensively, and at times psychotically. Against such stasis, Britton addresses the specific nature of discrete movements in and around the liminal spaces between paranoid-schizoid and depressive relating. He acknowledges a specific debt to Betty Joseph's (1985) work on the fine-grained movements within the totality of transference situations, and stresses the ways in which analytic sessions enable the observation of miniscule and discrete movements between largely paranoid-schizoid relating and greater integration of the self, as closer relating to the depressive position emerges. In turn, such movement tends to result in fuller and richer contact between the analyst and the patient.

Later, with specific reference to our work on submerged aspects of shared hermeneutical readings across the psychoanalytical canon (Miller & Sweet, 2017, here revised as Chapter 4), we give a fuller outline of how we initially came to develop our thinking on the discrete movements and iterations between paranoid-schizoid and depressive relating, and their emergence as landmarks (Macfarlane, 2015), or footholds, along the therapeutic journey. We recognise, of course, clear echoes and resonances with those thinkers who have charted similar territory, many of whom are referred to above.

We offer the observation that, in our experience, arrivals at a momentary conception of D are in actuality, idiosyncratically fine-grained, and invariably transitory movements involving d elements. These arrivals are often repeated many times during the process of therapy. They seem to be based on an accretion of experiences, dyadic in nature between therapist and patient; and may, in the longer term, cement more fundamental structural change, in terms of the psyche and global personality. To designate and symbolise the oscillating nature of these communications, both intrapsychically and interpsychically, between patient and therapist we deploy a lower-case d.

This is a form of shorthand that we hope, rather in the same sense that Bion's choice of the terms beta elements (β) and alpha elements (α) are designed to do, avoids over saturation of the concept, leaving scope for further development.

On psychopathology: fusion/de-fusion and d elements

Developmentally, from the perspective afforded us by the psychoanalytic frame of reference, personality growth and development is based upon ongoing interaction between a range of external and internal objects. These include: core self imagoes; affectively imbued objects; and combinatory self/objects that exhibit a broad and diverse range of affective states (Bion, 1962a, 1962b; Fairbairn, 1952; Freud, 1917e; Kernberg, 1992; Klein, 1946; Kohut, 1971; Winnicott, 1958). Conceptualising object usage and the quality of the object as either evocative or destructive (Bollas, 1992, 1995) is also an important consideration in the psychotherapeutic treatment of those patients who present with complaints of stuckness in their lives, a sense of futility, or, in more extreme cases, thoughts of life not worth living and active suicidality.

In the course of early development, the reciprocal relationship between the child and the child's caregivers is pivotal if the individual is to develop an internal world that can progressively and healthily accommodate a range of affective states, linked to healthy and realistic self and object representations. Within the British school, Wilfred Bion (1962a) explored this relationship, and its implications for both healthy development and for the development of later adult psychopathology, in his influential paper *A Theory of Thinking*. Although some of the ideas expressed in this paper may at first reading appear counter-intuitive and recondite, such as Bion's concept of *thoughts without a thinker*, he imaginatively and creatively described the dyadic relationship between the child and the caregiver, and the sense in which a thinking apparatus emerges as a direct result of the containing function that the parent offers the child. What is particularly prescient in Bion's model of containment, or the lack of it, specifically in relation to the later development of psychopathology, is the way in which he describes the evolution of thinking in terms of the young child's capability to endure frustration. In the schema presented, if the experience of the absent object, the breast, can be tolerated and endured, then this experience may be turned into ideation as thought, which is initially ideographic. The capacity to develop and hold, however temporarily, such inchoate thoughts helps to sustain the infant until the external object reappears. Over time, an ability to delay gratification of intense impulses develops and the capacity to endure waiting for a need to be satisfied evolves. In effect, the individual internalises a personal containing function.

In the absence of an ability to tolerate frustration, the absent object is felt to be persecutory and, in Bion's language, fit only for evacuation from the psyche. He contends, "Incapacity for tolerating frustration tips the scale in the direction of evasion of frustration" (ibid., p. 113). Under such circumstances, Bion suggests that the infant, rather than developing a capacity for thought, seeks urgently to expel hostile and aggressively imbued internal objects, through the persistent use of projective identification. The evacuative expulsion of objects that could, under different circumstances (transformation through containment) act as the foundations of thinking, leads to the operation of what Bion terms "minus K" (–K). As the name suggests, the operation of the –K function is deployed in order to evade knowing and truth. In essence, as Bollas (1987, 2008) has commented, the transformative function of containment fails and an object is experienced as destructive rather than as evocative. Issuing from the psychotic part of the mind, –K distorts reality. It denudes experience of meaning and is implicated in the pervasive "attacks on links", earlier discussed by Bion (1959). Under –K, painful and disturbing mental contents, implied by combinations of objects, self, and affects, are felt to be intensely threatening and potentially annihilatory. A vicious cycle develops, in the absence of an ability to symbolise experience (see Chapter 3), leading to the creation of an internal psychological world of *nameless dread.*

Under such conditions, the experience by the infant is not only of intolerable feelings of anxiety, but also that there is *no way* that such sensations and feelings can be made tolerable. In fact, if Bion's line of thought is followed closely, there is not even a context in which to situate affects—spatially or temporally—because coherent internalised object relations connected to affect states, that would give meaning to these ideas, however inchoate and primitive in the case of the young infant, have neither developed nor been internalised. It is under such conditions that the young child resorts to what Bollas (1992) has termed *binding*. This primitive self-protective process is a means by which the child attempts to desensitise the self, both to control the damage inflicted on the self and to expel painful affects. This primitive level of visceral sensory experience has also been discussed by Thomas Ogden (1992), who coined the term "autistic contiguous position" for this stage, and suggested that such functioning predates Klein's paranoid-schizoid phase.

Earlier still in the historical development of psychoanalytic ideas, with reference to intrapsychic object representation, Money-Kyrle (1968) delineated three distinct levels of representation. He described the first level as *concrete representation*, akin to Segal's (1957) concept of symbolic equation. At this level, no differentiation is made between psycho-sensory representation and the object or a particular situation coterminous with it. According to Money-Kyrle, concrete representation operates at a primitive and deeply unconscious register. The second stage of symbolisation, mirroring Bion's concept of alpha function, is called ideographic representation and includes dreams. The final level of representation is conscious, predominantly verbal representation. In a schematic way, one can consider the development of verbal representation as deriving from an initial state of psycho-sensory unformulated experience that becomes modified progressively through the experience of ideographic illusion and the later acquisition of language.

In both Bion's and Money-Kyrle's terms, the processes of cognitive construction and formulation require mental work. This requires the development of an ability to tolerate frustration, in the movement from a pleasure-seeking narcissistic ego to one that is oriented towards the demands of reality. Some contemporary authors, drawing on Gadamer's (1975) hermeneutical theory, have extended such ideas to suggest that dissociation represents, primarily, a defence against the formulation of deeply unconscious and unformulated experience (see, for example, Stern, 2009, pp. 635–662). In such models of mind, unformulated experience and non-understanding reflect the primitive and natural order of the psyche. Indeed, in clinical conditions such as the addictions, we meet with individuals who self-administer dissociative states (Somer, 2009) and, in extreme circumstances, pursue the obliteration of verbal memorial thought in its entirety.

These patients report blackouts after alcohol and other drug binges and often experience intense anxieties as islands of memory, often fragmentary, which re-emerge post-intoxication. This pattern of behaviour, which at base appears to indicate an overwhelming impulse to annihilate awareness and understanding, affords the clinician an opportunity to witness the force of deep unconscious object imagoes and the gravitational pull that they exert upon a very fragile ego, the so-called black hole within the psyche, which has been described by a range of authors (Eshel, 1998; Glasser, 1979; Grotstein, 1990; Hopper, 1995; Sweet, 2012; Sweet & Miller, 2016). In severely disturbed patients, as Bion (1959) observed, rather than refer to the self by use of the first person pronoun "I", such individuals often employ the word "it", for example: "It seems that …" or "It's driving me crazy." The use of the word "it" conveys the sense in which the patient feels dissociated from a part object that has not been structurally integrated into the ego, and this is an idea we had initially outlined elsewhere, in relation to graduated transitions in awareness connected to a move from predominantly paranoid-schizoid impulses and thoughts towards depressive (d/D) thinking proper (Miller & Sweet, 2017; Sweet & Miller, 2016). The "it" part of the personality can also readily be associated with superego nuclei (Britton, 2003; Riesenberg-Malcolm, 1999), split off in the deep unconscious, as is clear when objects appear aggressively punitive and sadistically harsh.

An example comes from work with a middle-aged female patient who experienced her mother as a constant spoiling presence in her childhood. The patient began to suspect during middle childhood years (aged eight) that her mother's chief concern was to restrict the child's contact with her father. She came to believe that her mother was jealous of her. When the father experienced a psychotic depressive breakdown during the patient's last year of junior school she felt herself to finally be, as she said "… parentless." Identifications with an idealised father and a sadistically attacking and spoiling mother were repeated through the patient's later development of drug dependency on benzodiazepines and a propensity to binge-drink alcohol. Commencement of psychotherapeutic treatment had also been advised following a suicide attempt, by overdose. Most markedly, and reflected in the lack of a meaningful or containing and contextualising psychological space for this patient, was her use of the word "it" to describe her inner world. During the early months of attendance she would often begin sessions by saying: "… I don't know what it's about today" or "… it doesn't matter anyway" after recalling a recent experience. Here, we would contend, there is evidence of a fusional state between the self and its objects, with the implication that a viable potential or transitional space (Winnicott, 1953) that may facilitate the emergence and development of d elements is grossly restricted.

This sense of being invaded by alien objects that cannot be assimilated in any meaningful way appears to develop when differentiation of self, object, and affective states fail. Such difficulty in assimilating internal objects, which cannot be in part or more fully psychologically metabolised, often leads to extreme defensive strategies. Reactions to such experience have been described in various ways by a range of psychoanalytic thinkers, for instance: internalisation of a pathological organisation (Steiner, 1993), failure of mentalization (Fonagy, 2001; Fonagy & Target, 1996a, 1996b), defensive dissociation as a reaction to chronic relational trauma (Howell & Blizzard, 2009), and as a reaction to the impact of invasive objects (Williams, 2010), and as mimetic fusing (Sweet, 2013). In extreme cases of psychological distress, psychosensory impingement and/or deprivation, and when manic defences break down, the individual may feel that the sacrifice of the self is the only way to rid the mind of hostile and persecutory objects. Here, we suggest, that the failure of splitting per se, in the face of overwhelming annihilatory anxieties, leads to the defensive use of fusing the self, in part or in whole, with a range of deadly and terrifying objects. Dimensions of such fused experience with internal objects, replayed in the transference on to the analyst, and often experienced with intensity through the analyst's sense of countertransference phenomena, come to inform the sense of not only stuckness and stasis within the therapeutic relationship but also progressive and fine-grained movements intrapsychically and interpsychically, between patient and therapist. We have further developed our thinking, in relation to such psychopathological states and their emergence in the clinical encounter, with reference to the interrelated concepts of fusion, mimicry, and automatism. It is to these ideas that we now turn.

Mimicry and automatism

Eugenio Gaddini's (1969) concept of imitation, a form of mimetic identification that involves attempts to fuse the rudimentary self with objects, has previously been described by one of the authors (Sweet, 2013), with particular reference to severe forms of addiction and associated behaviours.

In essence, this concept of mimetic fusing, as it became known, had been offered as an augmentation of the traditional Kleinian view in which excessive projective identification *creates* bad objects. It was suggested that the invasiveness of bad objects may also lead to a form of primitive defensive identification, in terms of *mimetic fusing* of the self and its object. Subsequently, in the absence of effective mutative containment during the mimetic phase, there appears to be a forestalling of developmental processes, including the healthy use of projective identification through which the self may differentiate from its object. The resultant states that tend to emerge as complaints later in adulthood run on a continuum from mild, moderate, to severe difficulties though ubiquitously featuring somatisation: a sense of stasis that feels, at times, paralysing; and rapid decompensation defensively leading to enactment when a threat to the sense of fusion with the object—thus potentially separated from it—is felt.

We observe that there are two clear markers for the severity of such fusion in clinical assessment: 1) the level and extent of impulsivity and 2) a lack of insight, evidenced by the patient. The former marker is the dominant feature in the borderline case and represents the individual's repeated attempts to escape the intense gravitational pull of a rigidly internalised and automatic mimicry. Paradoxically, such impulsivity may also represent the last viable defensive strategy available to the patient against fusion with the object.

The latter marker, lack of insight with its hallmark, the wholesale elimination of thinking, indicates that fusion has become practically total, leading to a psychological structure that is predominantly psychotic in orientation.

In clinical day-to-day work, with a range of patients, the sense of alternation between periods of aliveness and deadness in the countertransference is an essential reference point for therapists in their work with mimetically fused patients. We now offer, through presentation of the following necessarily compressed clinical case examples, our sense of some ways in which to better understand and assist such patients, who appear rigidly fused with their internal objects.

Mimetic fusing in the clinical setting

Clinical case 1: Mr J

This clinical case features a patient, Mr J, a fifty-six-year-old unemployed financial analyst who is divorced with three children. His ex-wife and children live in another part of the country and Mr J, at the time of psychotherapy with one of the authors (AS), was living with his elderly parents. He was referred, ostensibly due to a history of heavy drinking, by an alcohol liaison nurse. The referral note stated there had been "… a very heavy pattern of alcohol consumption which has resulted in hospitalisation. When admitted he was suffering from hallucinations, loss of mobility and deranged electrolytes. Psychiatry would ask that you assess for treatment."

We hope to convey in the clinical vignette presented, some sense of the rather dislocated dialogue of this patient, and the ways in which splitting led to various types of dissociation, manifest by attacks on linking (Bion, 1959). This is particularly relevant in the case of Mr J in terms of the disjunction between the content of his associations and the apparent lack of emotional affect attached to them. At the time of this session, he had been abstinent from alcohol, by self-report, for around six weeks.

Mr J began his fourth therapeutic session by associating to a phone call that he'd made the previous weekend. His eldest son Harry (fourteen) had answered, and Mr J asked him what he had been up to. Harry replied, "Nothing." Mr J then asked his son what he'd been doing at school. Harry again responded, "Nothing." Persevering, Mr J then enquired what Harry had been getting up to between his school lessons. The boy again responded in the negative, simply stating, "Nothing." Without communicative signal or punctuation indicating a change of subject, Mr J continued, "Of course father has been quite unwell this week. He suffers from Crohn's disease. Some of the time he's quite alright but this last week he hasn't wanted to be more than twenty yards or so from a toilet." Again shifting ground (and initially confusing to the therapist until he was able to "catch up" with the thread of Mr J's narrative) he continued, "Although they were both fine this morning and off to Tesco for groceries when I got up to have my breakfast."

Next, Mr J paused briefly. Then, quite softly in an almost whispered voice said, "Well I don't know. Is this the sort of thing you want me to talk about?" Again, he paused briefly, after which I (AS) said: "It seems there may be a communication problem. I want to be clear that I can only suggest this to you but I wonder if you are feeling frustrated because the people you are trying to reach seem not actually to be there."

Mr J looked ponderously and quizzically at me before speaking again. He said, "I left my Zimmer frame at home today. I thought I could manage the road without it and besides it was only taking up space in the waiting room. When I'm walking home, if I get stuck, I can always get on a bus or telephone for someone to rescue me."

I said, "You felt as if you were strong enough because what you previously leant on, the frame, had become a sense within you rather than an object outside of you. Now you doubt the strength of what you took in to yourself." Apparently oblivious to what I had just said to him, he continued. "I remember," he said. "Harry asked who would die first, Grandpa or Grandma." I drew his attention to a further theme in his associations, that of death, disease, and distance. "That's right," he said. "Father was talking about wanting to be cremated the other day and I said we could break the concrete in the plot and have his ashes buried underneath, but he said he wanted them scattered on the plot." Mr J began to chuckle and giggle, and then said, "I've always thought that could be quite farcical. What if the ashes were to be blown back in your face by the wind?" It seemed, though I didn't say it, that the emergent though fragile sense of his self-agency had become no more than ashes that were being blown in the wind. Could my interpretations, as the father analyst, also be experienced not as words that could penetrate the hard concretised mind he presented but rather as words that had become dust and ashes being blown into his face?

Now the earlier associations seemed more resonant. By projecting his resistant and recalcitrant self into Harry, and becoming the non-engaging negative adolescent, Mr J attempted both to placate and irritate the aggravating and aggravated father analyst, at one and the same time. In so doing, he also managed to reverse the analytic perspective by quizzing a resistant and negative childlike part of himself. He had, in effect, transformed a dynamic process into a static one. Bion (1963) might have described such a procedure as evidence of the dominance of –K in this particular patient's psyche. In this sense the potential aliveness, vibrancy, and spontaneity coalescing within the d elements are drained of their vivacity and deadened. Now the therapist is faced with the dual tasks of both understanding the effect of the patient's communications and actions and also sustaining and maintaining a thinking and containing capacity in the face of such an onslaught.

One can also speculate that at the unconscious level, in terms of phantasy, we see the enactment of murderous rage directed both towards the father, and in the transference through effective elimination, towards the therapist. Indeed in the broader context of my countertransference responses, allowing for these in the conscious perceptual and unconscious sense, I felt a strange mixture of affects and emotions while listening to Mr J. It was difficult to find a balance between, at times, a sense of nagging irritation, sadness, *Fawlty Towers* (a popular British sitcom referred to at times by Mr J) hilarity, and frankly, bafflement and despair.

Mr J, after a brief pause continued. "Mother and Father like to watch *Gogglebox* [a popular TV programme]. They watch it in bed but I watch it on the iPlayer. My children like that programme too. I think its rubbish." What struck me at the time about this rather enigmatic statement was the fact that he communicated his habit of "watching" a television programme he considered rubbish, on his iPlayer. One can only presume that there was no practical reason why he had to watch this *rubbishy Gogglebox* programme on his iPlayer, and yet he appeared compelled to do so.

Linking to earlier material in the session it again became clear that there was a critical lack of separation between Mr J and his parental objects. Previously, they had gone to the shop to buy "groceries" and he had been left to fend for himself; *to make his own breakfast*. Now, he appeared to have been left alone with "rubbish" and his iPlayer while they were comfortable in bed together enjoying *Gogglebox*. Further, he stated that his children "… like that programme too." Connection with his diseased, dying, and fused objects seemed only possible through the relationship he had with his iPlayer. Such a connection could be read with reference to a thick-skinned narcissistic psychic retreat (Rosenfeld, 1987; Steiner, 1993), subsumed under a more general pathological defensive organisation. However, a pathway to better understanding much of what appeared to have been going on here, we would contend, is to be found in a rigorous examination of the countertransference, and its emergence relative to fusional states between therapist and patient.

By this stage in the session, it had become difficult as therapist to maintain either a cognitive or affective link with the patient, or at least to maintain links at those levels that in any sense felt meaningful or integrated. Indeed, it had become increasingly difficult to organise thoughts into linking patterns that might produce intelligible constructions or, perhaps optimistically, interpretations that might reach the patient, based on "elements" in flux across the PS ↔ d (D) continuum. All of this perhaps becomes more intelligible if we consider Bion's (1987) sage observation in his paper, "On Arrogance", with regard to the interactions between patient and analyst, when projective identification is the patient's primary mode of communication, that:

> In this phase my employment of verbal communication was felt by the patient to be a mutilating attack on his methods of communication. From this point onwards, it was only a matter of time to demonstrate that the patient's link with me was his ability to employ projective identification ... On this depended a variety of procedures which were felt to ensure emotionally rewarding experiences such as ... the ability to put bad feelings in me and leave them there long enough for them to be modified by their sojourn in my psyche, and the ability to put good parts of himself into me, thereby feeling that he was dealing with an ideal object as a result. Associated with these experiences was a sense of being in contact with me, which I am inclined to believe is a primitive form of communication that provides a foundation on which, ultimately, verbal communication depends. From his feelings about me when I was identified with the obstructive object, I was able to deduce that the obstructive object was curious about him, but could not stand being the receptacle for parts of his personality and accordingly made destructive and mutilating attacks, largely through stupidity, upon his capacity for projective identification. (pp. 91–92)

Though there is no sense, necessarily, of ordered sequence, in which the type of projective identifications here described by Bion tend to unfold, one learns through clinical experience that good parts of the self are often ejected during the early phases of contact between patient and therapist. This can be thought of in terms of the longer duration of psychoanalytic psychotherapy, though it is perhaps more helpful clinically to monitor and observe such communications at the micro level, in terms of what is happening in the immediacy of the session (Britton, 1998; Joseph, 1985; Miller & Sweet, 2017; Sweet & Miller, 2016).

In Mr J's case, it was notable that he had begun his associations with reference to his fourteen-year-old son, Harry. Here, the frustrated and frustrating self appeared so intimately conjoined and mimetically fused (Sweet, 2013) with its objects, that it was difficult initially to gain clarity on the nature of the unconscious communication. Fusion of this type can be thought of as a means by which internalised persecutory object representations can be fused with the fragile and inchoate self, defensively. Remnants of the self and its objects may subsequently be eliminated into the analyst's mind, and then further sifted and monitored by the analyst, before being modulated and made meaningful, in the process of working through.

In essence, we would contend that this is what Bion is referring to when he uses the phrase in relation to the patient's projections "... *modified by their sojourn in my psyche.*" We would further offer that modification through sojourn in the analyst's psyche represents an iterative stage involving movements in d, and the putative emergence of d elements. And this may be a particularly trying phase of treatment—precisely because dawning awareness on behalf of the analyst may in no sense be mirrored by or shared by the patient. The implication here is that the analyst may be required to carry, for lengthy periods of time, a range of intense thoughts, feelings, and affective states directed towards the patient, before these become more realistically oriented, through the progressive working through of split-off d elements.

It is helpful to recall, during such periods in psychotherapy, that Bion (1970), in his later work, described three particular forms of projective identification: commensal, symbiotic, and parasitic. Modification of projections is considered to take place both in the commensal and symbiotic forms of projective identification, though not when projective identification is of the parasitic type. In this type of projective relationship, the third object produced is destructive; precisely because reciprocity between self and object is lacking and envy (Klein, 1957) predominates, forestalling and preventing genuine reparative movement within the depressive position. Alternatively, these "attacks on linking", as Bion so adroitly observed in his 1959 paper of that name, are primarily directed against the emergence of thinking and the genuine emotions that may therefore ensue: "In this state of mind emotion is hated; it is felt to be too powerful to be contained by the immature psyche, it is felt to link objects and it gives reality to objects which are not self and therefore inimical to primary narcissism" (p. 108).

Our second clinical case in this chapter contextualises some of the demands made on both therapist and patient as processes involving movements within d relating begin to evolve. It should be noted, as the case evidences, that movements within d involve periods in the work testing the capacities of both patient and therapist—akin to transitional gestations spread out over months, and at times, over several years of psychotherapeutic work.

Clinical case 2: Tom

The patient, a forty-two-year-old single man whom I shall refer to as Tom, was referred for weekly psychotherapy by his consultant neuropsychologist. Three years before entering treatment he had suffered a traumatic brain injury involving a subdural haemorrhage and it had also been observed, on scans, that he evidenced cerebral cortical atrophy, most likely as a result of a lengthy history of heavy alcohol consumption. The manifest symptoms of these impairments included: both remote and short-term memory amnesias; limited ability to contain affects and volition; a slowing and slurring of speech; acute sleep disturbances, and restricted motility on the left side of the body. At presentation for assessment he struggled to recall details of his life both before the brain injury and during the intervening period. Significant gaps were, to some degree, filled in by informants, including the mother with whom I met on a number of occasions during the initial assessment interviews, and again intermittently. Tom's version of contemporary events in his life week to week, as therapy progressed, were often at considerable variance to those reported by the informants within the family, and indeed other members of the multidisciplinary healthcare team. He appeared, initially at least, to airbrush events, omitting mention of heavy drinking episodes, verbal onslaughts against the parents, and periods when he took himself off and was, as he later described, "… missing in action." This behaviour led to feelings of considerable anxiety within the wider family, who viewed Tom as a recalcitrant child who, at all costs, had to be monitored and managed. To some degree their anxiety was understandable given the impairments, both psychologically and physiologically, that Tom suffered.

The childhood history, as may have been expected given the neurophysiological impairments that underscored amnesia, was difficult to establish. I was able to glean information from the mother and, less reliably, from Tom. He was an only child and had been carried to full term with no apparent complications. There were no separations post-partum from the parents and no childhood hospitalisations. There had been intermittent enuresis up to the age of seven and pickiness with food during early childhood. The impression was of a little boy who was often left to amuse himself whilst in the company of adults, who seemingly had other tasks to get on with. There was history of alcoholism on the mother's side (maternal grandfather), though the parents themselves were only moderate drinkers. Tom's difficulties with alcohol had evolved from teenage years within a socio-economic culture where heavy drinking was the norm. After the breakdown in his late twenties of what appeared his only longer-term intimate relationship, with a somewhat younger woman, he began to drink dependently. Drinking was accompanied by a range of self-destructive behaviours, for example driving while intoxicated, attempting paracetamol overdose on at least two known occasions and drinking to the point of paralytic immobility resulting in fractures, bruises, and lacerations. It was in such a condition that he suffered a fall down a steep stairwell, leading to the traumatic brain injury previously mentioned.

In the early months of psychotherapy, Tom's material and behaviour during sessions exhibited a predictable and static pattern, so much so in fact, that I identified with Bill Murray's character Phil Connors in the movie *Groundhog Day* (Ramis, 1993), who lives through the same day over and over again, in the Pennsylvania town of Puxsutawney, and believes himself to be going mad.

There was an eerie quality to sessions that began with exactly the same joke and were punctuated by the same aphorisms and stories that I soon came to know verbatim. The central theme in these early months seemed connected to rather desperate attempts by Tom to defend against any awareness of a desolate and terrifying internal world, apparently denuded of meaning, in which an incredibly fragile part of his ego seemed to be trapped. The presenting personality was excessively jovial, constantly cracking jokes and deploying acerbic witticisms. However, clues to more obviously malevolent, violent, and aggressive internal objects were suggested by both my countertransference affects and Tom's behaviour outside the therapeutic hours.

An accretion of bizarre objects minutely fragmented, as Bion (1962a) has described these, and fit only for projection, appeared to be indicated by the static and lifeless quality of the patient's virtually robotic interactions with me during the therapeutic hours. This had the effect of leaving me feeling bombarded for fifty minutes with the certain conviction that the process would be repeated, in a virtually identical manner, at the next meeting. In the transference, I appeared to stand for a dry and empty breast, or perhaps more accurately nipple, that was mercilessly chewed upon, swallowed, and then regurgitated. Indications of this very primitive and destructive relationship to internal objects were also evident in the patient's behaviour between the sessions. He drank heavily, literally making himself physically sick and becoming incontinent, before a member of the immediate or extended family would find him in a semi-conscious state, and assist in "cleaning" him up.

Interpretations of these behaviours, which were made in simple terms, for example by attempting to draw the patient's attention to the acting out of his feelings of hopelessness, impotence, and futility, were met with short and didactic acknowledgements, grunts that were then further diluted by laconic witticisms. The panoply of manic defences that were deployed seemed impenetrable. My own feelings of therapeutic impotence, futility, and hopelessness appeared to suggest an identification with the projections of the patient and I became concerned that at times I could be drawn to enact my aggression towards Tom in various subtle, and sometimes not so subtle, ways. For instance in speaking to him in a rather stern and condescending manner and by failing to, at times, pay the level of attention to the fuller range of his communications, that one would expect in psychotherapeutic work.

My attention was drawn to a triadic relationship with the mother; and I considered that I had used her to, in a sense, *take revenge* on Tom after particularly trying sessions. She accompanied him to every session and remained in the waiting area. When I saw her it was typically after the session, Tom having excused himself to go to the lavatory, possibly communicating his need to further expel dangerous and threatening internal objects. After a time, I was faced with a therapeutic conundrum. Should I continue to meet the mother to gain more accurate information about what was going on outside the sessions, with the attendant risks of stimulating further acting out by the patient and by me (not to mention the mother), or should I restrict my contact to the patient only? After consideration, and with the benefit of supervision, I decided on the latter course.

Looking backwards, I believe that this situation marked a turning point in the case. Unarticulated clinically, and requiring the second opinion of a senior colleague, I was able to discern a tightening impasse in which I had felt myself forced through numbingly repetitive immersion with Tom towards the aliveness of human contact. Momentarily, this was stolen in the waiting room, with Tom's mother.

However, Tom was present too: and, busying himself in the toilet, without speaking, was also active in this somewhat illicit pairing. Adaptively, the shift of my attention away from Tom in this moment also signalled a fissure in my capacity to contain what he had brought earlier to session; and, turning from this activity to focus yet again on Tom alone seemed to resound within him as if I had participated with him in his evasion of therapy—my own facilitation of a dyadic psychic retreat within our work; and now again, faced him alone. Tom remained unfocused but increasingly livid.

Over the next three months, there was a change in the rhythm and tempo of the sessions. New verbal material emerged in which splitting more obviously appeared. Money became a central concern for Tom and he would launch into bitter tirades against "... filthy-rich doctors and lawyers, petrol companies, and phone companies." The prices in shops were considered "... extortionate" and he complained ceaselessly about the state of the economy. I noted the obvious transference dynamics implied by his reference to "... filthy-rich doctors ..." and in fact he made a number of references, all in a jovial manner, that further highlighted this evolving dynamic in his relationship with me. However, in reality the shift felt like a relief—at last in contradistinction to the initial phase of fused static impasse: there seemed to be movement intrapsychically and material that seemed to offer potential for greater exploration, construction, and, ultimately, interpretation. These fine grain movements, across the PS $\leftrightarrow$ d (D) continuum, had evolved; but slowly, over several months.

Tom also developed, around this time, a compulsive pattern of buying mobile phones, often not being able to keep up payments on them; and also forgetting where he had actually purchased them. This resulted in a barrage of calls from mobile phone companies, either demanding outstanding payments, or offering to sell him the latest model of their phone. I was struck by the externalisation of the fragmented, and deeply split, inner world. The phone companies' credit controllers representing persecutory internal objects on the one hand, and the "... silver-tongued sales people" offering immediate access to the idealised object on the other. Here too, I regarded such references as indicative of his ambivalent attitude to treatment. I could be perceived as the mean credit controller at times (restricting his access to alcohol) whilst at other times I was the silver-tongued salesman offering slick and ready interpretations that appeared seductive. More straightforwardly, the choice of obsessional object, mobile phones, appeared to indicate both movement and a desire to communicate, however obliquely at times.

When Tom achieved, over several months of therapeutic work, a longer period of abstinence from alcohol, consolidated his move to fuller independent living through supported housing, and appeared receptive to trial interpretations which linked past experience with both contemporary events and the relationship in the transference/countertransference, the decision was made to proceed to insight-oriented therapy. It was decided that a central focus should be on Tom's apparent repetition in adulthood of earlier childhood conflicts—namely, self-isolation as a defence against dependency on others and on fears of separation anxiety. In part, these anxieties appeared to be stirred by a genuine experience of claustrophobic engulfment by his primary objects that alternated with sudden abandonment, when he would be left to "amuse himself".

One could speculate about the deeper unconscious impulses that influenced dangerous self-injurious behaviours, including the severe head trauma, suffered after a fall while intoxicated. In essence, these had resulted in Tom becoming once again dependent on his parents, particularly his mother. However, such dependency and need produced feelings of uncontrollable rage, often resulting in drinking binges, when Tom felt claustrophobically engulfed and trapped, particularly within the orbit of the maternal object.

The final phase of treatment involved linkage of recent and current behaviours to underlying core conflictual experiences engendered in relation to alternating fears of engulfment and separation/abandonment. An enactment that occurred three weeks before the planned ending of treatment was interpreted and situated accordingly. Tom missed a session, following a drinking binge with a neighbour, and subsequently having fallen asleep in the neighbour's house. Despite this brief lapse to drinking it was felt by all involved in this case, including Tom, that real progress had been made over the months from stabilisation and consolidation of gains to insight-oriented therapy.

The complexity of the cases here discussed, along with the primitive and trenchant defences and resistances, deployed in order to eliminate the possibility of thinking and so to evade emotions, deserve further exploration and illumination in the context of the challenges faced by both patient and therapist, in the therapeutic encounter. In order to do so, we now turn to a consideration of those factors that contribute to the development of capacities to symbolise experience and the implications when these capacities are limited or break down.

CHAPTER THREE

Symbol formation and movement within d

It is our contention that movements within d significantly contribute to and enable symbolisation proper to develop from the original "matrix of the mind"; and that the development of these symbolising processes is intimately linked to the dawning awareness, initially at a sensory-psychological level, of form in relation to the self, its objects, and the spaces that exist between them. This awareness of form has, we contend, a trajectory based on initial representations of the bodily self, a sense of fusion with the object and separation from it; and, ultimately, representation of the self and its objects as separate entities available for both reflective and anticipatory thought, within a facilitative space-time system. The discrete and idiosyncratic movements, or oscillations, that we mark as d phenomena may be thought of as elemental processes (Bion, 1963; Waelder, 1951)—akin to quanta, or quantum particles at the mental level, fundamental to both individuation and later symbolic representation of that which is external to the self.

The model that we propose may be viewed as a natural extension of the impressive body of work carried out on symbolisation, and the development of symbolising capacities, by a range of psychoanalytic practitioners, beginning with Freud and Breuer (1895d). In this tradition, further elaboration and application of theory in the clinical setting have been recognised by Freud (1900a, 1911c), Jones (1916a, 1916b), M. Klein (1923, 1930), Segal (1957, 1979), Bion (1963), Money-Kyrle (1968), and more recently by Ogden (1992). Those working in the cross-pollinating fields of both attachment studies and psychoanalysis (Bateman & Fonagy, 2006; Fonagy, 2001; Nahum, 2002) have also considerably added to our understanding of the internalisation of symbolising capacities among infants.

Psychodynamics and symbolism: early conceptual developments

Freud's early references to symbolism, in both "A Project for a Scientific Psychology" (1950a), which dates from 1895, and with Joseph Breuer in *Studies on Hysteria* (1895d), initially contrasts normal symbol formation with hysterical symbol formation; and then in the *Studies*, more fully develops the notion of associative determinants of symptoms and their symbolic representation (see particularly the cases of Anna O and Fraulein Elisabeth von R).

Throughout his life, as he meticulously revised the four editions of *Die Traumdeutung* (1900a), Freud stressed the importance of dream symbols and their translation: so much so, that the entirely new section of the dream book added to the fourth edition is devoted to an exploration of symbolic representation (pp. 350–404).

The universality of fixed meaning within symbols across a range of cultures and for a diverse group of individuals is stressed by Freud; and it echoes ideas which also influenced Jung's description of the archetypes. Freud suggests, in the *Introductory Lectures on Psycho-Analysis* (1916–1917), that in the interpretation of the patient's use of symbolic expression, the analyst should be mindful not only of the dreamer's associative links to symbols but also of the fixed meaning of symbols, deriving in the main from his theory of phylogenetic transmission through inheritance. These latter, he contends, are not a product of personal creation by the dreamer.

Ernest Jones's contributions on symbolism, originally published in 1916 though expanded and reissued in 1948, stress both the primitive and defensive nature of symbolisation, in contrast to his more elevated view of sublimation. Jones observes:

> Symbolism thus appears as the unconscious precipitate of primitive means of adaptation to reality that have become superfluous

> or useless, a sort of lumber room of civilisation to which the adult readily feels in states of reduced or deficient capacity for adaptation to reality, in order to regain his old, long-forgotten playthings of childhood. (1916b, p. 109)

Even at this distance across the century one can see, in rough outline within Jones's limited view of evolving symbolising capacities, the movement in differentiation between the self, its object, and the environment. It was, however, Klein and her followers who were to embellish and to develop psychodynamic approaches related to symbolisation and its development, as a series of intricate mental processes based on the relationship between the self and its earliest objects. For instance, challenging Jones and eschewing a strict distinction between symbolisation and sublimation, Klein sees the two processes to be intimately related. Beginning from a position that stressed bodily sensations to be the fundamental constituents of unconscious phantasy, in ongoing relationships with objects, enabled Klein (1923, 1930) to situate the beginnings of symbolisation within the crucible that is the infant's psyche, during the earliest stages of life.

Within Klein's (1929, 1930, 1931) recognitions during this early period of her work is a potentially rich though subsequently underdeveloped **d** concept, that we see as important in furthering our understanding of symbolising capacities and their developmental constituent elements. We refer to Klein's notion of the *epistemophilic instinct*, or the wish to know. The richness of the concept lies in the duality suggested by the child's strivings towards knowing; and we further suggest that this dual nature of the child's epistemophilic instinct, though not always fully recognised by subsequent writers, has significantly influenced those contributions offered by them (Bion, 1962b; Money-Kyrle, 1965; Ogden, 1992; Segal, 1957).

Klein's critical illustration of this epistemophilic **d** in the evolutionary development of psychoanalytic ideas 1) begins with an elaboration of Freud's idea of the desire to know as a partial sexual drive anecdotally described within the domain of infantile sexuality (1905a); and 2) elevates or elaborates this concept as useful within her own (and future) psychodynamic elaboration. In this move, she illustrates the shift observed by Bergmann along the continuum of "extenders, modifiers, and heretics" within the advancing lines of psychodynamic thinking (1999, p. 200). In this sense, **d** represents a non-heretical outcome of acceptable vernacular analytic expression, and the recognition, through a rough consensus of the psychoanalytic movement at a given moment in historical time, of a legitimate, verbalised and verbalisable analytic "form".

Returning to the particulars of Klein's epistemophilic instinct, a paradox is revealed. The instinct, while being exploratory and necessary, is also driven at times by the insatiable need to know, which inevitably becomes aggressive and potentially destructive of the object and, in tandem, the self. Thus, one might say, curiosity really does kill the cat! Klein's graphic description of the infant's phantasies of getting inside the maternal body and robbing it of its rich contents, including of father's penis, is often presented without a fundamental qualification—it is the child's greedily burning desire to know what is happening inside the mother and to find the objects of his phantasy that propels and fuels the cauldron of inner wishes and phantasies which predominate during the paranoid-schizoid stage.

However, the therapist's verbalisation of such conceptual recognition may overwhelm the patient who is incapable of assimilating its linguistic plausibility. That is, articulation of such a dynamic might become reduced to just so many intrusive, destructive words rather than as a prompt for the patient's own thinking capacities, experienced by the patient as an aggressive and potentially intrusive counter-attack, emanating from the therapist not only as transference object but also experienced as an intrusive external action in real time.

That the child's epistemophilic drive acts as a two-edged sword may enable us to better understand the oscillatory nature of movements within the depressive position, which we will return to and expand upon shortly. It is worth noting here that we consider the relative fusion and de-fusion of the exploratory wish to know with and from aggressively imbued destructive phantasies to be a vital function in the formation and proliferation of the primary elements which constitute symbolising capacities—akin to the quantum particles, mentioned in the introduction to this chapter. Disturbances in the processes of fusion and de-fusion with the object ultimately impede and/or erode symbolising capacities; and such disturbances may include defensive misrecognition of the therapist's proffered intuitive interpretations. Gaps therefore present themselves within the fabric of the therapeutic relationship, with vital terms in the patient's vocabulary of thought either not formed or expunged from awareness, but which may be palpated in direct clinical experience by the therapist.

Mid-twentieth-century developments and beyond

Hanna Segal's classic paper, "Notes on Symbol Formation", was originally published in 1957, though the author added an important postscript to the work later, in 1979. Drawing heavily on Klein's (1946) concept of projective identification, along with her own psychoanalytic work with psychotic patients, Segal makes a vital distinction between what she terms symbolic equation and the symbol proper. In the former, symbolic equation, she considers *the symbol-substitute to be the original object*. The symbol proper, conversely, *actually represents the object*.

Segal contends that the symbolic equation is used to evade or deny the absence of the ideal object, or in contradistinction, to control a persecuting object. True representation of the object, through internalisation of the symbol proper, develops as capacities for tolerating guilt, loss, separation from the object, and ambivalence towards the object are more fully integrated, when depressive feelings predominate. Segal makes a salient point, and one familiar to all practising analysts, when she observes:

> Symbols are needed not only in communication with the external world, but also in internal communication. Indeed, it could be asked what is meant when we speak of people being in touch with their unconscious? It is not that they have consciously primitive phantasies, like those which become evident in their analyses, but merely that they have some awareness of their own impulses and feelings. (1957, pp. 57–58)

This observation goes to the heart of Segal's later emendation to her paper, offered in the postscript that appeared some twenty-two years after initial publication. The revision concerns Bion's influence on Segal, in light of his very significant contributions in the late 1950s and early 1960s. These contributions concern: the nature of the psychotic and non-psychotic aspects of the mind; the emergence and development of thinking; and, particularly, Bion's model of the container/contained. Segal takes up Bion's model of the container/contained and develops her thinking on symbolisation accordingly. Recognising that the infant deals with discomfort and anxiety by projecting these into the mother, Segal also notes the role of the mother in either being able or unable to contain and modulate such feelings. Here, she retraces Bion's outline of the process, offered at greater length in his works on thinking (1962a) and learning from experience (1962b). The good mother, capable of containing and modifying the child's projections, and of transforming them through her reverie and thus imbuing them with meaning, is in turn introjected as the prototype of an internal containing object. Crucially, Segal points out, through this process the internalised container provides the foundations for a mental space where Bion's alpha function may more permanently develop and operate. Elegantly, Segal states:

> Another way of looking at it would be that it is in this container, in which alpha function can occur, that primary processes begin to be elaborated into secondary ones. The failure of the container and alpha functioning results in the inability to perform the dreamwork and, therefore, the appearance of psychotic, including concrete, dreams. ("The Function of Dreams", reprinted in Segal, 1986, p. 93)

Developing Bion's container/contained model also assisted Segal in describing and outlining her thoughts on symbolisation, verbalisation, and language. In this, we detect a conceptual bridge between what is essentially unconscious and internal to the self, and those external processes that more obviously act upon and influence the developing symbolising capacities of the child. Speech, for instance, has to be learned. The inchoate sounds of the infant are the raw materials from which language acquisition can proceed, though only in the presence of another who can take up sounds, bind them, and thus give them meaning. The object, in this case, more directly as Segal points out, contains, encompasses, and expresses meaning, and in so doing provides a container that shapes the infant's primitive attempts at verbalisation.

Containment of this order then assists the developing infant, by integrating processes at the psycho-physical level that not only promote awareness of meaning, but that also lay the foundations for its generation. Conversely, when there is a lack of adequate containment, such awareness both of intrapsychic and interpsychic meaning, that facilitates mentalization (Bateman & Fonagy, 2006) and the generation of meaning, appears to be forestalled. However, the complexity of interactions that foment both awareness of meaning and the generation of meaning should not be underestimated.

In his seminal and groundbreaking paper *Cognitive Development*, Roger Money-Kyrle (1968) outlines intricate processes that underscore conceptual development, and notes three key stages in the evolving capacity to both symbolise and cognise experience. Preliminary to this understanding is Money-Kyrle's linkage of two other thinkers' ideas. First, Money-Kyrle draws upon Bion's notion (1962a, 1963) of an "innate preconception mating with a realisation to form a conception". Next, he links Bion's idea with an idea he attributes to Moritz Schlick, the founding father of logical positivism. Money-Kyrle emphasises Schlick's recognition that the acquisition of knowledge depends: 1) upon awareness of sensory-emotional experience, but more crucially, 2) upon the *recognition* of what that sensory-emotional experience is. Here, Bion's model varies from Schlick's in that Bion posits preconceptions he considers to be innate.

Building upon this conceptual foundation, Money-Kyrle describes a first phase in the infant's life in which he operates at the level of concrete representation, akin to Segal's stage of symbolic equation. Following Bion, he notes a subsequent stage of ideographic representation, as is found in dreams. Lastly, he denotes the stage of conscious, mainly verbal thought. This sequence approximately tracks Rapaport's (1950) distinction between ideation and thinking with the intermediating level corresponding to hallucinatory gratification.

Money-Kyrle stresses that this rather compressed list of developmental phases is meant to convey a progression, not so much in sophistication, as in degrees of consciousness. He further asserts that these degrees of consciousness are only possible if recognition, the predominant quality of consciousness and cognition, has the opportunity to evolve phase to phase across the three domains, in an appropriate and timely sequence. He writes,

> I am suggesting that the development of … thought normally goes through three stages: concrete identification, unconscious ideographic identification, conscious, predominantly verbal representation. If the last stage is reached as it were theoretically, without going through the other two, the resulting concept would seem to be unserviceable for emotional development. (1968, p. 423)

What Money-Kyrle is alive to, and intimately aware of, is that the evolution of symbolising capacities depends on the unfolding of processes that are appropriate to the child's capacity to move through the stages, as he has described them. Delay or impediment of such movement in development may be extremely damaging for the child; similarly, development cannot be hurried or rushed in a way that is beyond the child's capacity, in terms of both learning from experience and, in addition, to more fully integrate such experience. In parallel, the same can be said of the therapeutic work undertaken between the analyst and the patient, given the allowance for, and development of, an appropriate space and time frame in which such work may evolve. This movement through moments of distortion, misrecognition, and clarification was anticipated forty years earlier by T. V. Moore in his concept of parataxic distortion within the therapeutic encounter. Moore expands the originally idiosyncratic linguistic patterns discerned by George Herbert Mead (themselves based in Wundtian psychology) into the full range of expressive emotional actions discerned within psychotherapy (Mead, 1904; Moore, 1921).

Interestingly and importantly, on this note, Money-Kyrle stresses that in addition to developing the capacity to form and contain a number of basic concepts upon which a dawning awareness of the "facts of life" may be based, the infant must also be able to arrange these inchoate elements of experience within a durable and consistent space-time system. He takes as the prototype for this, the initial introjection of the object, in concretised form, without a degree of differentiation between the self and its object. Succinctly, Money-Kyrle describes such a process of concretely containing the lost object as a precursor to the emergence of the unconscious ideograph, and finally its conscious verbal representation. Where Money-Kyrle struggles (and has the humility to admit so in his paper) is in trying to more accurately account for the elements which are implicit in and to a degree become separated out, as the division between concrete pre-representational thought in terms of internal objects and the stage of representational thought evolves.

We will return to this problem of division presently, in order to more fully illustrate our understanding of the processes involved, in relation to discrete and idiosyncratic movements within d, while in addition, contextualising these with reference to clinical casework. However, before doing so, we turn to Thomas Ogden's (1992) work on what he terms "the primitive edge of experience", with particular reference to his description of "the autistic-contiguous mode", and ways in which this concept may assist in furthering our understanding of symbolisation and the development of symbolising capacities.

Ogden, introducing this important and innovative work, begins with a relatively simple observation. He recognises a core aspiration in the psychotherapeutic endeavour, from the analyst's perspective at least. This involves an attempt to assist patients in achieving freedom from those forms of conscious and unconscious aspects of organised experience that entrap and restrict them in terms of further development. In order to create a setting and experience between analyst and analysand which may permit such growth and development, he succinctly and adroitly states that the analytic setting, interaction, and discourse must act as containers for the experience of, at times, confusion and not knowing.

Acknowledging his debt to the British object relations school, and in particular to Klein, Winnicott, and Bion, he sets out to describe a "primitive edge of experience", building on the significant contributions made theoretically and clinically by those analysts interested in both earliest infantile stages and severe early disturbances of psychological functioning (Bick, 1968; Meltzer, 1975; Tustin, 1972). Echoing, in particular, Esther Bick's (1968) work on the skin as the formative ego boundary, Ogden cogently defines his concept of the autistic-contiguous mode of development, as follows:

> The autistic-contiguous position is understood as a sensory-dominated, pre-symbolic area of experience in which the most primitive form of meaning is generated on the basis of the organization of sensory impressions, particularly at the skin surface. A unique form of anxiety arises in this psychological realm: terror over the prospect that the boundaries of one's sensory surface might be dissolved, with a resultant feeling of falling, leaking, dropping, into an endless and shapeless space. (1992, p. 4)

Ogden portrays this autistic-contiguous mode of experience as intimately related to the paranoid-schizoid and depressive positions, as described and applied clinically by Klein (1935, 1946). Each mode, he contends, "... creates, preserves and negates the other," and further "... is the negating context for the other" (Ogden, 1992, p. 4). In essence Ogden asserts that human experience, including the generation of meaning, is dependent upon the dialectical interplay between the three modes of being and experience. To apply the familiar Bionian (1963) algorithm one might denote, initially at least, the process thus: AC ↔ PS ↔ D. More accurately however, given the intersecting poles of experience and their generative and degenerative qualities, and grafting Ogden's concept onto Bion's original model, diagrammatically the dialectical interplay may be represented thus:

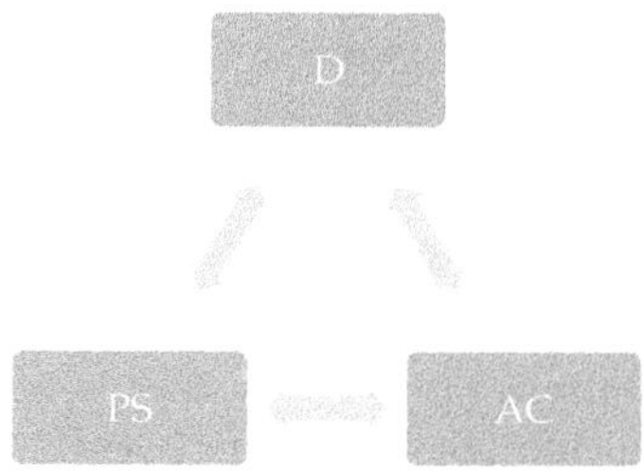

The model also elegantly underscores Ogden's conceptual depiction of psychopathology and its emergence. He sees psychopathological phenomena and resultant mental states as directly arising in relation to the collapse of the dialectic between one and the other modes of "generating experience". Such collapse into the autistic-contiguous mode may result in a restriction of growth, with the individual horribly trapped in an asymbolic and tyrannising series of bodily sensations. Or, in the paranoid-schizoid mode, entrapment may involve internal objects interlocked in battles dominated by concretised omnipotence. Finally, entrapment at the depressive level may relate to a self isolated from the genuine aliveness of experience.

Evidence for restriction in the capacity to both internalise symbolising abilities and subsequently to live in such a way that life appears hollow and devoid of meaningful emotional contact with others is frequently found in our daily psychotherapeutic work. The following two clinical cases are, we hope, illustrative types of presentation one may encounter in practice.

Clinical case 1: Mr M

The first clinical vignette is narrated across two years of three times weekly psychotherapy. Mr M, while admittedly "chained" within a soul-destroying marriage of many years, was nevertheless "crushed" when he discovered his wife's infidelity and subsequent petition for divorce. The progressive and painful work within therapy would link early childhood attachment, still active, to a psychically unavailable and often critical "dead mother" (Kohon, 1999), whose active presence continued to colour Mr M's relation to his several children, his deadened relation to work, and his frequent somatic complaints concerning heart attack and potential for stroke, though according to his medical report, his physical condition remained robust. Frequent panic attacks and immobilising anxiety caused him worry that he would lose his academic livelihood; and he "secretly" confided that since receiving the notice of divorce, he had lost the capacity to retain written information. He was devastated at no longer being able to read; and guilty that he continued as if he were "busking", getting by through consciously reminding himself that he should "act the competent and dutiful" father he believed himself to be. Mr M seethed at the idea that his dedication to duty in his role as husband had not secured him his wife's love; yet was unable to link this inability with his actively living enmeshed animosity for his "dead mother", herself physically dead for many years.

Therapy proceeded through Mr M's enduring attacks upon the therapist. Occasional interpretation, translating Mr M's expressions into therapeutic attempts at approximations of d were frequently scoffed at; but Mr M continued to attend sessions regularly for two years. Throughout, he complained that this work could not compare to earlier, if failed therapies; yet could not account for the "glue" which seemed to bind him within the therapy, itself experienced as a hateful exercise, not unlike his endurance of marriage.

Withstanding the withering attacks over the years was paired with the therapist's recognition of his own learning within this work relative to: psychotic regression; the inchoate violence of Mr M's emotional world, despite his protestations that he did not feel angry; the active destruction of thought linkages; and the conceptual form of the "dead mother", all within a negative form requiring the therapist's intuitive leaps. These however, were themselves sharply recognised and demeaned, as Mr M commented, "One of the things I hate about your smug judgements is that you listen for long periods of time and then come to some conclusion which I always tire of because it is inevitably incorrect."

By the time of Mr M's trenchant attack on the central dynamic of containment and reflection, eventuating in attempts at d together with his rejection of any possible transferential relationship, the sense of the work from the therapist's side was of a destructively dependent fusion, a battle to joint oblivion, such as was represented in Mr M's depiction of his marriage, his relation to children who hated him, to work, and ultimately to his internalised dead mother. He was not angry; rather, he was hollowed out, a male Medusa-head radiating enormous constraint under a blank funereal stare.

Working backward over time to this impasse, patient and therapist seemed to pass from Mr M's telling of his narrative, to the automatic and formulaic death-grip of a lifeless therapy session. His expressions of life accomplishments took on the look of the mimetic (Sweet, 2013) in that they lacked life, imitating earlier templates as examples of what Mr M could copy; but like his temporary loss of the capacity to read, affording no joy or depth in ownership as accomplishment or skill. He continued to "fake it", to "busk", at a conscious and anxious level, betraying the more fundamental mimicry that underlay his adaptation to living.

Finally then, his therapeutic regression led to the session-by-session enactment of a malignant fusion; its only aliveness was evidenced in his periodically sadistic wish to "unsettle" the therapist, who, inured to the brutalisation, felt only sadness and a clinging onto life in dull obedience to the Winnicottian notion of the therapist's survival of the patient.

Conceptually, within this two year analytic treatment, patient and therapist had worked backward from attempts to bridge Mr M's "black hole"—themselves permitting the patient's gleeless attack on the therapist's intuitive interpretation while 1) accurately observing what the therapist was "doing" over time and 2) at the same time, denigrating it as inconsequential—and 3) moving towards the revelation of a life lived both as automatic and in mimicry, except for the actively vibrant insistence on a relationship to the other of assured mutual destruction, a malignant battle throughout life with all others, equivalent to his mother's shiva-like malignancy. The final act of analysis would be to offer the possibility of considering the fantasy (and enactment) of destructive fusion as yet another d with the possibility of its aliveness as potentially useful in shifting the regression to the often-desired quiescence of death. It would be for Mr M to recognise such utility or not.

Clinical case 2: Mr G

Mr G arrived for an appointment during the second year of weekly individual psychoanalytic psychotherapy and seated himself anxiously, ensuring that his gaze remained fixed upon me until I too had sat down. Following this he coughed and sneezed two or three times, took his glasses off and replaced them several times and then concluded with a pronounced belch of flatulence and a loud hollow gargle from his stomach. This visual and sonic concerto, which apparently involved various forms of tension and release, had become familiar to us, over many months, as one way in which Mr G seemed to attempt to control minutely fragmented and split-up thoughts. He appeared to attempt to bring these proto-thoughts together and try to arrange them into a coherent pattern which gave the impression of semblance and sequence.

His apparent experience of his therapist, at such times, as an intrusive or invasive object (Skogstad, 2013; Williams, 2010), meant that upon seeing the therapist again after a week's separation he most immediately took the therapist into himself—through his eyes, mouth, and nose—and then automatically and unconsciously attempted to evacuate the split-up anxiety-provoking object(s). Momentarily, it appeared, as the therapist was to come to suspect during the course of therapy, that the therapist had been converted into wind to be cleared through the throat, the nose, or as flatus in the stomach—and as sight to be denied by the removal of the glasses as a visual aid.

A few moments of relative silence passed during which the therapist noticed a rather bashful smirk appear on Mr G's face. It appeared he might have privileged access to important information denied to the therapist. It seemed that the expulsion of broken up parts of his mind, merged with aspects of the intrusive object at the bodily level, had provided at least temporary relief. There was an attempt to convey this to him by commenting that he seemed relieved. This observation led to something of a change in his demeanour: the smirk gave way to a more thoughtful, considered, and somewhat concerned look. One might suggest, in retrospect and with the benefit of hindsight, that pointing to the ways in which he attempted to relieve himself of anxiety, however obliquely, brought a range of previously concealed and narcissistically oriented behaviours into sharper focus.

There followed another brief period of silence, which lasted perhaps a minute and a half to two minutes. Then there was a sideways movement in the chair and a pronounced twitch above the left eye, at the temple. Crucially, these bodily communications acted as a prelude to verbalisation, reminiscent of the demands made on the infant at the oral, olfactory, and pulmonary levels in the transition from the liquid environment in-utero to a post-natal gaseous one (Bion, 1994). Above all, the dominant need appeared to involve the expulsion of painful and irritating sensations by which Mr G seemed to be claustrophobically assailed. The sense of this in the countertransference was of experiencing a mild degree of irritation, in essence feeling under attack from a range of bodily functions and gestures and not knowing how these would unfold on a given day or for how long they may continue.

Finally, when he spoke, there was a return to a familiar subject. One that had dominated the verbal material from the very first session, almost two years previously. "I don't like grannies," he said. And then he further offered: "I don't like their white hair." He continued: "I don't like black cars and there were a lot of them around in the city today when I was coming here." The therapist reflected with Mr G on his dislike of both white things and black things and said that he seemed somewhat relieved to have got rid of these images from his mind and further added that he seemed to feel an urgent need to get rid of these images from his mind. He replied: "That's right." The sense was that though the therapist had offered an interpretation of sorts, it had perhaps failed to capture the essence of Mr G's communication. The interpretation seemed, on reflection, to be something of an analytic cliché which felt rather tired, heavy, and predictable. Mr G's response seemed to echo this sense.

Mr G then yawned loudly, in a rather exaggerated manner. Following this he relaxed back in the armchair as if he might drift off into a snooze. Shortly afterwards he became animated once more and began to twitch and move about in an agitated fashion. He then said: "The T ….. s [name of family neighbours during his childhood] used to call me names and I got mad about it." The therapist now more directly interpreted his wish to sleep so that he could eliminate the T ….. s from his mind as he felt tortured by them. A link was also made to the idea that he felt he might get mad with the therapist and so he wished to fall asleep. It might be added that perhaps what was missed here was propensity to anger and frustration that had been stirred in Mr G by the therapist's rather hackneyed interpretation, and the sense in which it may well have been more productive to have waited before offering any form of interpretation at that juncture.

The short and brusque verbal statements from Mr G appeared to indicate his sense of this. The therapist had learned from monitoring his cognitive and emotional reactions that any attempt to press for further detail or organisation of such statements was futile. In point of fact, such pressings simply aggravated Mr G and he would tend to withdraw into a silent and unreachable psychic retreat (Steiner, 1993), generally thickly overlaid with psychosomatic elements, reminiscent of Ogden's description of life in the autistic-contiguous mode. It also became apparent that the enactments outside the therapeutic hours, such as verbal outbursts towards family members or strangers and his greedy smoking, drinking, and eating, represented substitutive attempts to anaesthetise the fragile self against fears of annihilative breakdown and further disintegration, as even quite primitive symbolising capacities began to give way.

At such times, it appeared that the accretion of concretised and non-metabolised thoughts, or beta elements to use Bion's term, required urgent and insistent action, either by projective or introjective means. Malignant and persecutory intrapsychic bizarre objects could thus be identified with a range of apparently innocuous objects—from white-haired grannies to black cars—facilitating intensive projective identification. In the absence of either a reliable internal or external container there appeared to be an urgent and predominant need to resort to such projective identification, as the fragile self felt assailed and threatened by annihilation. On the other hand, a range of substances could be binged on—alcohol, cigarettes, or junk food—to provide a temporary emotional balm not unlike a second skin, through introjective identification. However, such behaviours also reinforced powerful splitting mechanisms, with these substances both idealised for their intoxicating effects, then later experienced as persecutory when the self was felt to be both psychologically fragile and physically ill, post bingeing. In this way, a complex range of alexithymic behaviours were deployed defensively in the form of direct action and/or somatisation and scotomisation (Segal, 1957).

It had also become apparent that between the poles of immediate action, to discharge proto-thoughts, or their bodily conversion through somatisation in the form described at the beginning of the session above, there existed an ominous third alternative course, namely destruction of the self and the internal persecutory objects, by recourse to suicide. Mr G's conscious fantasies in this respect involved obsessive ruminations involving throwing himself off high bridges, and he had gone as far as looking for suitable structures from which he could jump. The question of seeking hospitalisation for Mr G at this stage in his treatment naturally arose in the therapist's mind. However, at the same time, the therapist was conscious of identifying with the patient's sense of uncontainable anxiety and seeking a "magically" transformative and immediate therapeutic/medical solution, by recourse to a referral for inpatient treatment.

Such a reaction on the therapist's behalf could be read as a corollary to Mr G's wish to expel intense latent anxiety, by jumping to his death from a high bridge: thus at one level, satisfying the unconscious desire to silence a range of persecutory and unintegrated internal objects. Experience tends to show the malign and aggravating influence of these unintegrated internal persecutors, particularly when there is a period of relaxed quiescence after the decision to take one's life has definitely been made. One is reminded of the power exerted by an ego destructive super-ego (Bion, 1962a, 1962b; O'Shaughnessy, 1999), internalised on the basis of dissociative identifications rather than projective identifications that have been helpfully modified by their sojourn in the object before being re-introjected.

The therapist came increasingly to view these dissociated internal objects as proto-typical superego lacunae. The lack of a more fully integrated superego structure suggested again both an absence of an internalised containing object and an inability, at this stage, to contemplate higher-level feelings of mourning and guilt in relation to these damaged primary objects.

It might also be suggested that in work with patients evidencing such paucity of psychological integration, the lack of temporal awareness with regard to the acceptance of time and transience means that death neither signifies limit nor finality. Rather death or deadliness may evoke, unconsciously, the possibility of transition, rejuvenation, rebirth, or more generally, new beginnings for the beleaguered self. In this sense death, and deadly behaviours, take on an addictive quality (Joseph, 1982) precisely because in phantasy they offer relief from a range of persecutory internal objects and consequently the narcissistic inflation of a beleaguered self, which anticipates through such triumph confirmation of its omniscient and omnipotent superiority.

Such phantasies may be overwhelmingly seductive in light of a self that is felt to be agonisingly imprisoned within the maternal object, or in Meltzer's (1992) terms, within the claustrum. The dominant themes expressed by these suicidal patients, whether directly or indirectly, tend to involve attempts to relieve a sense of breathless claustrophobia based on a suffocating engulfment, or entrapment, by and within the maternal object. Psychotherapists working with acutely suicidal and/or violent patients invariably experience, at times, very intense and pervasive thoughts and emotions, infused by projective and counter-projective processes. In Mr G's case what appeared most challenging, at times, was the therapist's capacity to retain thinking in a measured and creative way, rather than resorting to "technical enactments", largely to assuage both conscious and, more perniciously, unconscious anxieties stirred in the therapist.

One might go further however and contend that being with patients like Mr M and Mr G, who are developmentally arrested at a pre-symbolic and prelinguistic level, reminds one, at times, of being in a rather two-dimensional dream space that appears to be ego-destructive, claustrophobic, and agonisingly impinging. The very difficulties that such a shared space present for the analyst, in terms of linking thoughts and thus preserving a thinking capacity, alerted Bion to the fundamental attacks on linking (1959) that dominate and underscore psychotic thinking and functioning.

Conclusion and summary

We have emphasised that movements within d significantly contribute to and enable symbolisation proper to develop and we have linked such movement to the dawning and inchoate awareness, initially at a sensory-psychological level, of recognisable form. The internalisation of capacities to experience form is also considered to be co-constructive of and only possible within a facilitative space-time system. To reiterate what we observed in the introduction to this chapter: the discrete and idiosyncratic movements, or oscillations, that we are marking as d phenomena may be thought of as elemental processes (Bion, 1963; Waelder, 1951)—akin to quanta, or quantum particles at the mental level, fundamental to both individuation and later symbolic representation of that which is external to the self. The impressive body of work offered within the psychoanalytic tradition, from Breuer and Freud to Ogden, has deeply influenced the ideas presented here and may be viewed, we suggest, from such a perspective. We now turn to a consideration of the practicalities of recognising d elements and further understanding and mobilising them with patients, during the daily work of psychotherapy.

CHAPTER FOUR

On d*

So far, a compression of this book's serial chapters leads from: 1) the general recognition of clinical forms or concepts to 2) the specific recognitions of clinical forms within the realm of significant psychopathology; and to 3) the centrality of symbolisation within the daily practice of psychotherapy. Such compressed statements might also be taken conceptually, as **d** elements, themselves recognisable within a given clinician's cognitive-emotional matrix of clinical expression. The present chapter examines the intersubjective dyadic interaction at the heart of psychotherapeutic action and through its back-and-forth, the practical emergence of workable d structures. Conceptually, we anchor our discussion in W. R. Bion's articulation of Melanie Klein's recognitions of P/S and D, together with the dimension of time and the therapeutic action of that which is contained within therapeutic space, time, and event causality. In this sense, d structures operationalise Freud's desideratum regarding the therapeutic task, of "learning from

*Originally published in 2017 as "Psychic rigidity, therapeutic response and time: Black holes, white holes, 'D' and 'd'" by Ian Miller & Alistair Sweet in *International Forum of Psychoanalysis*, 26(2): 97–104, copyright © The International Federation of Psychoanalytic Societies, reprinted by permission of Taylor & Francis Ltd, http://www.tandfonline.com on behalf of The International Federation of Psychoanalytic Societies.

the patient something that I did not know and that he did not know himself" (1910a).

We note that what is new in our recognition and articulation of d, is its explicit notation and naming. Its derivation is from within Klein and Bion. And, from another worker's vertex, it is a vocalised arrival at what André Green (1975) terms a "ventilated space", transitory in meaning, and non-definitive, that allows the "presence" of absence necessary for the generation of reflective perspective. Here, the significant fact is in a convergence of particularised observations across the developmental history of our discipline, articulated in different conceptual tongues, but pointing towards a similar generality, consensualised or objectified as utilitarian, from within the clinical practice of multiple therapists.

We begin this chapter with an observation of an earlier convergence between multiple therapists across historical time. Robert Waelder's article, "The Structure of Paranoid Ideas", written in 1950, performs a responsive, elegant dance across time together with W. R. Bion's later psychoanalytic formulations on thinking (Bion, 1959, 1962a, 1992; Waelder, 1951). These two theorists are prominently linked by three significant landmarks in **d**.

The first convergence is in striving for what Waelder terms an "alphabet" and Bion terms "elements", that recognise and describe clinically empirical landmarks of psychoanalysis. This is the universe of landmarks encompassed by what we call recognitions in **d**, the clinical markers by which psychodynamic clinicians steer.

The second linkage is in the tension between what both Waelder and Bion term "learning from experience" against the obdurate attacks upon thinking represented by paranoid ideation. Here, the individuals engaged in therapy continuously fall from and reconstruct a precarious balance between the dread of anxious uncertainty and hopeful, if transient, clarities in new learning. Three decades earlier in psychoanalytic development, this process was indicated by Sandor Ferenczi and Otto Rank as "experiencing and living through" within the analytic situation (Ferenczi & Rank, 1923, p. 16).

The third linkage is in Waelder's and Bion's joint conviction that the contemporary field of psychoanalysis, both within the therapeutic dyad and in its application beyond the consultation room in observation of historical currents in the world, is characterised by the rigidity of primitive ideation in continuous conflict with the human struggle for clarification, understanding, and freedom within the larger psychological systems which determine human history. This recognition in **d** entails the humanistic conceptual range of psychoanalytic thinking in its imminent recognition of conflict within peoples' dynamic behaviours, with its effects upon themselves, others, and the external world. Looking beyond the clinical dyad to systems of thought, including the psychoanalytic system itself, Waelder writes:

> Any systems of thought which have profoundly influenced the course of history have been more or less akin to paranoid systems. One may even say that history, is, to a large extent, the outcome of two forces, viz, on the one hand the process of learning from experience, the struggle for a better adjustment to, or a better mastery of reality, both natural and man-made, and on the other hand the ever-continuing rise of paranoid structures. (1951, p. 167, fn. 3)

Given their joint attention to similar dimensions of rigid and primitive forms of thinking, it may seem paradoxical from our own, generalised perspectives in psychoanalytic history that these theorists/practitioners are located within different schools of metapsychological orientation. Waelder's location is within the American development of ego psychology and Bion's location is within the British post-Kleinian tradition. Yet, psychoanalytic literary proof suggests differently. Cross-germination of ideas across institutional splits in the historical development of psychoanalysis is incontrovertible. Against barriers to linked thinking, represented in the fiercely defensive, protectively exclusive positions of basic assumption group behaviour (King & Steiner, 1992; Tuckett et al., 2008), the evolution of psychoanalytic technique and theory nevertheless proceeds collaboratively through pluralistic reading, rereading, and amplification of comparative psychoanalytic expression, converging in discernibly new currents of conceptual development (see, for examples, Conci, 2009; Khan, 1963; Miller, 2015; Sandler & Dreher, 1996; Searles, 1965). Such concordances in the generation of a psychoanalytic "common sense" are to be noted and treasured against defensive and destructive attack. As Bion observes in passing, psychoanalytic common sense "is common only to some psycho-analysts who may be presumed to witness the same events and make the same deductions" (1992, p. 11). Indeed, it is exactly refusal to credit the plausibility of certain ideas while defensively barring the door against such plausibility that characterises paranoid expression.

Psychoanalytic history itself is unruly. It is fragmented into different scholastic traditions marked by fierce institutional splitting and emphasising the asynchronous development of multiple ideas, often tinged with the politics of institutional rather than conceptual development (Makari, 2008). Its world of potential influences upon clinical workers is often inexplicit, difficult to pin down in a clear linear manner. While typically, clinicians shelter among the determinants of their multiple schools, learning their traditions and conceptual markers, we display considerable anxiety in drawing outside the authorised lines in consideration of concepts, thinkers, and technique that differ from our own (Tuckett et al., 2008). Nevertheless, each clinician integrates her own clinical object in its evolution from within the day-to-day imperatives of clinical experience. We form individualised vernacular expressions of psychoanalysis (Miller, 2015) as a fusion of received discourse, direct clinical experience, and subjectively significant mentoring thinkers (often in the received form of published articles), in addition to the generally acknowledged triadic learning of personal analysis, supervision, and formal study. In so doing, we underline the significance of certain theorists, while remaining uncertain about others, less well known to us.

The present chapter begins in a convergence of mid-twentieth-century psychoanalytic thinking in relation to psychotic and non-psychotic states, centred in the parallel interest of Robert Waelder and W. R. Bion; and mediated for both, by Maurits Katan's studies in primitive ideation (Bion, 1992; Katan, 1949, 1950a, 1950b, 1954; Waelder, 1951). Waelder's integration both of Katan's and Tausk's reflections on psychotic process is hardly new within his writing. Twenty-six years earlier, his paper on the psychoses, subtitled "Their Mechanisms and Accessibility to Influence", was read before the Vienna Psychoanalytic Society. Waelder integrated Tausk's thinking in that presentation just as Freud has similarly referenced Tausk in "Mourning and Melancholia", published seven years earlier (Freud, 1917e; Waelder, 1924). Twelve years later, in remarks to a paper given by Joan Riviere, Waelder presented "The Problem of the Genesis of Psychic Conflict in Earliest Infancy" (1937) noting Katan's recent work and observing that:

> Something similar to everything that has been observed in psychosis occurs in normal life and in neurosis. The characteristic feature of psychosis, the irremediable disturbance of the function of reality testing, is still an enigma. It seems likely that we shall

> shut the door on the true explanation of psychotic phenomena if we try to account for them by assigning them to phases of normal development. (p. 452)

W. R. Bion is among the most popular and frequently cited theorists in contemporary psychoanalysis (Miller, 2015). His paper on the dynamics of thinking (1962a) presents his use of mathematical models that might today be called psychological algorithms. These concern internal arrivals at positions of fantasy and action modelled upon the dynamic structure of paranoid, schizoid, and depressive positions elaborated earlier by Melanie Klein (1946), in what is today the most frequently cited paper in psychoanalytic writing according to the statistics of the Psychoanalytic Electronic Publishing Archive (http://www.pep-web.org/). Bion observes the externalisation of these positions within the transitory activities experienced by patient and analyst in the therapeutic dyad. It is from the therapist's registration of such experiences, of paranoid (P), schizoid (S), and depressive (D) expressions, occurring at different moments of time within the course of therapy, that the therapist becomes able to formulate interpretation. The therapist's interpretive verbalisation refers to empirically shared moments in experience between patient and analyst, corresponding to the movement of the internal psychological algorithm intuited by Bion.

Bion's amplification of projective dynamics adds the dimension of time to consideration of psychotherapeutic engagement. The continuously iterative shuttle between paranoid/schizoid and depressive positions is seen also to yield temporary structures that require consideration within Bion's renowned calculus, PS ↔ D PS (n+1) ↔ D (n+1) (♀♂). Translated into words, this algorithm suggests a movement over time from a paranoid-schizoid moment to an achieved moment of the depressive position tinctured with paranoid-schizoid experience, itself transitioning over time to a depressive moment manifest in passive or active forms.

Bion amplifies Klein in demonstrating multiple points of temporal arrival at successive moments, suggested by his notations, (n) and (n+1). These are slow clarifications of paranoid-schizoid positions into persecutory moments of the depressive position before achieving the epochal depressive position. Later in this chapter, we address these quotidian moments of non-epochal arrival, designating them as lower-case d in contrast to the capital fonts of the Klein-Bion calculus.

Waelder's 1951 exploration of paranoid ideation leads to a clinical example provided by Victor Tausk (1934), which itself yields a surprising temporal dimension of recognition in what we term emboldened d (**d**) supported by Harry Stack Sullivan's then contemporary description of the clinical interview (1954). While Tausk's work and Sullivan's are not directly related except in their emergence within psychoanalysis at a given moment in its developing history, the similarity of these vernacular expressions demonstrates divergent workers' immersions in similar problems at similar times. Sometimes, as with Tausk and Sullivan, these suggest similar outlooks, the vernacular expression of a psychoanalytic zeitgeist, no matter how separate in physical location and psychoanalytic orientation. In the present example, the retrospective viewpoint of history allows us to recognise consolidations that could not have been perceived years before.

Following from these linkages between Waelder, Bion, Katan, Tausk, and Sullivan, the authors discern a clinical clue to the question put by Waelder: how does seemingly impregnable rigidity of thinking begin to clarify within the clinical dyad? Following Waelder (1924) we seek to discern the accessibility of such psychotic thought to therapeutic influence. We suggest that the path blazed by these early psychoanalysts leads to a clinical scaffolding or developing ideational matrix of therapeutically created d structures that address annihilative dread in therapy through reorientation and stabilisation of the therapeutic relationship along the dimension of time.

The following two sections, I and II, describe both the conceptual meeting points among psychoanalytic thinkers regarding primitive thought or emboldened d concepts and our present construction of these related concepts in the notation d.

Waelder, Katan, and Bion

The conceptual meeting point between Waelder and Bion is in their mutual recognition of Maurits Katan's clinical contributions to the study of psychosis (Bion, 1992; Katan, 1949, 1950a, 1950b, 1954; Waelder, 1951). Specifically, within Katan's linkage between clinical presentations of schizophrenia and his exegesis of Freud's thinking in the Schreber case, he focuses upon the therapeutically accessible matrix of "pre-psychotic" personality as well as upon recognition of personality's layers. The concept of multiple personality dimensions, today often associated with Bion's notion of simultaneous meaning at several levels of plausibility (Grotstein, 2009), are linked historically to the early psychoanalytic notion of symptom complexes, a Jungian contribution much in vogue during the early days of Bion's clinical training (Miller with Souter, 2013). Within the creative research of British psychoanalysis during the 1930s and 1940s, this notion of multiple sub-personalities was supplemented by the congruent relational construct of object relations, especially with Klein's fusion of her interest in the paranoid position with Fairbairn's research into schizoid phenomena (Sutherland, 1989). Within American psychoanalytic development, a similar contrast is recognisable in bound and autonomous aspects of ego functioning (Hartmann, 1939).

Katan similarly contemplates personality's divisions and fragmentations in contrasting patients' frank breaks in reality orientation to islands of "non-psychotic territory" within the same individual, towards which "the therapist attempts to increase the strength of the ego". When such attempts are successful, according to Katan,

> … the ego is able to surmount dangers which previously it was powerless to cope with. Because of this fact, energy which otherwise would reach the psychotic part may now remain within the more healthy part of the personality. (1954, p. 127)

Waelder illustrates this struggle between primitive thinking and reality through reference to psychoanalytic history. He rereads Victor Tausk's 1934 posthumous publication of "Ibsen the Druggist" as his example. There, Tausk describes an extra-therapeutic interaction effective in the momentary correction of a paranoid idea. Tausk portrays the links within the mind of his protagonist, Mr B, between a sculptural representation of the dramatist Ibsen, whose early training had been as a pharmacist, and another druggist with whose wife Mr B is concluding an extramarital relationship. Tausk's presentation is itself a matrix linking: 1) the manifest example of distorted thinking itself; 2) its separate preconceptions as 3) fused elements in compromise formation together with 4) the uncanny apprehension of a formerly recognisable object (the plaster sculpture of Ibsen), now stripped of immediate familiarity in the individual's experience; and 5) an effective intervention aligned with reality, a route Katan might later recognise as expanding the reality-related non-psychotic layer of personality. While illustrating the dynamics of primitive thought, Waelder unwittingly begins to solve the riddle of correcting misconceptions of reality, apparently resistant to clarification.

Waelder's retelling of Tausk's Mr B narrative concludes with a terse transformation, itself redolent of patients' sometimes unhappy moments of recognition. He writes:

> Tausk knew Mr B's personal circumstances. Mr B had recently been involved in a love affair with the wife of a pharmacist and the irate husband had threatened to beat him up. Mr B had used the threat to terminate a relationship of which he had already grown tired. It was an unsavoury affair. Tausk made a kind of short-cut interpretation and merely said: This is the pharmacist, and Mr B, who realized at once what it was all about, did not look too happy. (1951, p. 171)

What is remarkable here is the immediacy of Tausk's own intuition, his awareness of the contextual history of the situation, its characters, and circumstances, and his clear articulation of what Bion would later term the "significant fact" (Bion, 1992; Miller, 2015). Bion's own thinking in arrival at this concept is in consideration of the analyst's containment of the patient's verbal and non-verbal productions, always immediately present within a given session, but continuously emergent in different forms, so articulating different aspects of the patient's personality. These are reflected in the analyst's countertransference, across the timeline of the analysis. The substrate of this action is in the toleration of time: in a session's immediacy; in continuous emergence of narrative; in therapeutic repetitions of action, word, and emotion; in recognition of plausibility and in rejection of interpretation; in uncertainty; and of therapeutic containment itself as a necessary vehicle for therapeutic engagement.

Waelder's use of the Tausk example as illustrative of the dynamics of paranoia stops short of recognising its temporal dimension as a clue to the pathway by which the non-psychotic part of the personality is strengthened through the corrective shock of recognition. It resides within the immediacy of Mr B's response in minding the plausibility of Tausk's terse interpretation. Unnoted both by Waelder and Katan, but emphasised by Bion in his concern with the ongoing temporal dimension of psychotherapeutic action, is the relation between time, causality, and reality.

Clinical illustration parallel to Tausk's extra-therapeutic example is found within Sullivan's psychiatric interview (Sullivan, 1954). Sullivan describes, for example, his close listening to a journeyman electrician who has embezzled union funds. While Sullivan's interest is in illustrating how one listens to tonal differences within the clinical interview, he folds into his casual reconnaissance of the patient's situation the unrecognised contradictions within the patient's narrative such that the interviewee admits: "Well, as a matter of fact, early in my journeyship I actually did pocket a little of the percentage, and it has been on my conscience ever since" (p. 7).

Like Tausk's Mr B, Sullivan's electrician responds immediately. Tausk's implicit knowledge from his acquaintance with Mr B is the foundation of his comment's plausibility. Sullivan, by contrast, does not know his client. Rather, the careful listening and feedback from the clinical interview, appealing to the client's self-interested desire to have his story appreciated, forms the intersubjective substrate of the client's new awareness.

Together, whether in a single session or across the timeline of more extended psychotherapy, Sullivan provides a handhold in the shared history of a dyadic relationship, to which either of its participants might refer (Miller, 2015). Bion shares with Sullivan the articulation of one's personal experience of the other in the structuring of interpretation as "I call this X" which alerts the other to the dimension of experience to which the therapist refers (see Conci, 2009). Reciprocally, the patient may articulate what he or she experiences. Within Tausk's example, this is Mr B's unhappy acknowledgement of his amorous deeds and within Sullivan's it is the electrician's guilty admission of embezzlement.

From Tausk and Sullivan to d-constructions

Our examples from Tausk and Sullivan both illustrate a process in time at the level of the patient's receptive immediacy. This is facilitated in Waelder's example by the long acquaintance of Tausk and Mr B, facilitating interpersonal trust; and in the Sullivan example of the journeyman electrician, the clinician's non-judgemental reception and interest in his narrative presentation.

The "fact" within the dyadic relationship either of acceptance or rejection of such a venture, in which the therapist or patient attempts to name a dimension of experience undergone by each, suggests an interim resting point within the ongoing action of psychotherapy. The communicative verbalisation, "I call this X", signals a temporary arrival at a discernible point in the continuous and jointly creative work of psychotherapy. In our own evidence-based age, "I call this X" also stands as empirical evidence, the shared institutional memory of the therapeutic dyad. This is no trivial recognition. Rather, it is an unsurfaced dimension of Bion's own remarkable compression of the therapeutic process into a "calculus" or algorithm that expands the Kleinian movement between P/S and D. Under Bion's therapeutic abstraction, PS ↔ D PS (n+1) ↔ D (n+1) (♀♂), both Mr B's unhappy clarity with recognition that the bust of Ibsen signals his own unsavoury situation, and the electrician's admission that he has embezzled union funds, might be termed temporary arrivals at D (n+1). They are statements of arrival in understanding as a transformation within a process of therapeutic time. The elapsing of time relative to the movement of fixed ideas into receptive clarification varies broadly. Bion's own apprehension that a patient's "ice cream" was rather a parataxic expression of "I scream" occurs over long, long years of treatment, vast tracts of time (Miller, 2015). Arrivals at such d constructions, useful as consensual markers for subsequent therapeutic inquiry, are arrivals in time, dependent upon the patient's own capacities for the toleration of personal catastrophe as well as its momentary intrapsychic containment.

Our own observations are that the epochal arrival suggested by the capital D within the Bionian calculus seems to miss the quotidian regularity of such moments of recognition. These are easily overturned as they are superceded by other considerations in a deepening therapy, or swamped under destructive attempts of therapeutic resistance. Instead of crediting them with the epochal designation of "depressive position" suggesting Bion's own idea of a depressive position unflavoured by persecutory ideas, we see them as temporary constructions, small harbours along the Waelder-Katan-Bion island coastline of non-psychotic personality. Instead of representation in "capital" D, they are "lower case" registrations of d, which in the continuous process of at least one co-participant's desire to understand what is going on (Bion, 1992) stand as distinctly creative productions of the therapeutic enterprise, threads of possibility that remain within the institutional memory of the therapeutic couple, accessible by either.

As such, we wondered whether these "small d" moments might also be understood as examples of therapeutic scaffolding, extending the land mass of the Waelder-Katan-Bion islands of non-psychotic personality within the learning from experience at the heart of therapeutic process. Their utility, beginning with the significant pathology of psychosis and addictions, is traceable throughout the spectrum of clinical presentation. Both experienced and acknowledged or disavowed, the achievement of d as a momentary resting point can be recognised both in moments of construction and destruction.

d is a rather ordinary moment in a complicated therapeutic process. It is so ordinary that it is easily unseen. It is not so much a triumphant "Eureka" as a small grunt of acknowledgement, sometimes remembered, often not. But within it, we discern what Bion terms the "slow motion" of therapeutic action moderated by interpretation as:

> The patient grasps the gist of what I say. The totality of the statement, including the implication that I am the analyst is evacuated (the mechanism represented by the theory of projective identification). He identifies himself with the analyst and by virtue of his intuition is able to "see" the meaning of my interpretation. (1962a, p. 12)

Bion adds a second Kleinian dimension, beyond the continuous shuttle between PS<>D to his therapeutic palette. He extends Waelder's concept of paranoid ideation as verbalised communication to the implicit, gestural embeddedness in the non-symbolised, primitive communicative mode of projective identification. Here, the unpleasantness of Waelder's paranoid internal state, projected and then blamed externally, is heightened by the anal aggression of expelling mental contents into the other, as if, according to Bion (1992), the bodily wastes of faeces and urine. This evacuation also includes the dimension of time.

The following section, III, concludes this chapter with consideration of the relationship between the temporal domain within the conduct of psychotherapy, and the construction of the relational structures we term "white holes".

On time and white holes

Our relationships with reality are bound in awareness of time. We develop chronologically through infantile stages of omnipotence and magic to gain our sense of reality (Ferenczi, 1913); and through developing our grasp of causality along the dimension of time, we wrest consciousness from the unconscious, which resides in dreams and neurosis (Freud, 1915e).

Psychodynamic therapy operates along two intersecting planes. The first is interpersonal, with a therapeutic pair required for the action of mind upon mind that is the baseline of "psychical" treatment (Freud, 1890a). Even under Bion's construction of psychoanalysis as a dream-state, the particularity of the Bionian dream is that it corresponds to the intersecting contributions of two unique individuals engaged in joint creation, much like Winnicott's co-created Squiggle (Bion, 1992). The Bionian dream requires one mind minding the other; but in its reiterative therapeutic transit from omnipotence to the depressive position, the anchorage of psychotherapy is within the therapist's attention to temporal causality.

Bion is clear that the analyst's own reality sense with awareness of sequential time, awareness of causation, and awareness (and guilt) for insufficiencies and failures of personal agency, are required attainments for the practising psychoanalyst, the expected containing capabilities deriving from the analyst's personal psychoanalysis. These non-psychotic capacities are crucial within engagement of the patient's projections, with time their central thread. Under Bion's watch, the therapist is aware within the session of its fifty minute present: who says what, how the other responds, and the sequential contingencies that flow from this process, allowing that layering of experience from which, from within countertransference, the therapist intuits the singular fact to be conveyed in words to the patient, "I call this X" (Bion, 1992; Miller, 2015).

Within clinical process across the diagnostic spectrum, a number of salient patterns address pathologies of time. These include patients' attempts to: obliterate the boundaries between the present and the future so that desires and wishes are immediately gratified without having to wait; to annihilate transience and the experience of time passing; to extend experiences in time by creation of a static present; and to reverse time's arrow through regressive behaviours. The obliteration of time involves a complex set of interrelationships in which the bodily ego in its present state is experienced as unbearable. Together with this, there is a commensurate desire to transcend this state but with a refusal to either recognise or to accept limitation. Insatiable need is bound up with profound fear of self-annihilation related to a fragmented sense of self; and forms of waiting are invariably experienced as unendurable agonies.

Waiting is felt as a persecutory terminal state rather than a dimension of achievement in containment of what is possible and impossible, that expresses both disappointment with what is and an open-ended view to whatever future creative paths are available to the individual as a function of personal capability. Rather, for these patients, waiting signals direct contact between their position in the present and its distance from an anticipated idealised future. Activities or events which magnify waiting by highlighting the division between temporal points, such as travelling from A to B (particularly on trains, planes, and ships when control is vested in another), the weekend break separating Friday from Monday, or the anticipation of the months during a pregnancy up to term, may provoke crises and the urgent need to obliterate perception of this temporal division.

Such primitive states, as well as their effects upon others, have been likened to the cosmological "black hole" (Eshel, 1998; Grotstein, 1990; Sweet, 2012). In the same way that a black hole represents a region of space from which matter and energy cannot escape due to the gravitational field's intensity, such intrapsychic annihilative dread appears to collapse into sealed-over states of being. Like the black hole, which only becomes apparent due to the effects it exerts on objects around it, this patient's psychodynamic internal world emerges forcibly in the therapeutic relationship, through localised effects, including: splitting, projection, projective identification, ambivalence, denial, and disavowal (Klein, 1946). Such forms of transference issuing from the timeless dynamic unconscious described by Freud (1915e) seem to return the patient to a primitive psychological realm where objective time can be grossly distorted or even, in some cases, through the deployment of anti-time (Green, 2002), be effectively obliterated.

The implication of the intrapsychic black hole is that the primary object of the mind's attack is reality itself and its correlate, time. Therefore, the sense of waiting, based on a perception of the temporal division between a present and a future state, must be annihilated and obliterated. Absent from the patient's internalised containing lattice of object relations, self-representations, and affects that can be ameliorated and managed, the intrapsychic black hole develops, destroying islands of non-psychotic personality in its terror. Rather than having developed a durable capacity for the containment of negative affective states and cognitions, a toleration for internal catastrophe, the patient seeks immediate relief of the pain, frustrations, and negative affects as the therapist either battles the chaos now projected into himself, or else witnesses the patient's battle in an attitude of helpless compassion as his own sense of causality is challenged in the projected emotional storm.

In contradistinction, it is precisely the experience of internalising, over time, a containing psychological structure, composed of durable self and object representations in fluid relations with a range of affects, that leads to a structure, still permeable, that we would refer to as a white hole. The internalised white hole structure may be thought of as allowing the individual the freedom to fall, though still remain psychologically suspended. For the patient it now becomes possible to weave a sort of "trampoline" within her accustomed abyss; one falls, but remains suspended, if not bouncing.

The white hole as psychological landmark is a co-constructed hiatus achieved within the work of psychotherapy, reliant on the institutional memory within the therapeutic dyad of arrivals in d. If the black hole signals indefinite falling, then the white hole signals analogous experience, but attached to a bungee cord. It achieves a tolerable pause in the patient's lived terror. The fall is arrested in a sudden awareness of interruption that, if minded therapeutically, suggests the possibility of anxiety limitation and the generation of meaningful thinking.

Our attention to the white hole emerges from the intersection of the Waelder-Katan-Bion construct of non-psychotic islands of personality together with the same process of cognitive-emotional recognition suggested above, in the examples of Tausk and Sullivan. Based in the patient's allowance of the therapist's understanding and compassionate intention (or even his track record of such intentions at moments when persecutory darkness colours him as malevolent), the white hole develops from threads of reclaimed reality: when at some point "I call this X" was responded to with "I call this Y" and a form of tolerable mutuality was discernible. Or within a single session, when "this was good" becomes effaced with an avalanche of "these were bad" and the therapist wonders what has become of the earlier good in the patient's mind.

If the black hole signals the anxiety of annihilation, its turning point is in the immediacy of renewed temporal orientation in the here and now. The white hole is an element within the therapist's empirical alphabet, constructed incrementally over time by: multiple consensual agreements in naming the objects of the patient's interests; the creation of the therapeutic couple at many points in therapeutic time of mutative iterations of d, their facets allowing new and changing recognitions; and the empirical fact of a unique historical journey that is continuously present as a reference point for two individuals within the therapeutic dyad.

The white hole is a weaving under continuous construction. In moments of annihilative dread, a reminder of the other's continuing presence might facilitate a shift to dreadful disorientation, stabilised within the unfolding therapeutic process; so, later, capable of being "named" and itself becoming a referent for retrospective inquiry. The novelist Samuel Beckett (2006a) provides a literary example of self-analysis in expressing annihilative disorientation not unlike white hole experience within psychotherapy when one's stabilising utterances include, "Where now? Who now? What now?" as statements of awareness, at the edge of disorientation rather than as dimensions of inquiry. The verbalised question mark captures the moment's uncertainty, together with the individual's nascent articulations of personal agency. Yet, rather than meaningful questions, these uttered words are confused points of reference. In psychiatric terms, these are pre-orientations of person, place, and time, the murmurings of a punch-drunk boxer rising from the mat. Beckett's own terse articulation, "Keep going, going on, call that going, call that on" states well the fragile immediacy of this momentary stabilisation, made remarkable in a tolerated pause within a repetitive experience of dreadful annihilative plunging. "Call that going, call that on" parallels the therapist's continuous reminder of agency in his apprehension of the patient's presentation, "I call this X".

While the experience of the white hole cannot and does not preclude repetitive return to awful blackness, it provides, through its phenomenological demonstration within the intersubjective containing or holding of the therapist-as-other, a joint witnessing of possible stabilisation. No longer may the patient's story, both enacted and told to the other, remain wholly of dread. Through the process of signification, through demonstration, registered by the therapist as other, there exists the possibility of checking the repetitive real life descent into oblivion. The patient is reminded of time: of the present, of past history in a temporal binding. This is shared therapeutic reality, a fact of bearing tolerably what was a moment before intolerable; and its witnessing. In the language of W. R. Bion one observes the emerging capacity, by the patient, for K, in contradistinction to the predominance of –K, at an intrapsychic level.

CHAPTER FIVE

Recognitions in d

Having recognised the transitory emergence of daily approximations to the Kleinian depressive position in d, the vocalised, empirically demonstrable presence of d itself takes its place as a recognisable conceptual **d** element in psychodynamic thinking. As **d**, its transformation from clinical particularity to clinical universality, about which new, derivative particularities may be generated, achieves possibility. The present chapter links Chapter 2, on the recognition of pathological clinical forms, to Chapter 4, on the recognition of dyadically shared, d emergences.

In this chapter, we consider a clinical form emergent within the therapeutic dyad, so recognisable to the clinician, which we term "reverse splitting". In describing this **d** concept, we link together four chapter subsections. These include: 1) discussion of Kleinian conceptualisations about psychopathology; 2) discussion of the psychoanalytic **d** of splitting; 3) the idea of reverse splitting (RS) as a fundamental process in mental metabolisation and integration of the self, illustrated by three case examples; and 4) the chapter conclusion.

What strikes us as we "name" these recognitions is that often, in the documentation of psychoanalytic history, aspects of what we now observe have been seen and named differently at other times. For example, in discussing reverse splitting, we reference Betty Joseph's concept of "chuntering", presented in "Addiction to Near-Death" (1982). Chuntering itself becomes a useful **d** concept for us, aiding our articulation of reverse splitting. But there is more! Joseph's concept also appears to be hinted at fifty years earlier, in description of the resistant clinical situation in the opening pages of Wilhelm Reich's *Character Analysis*. Described there contextually rather than being highlighted and recognised by a "name" like chuntering, Reich quietly utters its recognition half a century prior to Joseph.

Here, we observe the replicability of such phenomena in our social science. The historical catastrophe of the Second World War fractured and fragmented the Berlin and Viennese centres of psychoanalysis, where Reich as a second-generation clinician perceived the clinical forms he would present both in Vienna trainings and in Berlin's fabled "Children's Seminar", training the third clinical generation (Danto, 2005; Reich, 1972). Joseph's rise too, is in the generations that succeed Klein, after the instantiation and firm rooting of the psychoanalytic tradition in the UK. Developing as one psychoanalytic generation builds upon the recognitions of the former generation, we recognise the significant fact of clinical development, rooted in the psychoanalytic founders' transmissions of clinical theory and practical direction, for extensions of thinking in **d**. Above, in Chapter 4, we noted a similar convergence relative to Bion and Waelder, in relation to Katan, Tausk, Sullivan, and learning from experience.

What is remarkable in the Reich-Joseph convergence, however, relates directly to our clinical recognition of reverse splitting as a **d** concept. Joseph's recognition, temporally, geographically, and metapsychologically distant from Reich's, is nevertheless rooted in the essential clinical practice of psychoanalysis. Her articulation reverses the fragmentation and splitting of an earlier **d** conception through its oblivion in catastrophic world events and dispersion of clinical workers, returning it (even outside conscious awareness or acknowledgement) to fullness within the daily work of psychotherapy. Conceptually in **d**, it parallels the clinical actions of reverse splitting we recognise daily in the ordinary dyadic emergence of d expressions.

On reverse splitting

The Kleinian psychoanalyst Betty Joseph, in her classic paper "Addiction to Near-Death" (1982), described what she called mental "chuntering" as follows:

> These patients pick up very readily something that has been going on in their minds or in an external relationship and start to use it over and over again in some circular type of mental activity, in which they get completely caught up, so that they go over and over with very little variation the same actual or anticipated issue ... Patients who get so caught up in these activities, chuntering, tend to believe that they are thinking at such times, but of course they are living out experiences which become the complete antithesis of thought. (pp. 451–452)

Joseph's observational description of chuntering can, of course, be seamlessly applied to compulsive disorders of all types, including both substance and non-substance based addictions. One suspects though, that there is also considerable room for extension of this **d** concept; and particularly in the case of psycho-somatised conversion symptoms, manifest by those that we work with and who persistently appear to feel assailed by medically unexplained physical symptoms and sensations. We might, for instance, speculate that the chuntering described by Joseph represents a last desperate attempt to hold on to the core elements of thinking (or thoughts) before they are further lost to immediate perceptual consciousness and cognition and become converted and lodged bodily, at a sensory-physical level, through somatisation; or indeed, give way to action and enactment in contradistinction to thinking. We suggest that the liminal spaces within the psyche that appear as, and have been described in the literature as, types of psychological reserves or retreats are the very levels at which we must work, in order to better understand complex processes of de-symbolisation, splitting, and psycho-sensory symptom conversion, in our daily and weekly psychotherapeutic work.

Further, in order for patients to endure the demands and challenges inherent in therapeutic work and so to eventually more fully emerge from the psychic retreats (Steiner, 1993) and psychological enclaves

(O'Shaughnessy, 1992) described in the psychoanalytic literature, a parallel though reverse process must occur. This process and the dominant preservative mechanism underpinning it we describe and designate as reverse splitting. We outline and exemplify, through detailed clinical material, the creation of self-preservative retreats and enclaves, in the service of the survival of an often seriously wounded and fragile self, often following experiences of chronic childhood relational trauma, environmental flux, separation from significant others, or bereavement.

(We also illustrate this process later in Chapter 7 with reference to the working through of trauma, as narrated by Samuel Beckett across thirty-three years of literary iterations (Miller, 2015).) We then further explore and demonstrate reverse splitting and its function in assisting integration of deeply split aspects of the self and the individual's internal objects.

We begin with a brief review of the more recent literature on pathological organisations and their clinical manifestations, with reference to a number of Kleinian writers, before developing our thoughts on reverse splitting and self-preservative retreats where individual core competencies may, for a time, be safely deposited.

The Kleinian development

The key Kleinian psychoanalytic papers which have developed the concepts of pathological organisations, internalised defensive structures, and psychic retreats span a period from the mid-1930s to the present. Spillius, Milton, Garvey, Couve, and Steiner (2011) provide a thorough and comprehensive review in *The New Dictionary of Kleinian Thought*, under the major entry of "Pathological Organisations" (section 11). In her overview, Spillius begins with an important and overarching observation. She highlights the two main strands, conceptually, in the descriptions given of pathological organisations, and to which we made reference in Chapter 2 above on aspects of psychopathology. The first, described by a range of Kleinian writers (Meltzer, 1968; Rosenfeld, 1971; Sohn, 1985), involves the assertion that in the evolution of a pathological organisation, a range of persecutory objects and self imagoes becomes dominant in relation to the rest of the personality. Here, it is argued, a fragile and dependent self may evidence a type of addictive bondage to intimidating and controlling intrapsychic imagoes; though most Kleinian authors also note the fundamentally sadomasochistic dynamics evidenced by patients caught in the grip of such a pathological organisation of the core personality structure.

The second conceptual strand that has been explored by a range of Kleinian analysts (O'Shaughnessy, 1992; Segal, 1972; Steiner, 1993), in their descriptions of pathological organisations, may be referred to as the *precarious equilibrium model of personality*. Such an intrapsychic organisation enables a degree of balance to be maintained, somewhere between paranoid-schizoid and depressive functioning. This position is strongly defended (by recourse to pathological splitting and projective identification at times), with the individual fearing a full psychotic collapse into the paranoid schizoid world on the one hand, while also experiencing anticipatory annihilative anxieties, in the face of the problems to be confronted in the depressive position on the other hand, including the pain implied by a fuller recognition of separateness, loss, and the unique individuality of the other.

Compressed exquisitely by W. R. Bion into an abstract algorithm, this dense construction becomes the royal road to contemporary psychoanalytic definition, receptive to multiple conceptual fusions of elements in **d** as demonstrated by Roy Schafer's (1997) evolution from ego psychology and action language to a contemporary Kleinian orientation. Implicitly affirmed through our contemporary vernacular expression of psychoanalysis (Miller, 2016a), itself a composite of psychoanalytic readers' interests, it is even more remarkable that it has been accepted without thorough exploration and understanding of the discrete interpersonal mechanisms requiring internalisation and identification, both by therapist and patient, which must underlie it. Our Chapter 4 demonstrates at a clinical level such fine-grain movements that occur between therapists and patients in the clinical setting reflecting vacillations between paranoid-schizoid and depressive functioning.

The question remains however, how does the healthy (however fragile) though beleaguered and entrapped self manage to survive attacks from the "bad" self and the full range of internalised destructive objects by which it so often feels mercilessly assailed? This question appears to have received considerably less attention in the Kleinian literature, particularly with regard to analytic "failures": in terms of the apparent interminability of some patients in analysis, the so-called eternal patient; or the sudden breakdown of the relationship and drop-out of patients from the therapeutic relationship. And yet, it is notable that for a patient to take on and endure the demands and emotional vicissitudes inherent either in a longer-term analysis, or long-term psychoanalytic psychotherapy, there must be a reasonable degree of self-resilience, simply to be able to manage the demands of the therapeutic work (Szalita, 1984).

In order to further develop our ideas in relation to reverse splitting we offer a brief review of some of the key ideas presented as the concept of splitting has developed and evolved in the psychoanalytic literature. Necessarily this is a selective review; and here, we concentrate on the line of development from Freud, through Klein, and on to Bion.

Splitting

The term "splitting" was used in a psychiatric context by Eugene Bleuler (1911), in his attempts to describe and explain mental processes to be found in schizophrenia. Even before this use of the term, Freud and Breuer had, in *Studies on Hysteria* (1895d), referred to the "... splitting of consciousness". Freud's intention in utilising the term, in the service of building a model of the psyche, appears to be intimately related to clarification of his ideas concerning repression, in which he emphasised the tensions between impulse and defence. However, his retention of the idea of a fundamental split or cleavage in the personality came to occupy a central place in his thinking, as he considered conflicts in the ego, engendered in relation to its various identifications; or indeed, the fusion of the self's elements in Freud's borrowing from Jung of the conceptual **d**, symptom complex, in representing the uniquely personal symptomatic presentations of different patients' distress (Freud, 1910a, 1914c, 1917e, 1921c, 1927e, 1940e). In Freud's major 1926 revision of the role of anxiety in the psychic economy, he goes as far as to suggest an earlier defensive alteration of the ego, based on splitting, writing:

> It may well be that before the sharp cleavage into an ego and an id, and before the formation of a super-ego, the mental apparatus makes use of different methods of defence from those which it employs after it has reached these stages of organisation. (1926d, p. 164)

In his last definitive statements on splitting, Freud (1927e, 1940e) echoes Bleuler's original application of the idea to schizophrenia, though also broadens the nature and function of the process as a primary defence to the wider field and spectrum of psychopathology. He writes:

> The view which postulates that in all psychoses there is a splitting of the ego could not call for so much notice if it did not turn out to apply to other states more like the neuroses and, finally, to the neuroses themselves. (1940e, p. 202)

The centrality of splitting as the key psychological defence mechanism, both in the psychoses and in the neuroses, is clearly indicated here in Freud's life's-end arrival at this final **d** formulation. Here, Freud affirms what his student, Waelder, had only three years earlier noted: the similarity of neurotic and psychotic structures. Yet Waelder took Freud's affirmation a step further, observing that psychotic phenomena must originate beyond the phases of normal development (1937).

Twenty years earlier, Melanie Klein had begun to outline her views on the fundamental role of splitting as an overarching and underpinning element in infantile and childhood development. Her later theories of both the paranoid-schizoid and depressive positions evolved from these earlier conceptualisations of binary splitting. Her theory of binary splitting, in terms of the infant's earliest stages of development, involve ideas of protection of the self in relation to persecutory and feared objects. In tandem, the strength and tenacity with which the child splits and divides both his ego and his good objects, in order to keep them sharply separated from hostile and persecutory self/object imagoes, propels the introjective and projective mechanisms that underscore development. Klein summarises this in *The Psychoanalysis of Children* (1932) writing:

> In dividing its mother into a good mother and a bad one and its father into a good father and a bad one, it attaches the hatred it feels for its object to the bad one or turns away from it while it directs its restorative trends to its good mother and good father, and in phantasy, makes good towards the damage it has done its parent-imagoes in its sadistic phantasies. (p. 222)

Explicit in this formulation is the idea that identification with the good object necessitates the need to repair the damage done to the object, a process which Klein here refers to in the context of the infant's "restorative trends". As we know, Klein always maintained, following Freud (1926d, 1927e), that a splitting of the object entailed a commensurate splitting of the ego, based on the processes of both projective and introjective identification.

It was however, W. R. Bion, particularly in his so-called schizophrenia papers of the late 1950s and early 1960s, who more fully developed an understanding of splitting and projective/introjective identification, both in terms of early infantile development and, crucially, in relation to the dynamics and vicissitudes of the therapeutic relationship during analysis. In doing so, Bion concentrated on the mental apparatus itself within a theory of thinking, in which he emphasised restrictions upon thinking and its development from primary to secondary process that fundamentally contributed to the evolution of psychopathological conditions.

It should be recalled that according to Bion (1957, 1962a), psychosis results from the fragmentation and later expulsion of the very means by which the self knows reality. This entails the pulverisation of and expulsion of the senses, consciousness, and thinking. Perhaps this is the missing ingredient conjectured by Waelder in 1937 that differentiates between neurotic and psychotic splitting.

Following Bion, the result is that individuals operating at a psychotic level (in the psychoanalytic sense of the term psychotic rather than the psychiatric) principally utilise three distinct means of defence in order to avoid potentially annihilatory anxieties engendered through contact with reality. These three means are: 1) somatisation; 2) hallucination; and 3) action (enactment). Underlying these three core defensive modes, we witness both the splitting of the ego and the object, as well as both projective and introjective identification.

If we follow the logic of Bion's argument, it becomes apparent that in the principal defensive mechanisms he describes, there appears an attempt to preserve both aspects of the object and the ego, through recourse to expulsion of psycho-sensory awareness, consciousness, and cognition. Therefore, the splitting of the ego results in the setting up of a fluid continuum of fragmented beta elements, reversible in essence, related to both projective and introjective processes. Most important, depending on the means of defensive evacuation deployed through projective identification in relation to inchoate preverbal thoughts—which Rapaport (1950) terms "ideation"—the capacity to reintroject what has been projected will critically depend on the reversal of the original pathway of evacuation.

Bion (1957, 1959, 1962a) is explicit and consistent in this regard. He argues that if, for instance, projection involved visual hallucination then reintrojection of what had been expelled from the psyche would only occur on the basis of the projected elements being taken back in, visually, through the eyes. This applies, *mutatis mutandis*, with respect to auditory, olfactory, vocal, or tactile hallucinations and disturbances. He described the conditions that led to the encystation of the psyche by psychotic forces as involving both environmental and personality related factors. Of the latter, he described, in his paper on the differences between the psychotic and non-psychotic personalities (1957): a preponderance of destructive impulses; a hatred of reality (both internal and external); a dread of imminent annihilation; and a premature and precipitate formation of object relations, most prominently recognisable in the transference relationship with the analyst.

A few years later, Bion turned to the consideration of environmental factors in his paper on thinking (1962a). In this paper, he delivered a fully evolved metapsychological theory of the evolution of the mental apparatus, based on the developing capacity to bear frustration and pain and thus to transmute raw ideographic thoughts into thinking. Crucial to this process, from the environmental perspective, is the role of the caregiver and her ability both to identify with and to moderate the infant's accompanying projections and identifications. Bion offers the following succinct observation, writing:

> Normal development follows if the relationship between infant and breast permits the infant to project a feeling, say, that it is dying, into the mother and to reintroject it after its sojourn in the breast has made it tolerable to the infant psyche. If the projection is not accepted by the mother the infant feels that its feeling that it is dying is stripped of such meaning as it has. It therefore reintrojects, not a fear of dying made tolerable, but a nameless dread. (p. 183)

Ultimately, under "good enough" conditions, what is introjected and more fully internalised at an intrapsychic level is both a containing and a durable object that underpins the development of the ego's capacity to bear frustration and pain, thus delaying immediate gratification of desire and encouraging adaptation to the realities of everyday life.

Reverse splitting as a fundamental therapeutic process in mental metabolisation and integration of the self

The nature of individual defences, their more global and complex interaction with a range of other defences, and the function of the psychic retreat has been summarised, adroitly, by Steiner,

> Sometimes we can examine the individual defences, sometimes it is helpful to recognise the complex system of object relations that the defences involve, and finally it is possible to conceive of the defensive structures as psychic retreats—that is as places where the patient can withdraw to seek relief from anxiety and pain. (2011, p. 2)

The reversal of the pathway, based on splitting that has, over time, led to the formation of the psychic retreat or enclave, involves the analyst's slow and sensitive work. Defensive systems inevitably coalesce into organisations of object relations, often long encysting the psyche, that are then re-mobilised by entry into the analytic setting through the relationship with the analyst.

The retreat or enclave viewed as a self-preservative creation means that often the most fragile aspects of the self structure, those felt particularly to have experienced shame, guilt, humiliation, and powerlessness in the face of an overwhelming threat, are deposited in the psychic retreat, particularly at times when they come close to exposure through relationships with others. In this sense, the establishment of a secure base upon which therapeutic work may develop is the pre-eminent task during the early weeks and months of psychoanalytic treatment.

It should be borne in mind, recalling Joseph's description of chuntering, above, that the fundamental splitting that tends to operate defensively in the formation of pathological intrapsychic organisations involves in the first instance an assault on the links (Bion, 1959) that might promote contact with and awareness of reality. Somatic conversion, in which literally unspeakable internal conflicts become lodged and stuck at the level of the physical symptom, are one of the most obvious manifestations of this process.

So too are the ways in which depersonalisations of the self are indicated by the language used by the patient. Strikingly, there is often a substitution of personal pronouns such as "I" or "me" by impersonal ones, so that one is faced with a description of something called "it", which appears to encapsulate innumerable conflicts and woes, and has a rigidity and fixity diametrically opposed to fluidity, creativity, discourse, or change.

The encapsulation of a living, vibrant though beleaguered self is paradigmatically indicated by the mechanical, automaton-like (Sweet, 2010, 2011) "it" object we describe above in Chapter 2, which stands in stark contrast to the "I" or "me" which has been expelled representationally and symbolically from perceptual consciousness. The gradient between the articulations of the inter-human (Buber, 1957) symbolised in the words, "I", "me", and "you" reaches an end point in such dehumanised "it-ness". The analyst's humanising, intuitive responsiveness to this "significant fact" (Bion, 1992; Miller, 2015), preparing the dyad for the potentialities of reverse splitting, are articulated within the contemporary literature in psychoanalytic psychotherapy through reference both to intuitive therapeutic "witnessing" of massive psychic trauma (Felman, 1992), and from within the dyadic, relational contributions of the psychoanalytic "third" (Ogden, 1994).

Clinical examples of reverse splitting

We now demonstrate how attention to relational rhythms and evocations, first felt by the analyst within the particular forms of personal countertransferential experience before clarification into the significant facts of intuitive, verbalised experience, approximate the "restorative trends" suggested almost eighty years ago by Klein (1932). We observe, beginning with our first example in the early phase of therapy, how such sensitivity may facilitate the reversal of intrapsychic splitting by a growing awareness in the therapeutic relationship of time shared together, between analyst and patient. This we see as a fundamental underpinning, for patient and therapist, of the sense of being joined together in a task, reminiscent of Bion's (1962b) early description of a "work group". The example also depicts the sense of encapsulation of the self (with the "I" replaced by an "it") as symbolising proper appears to have been foreclosed and to have been replaced by the sense of concretised equation, previously described by Segal (1957).

Clinical case 1: Mr K

Mr K, a forty-four-year-old single man living alone, presented for his initial appointment with one of the authors (AS) in a highly anxious and confused state. He had been referred by the psychiatric team involved in his case, with a long list of presenting issues. These included: a history of childhood sexual abuse, a more recent medical trauma which resulted in a diagnosis of PTSD; alcohol and drug (codeine) abuse; and "personality problems" particularly with regard to apparently unprovoked "verbal outbursts". Mr K found it difficult both to make and maintain eye contact during the initial consultation, searching the room furtively as if looking for something that both assailed him and of which he was inwardly terrified. Eventually he asked, "Is there a button under your desk that if you press, I will be taken away to the loony bin?" The question was posed in a non-humorous and deadly serious manner. The fantasy that I might alert security and have Mr K sectioned reflected the fragmentation and deep intrapsychic splitting that dominated his internal world. It was only months later that he was able to share with me how terrified he had actually felt in coming to see me during our early weeks together. Somehow, he also found the courage to begin to explore the raw emotions, thoughts, feelings, and fantasies engendered by repeated sexual abuse that he had suffered in a religious institution between the ages of eleven and thirteen years. What appeared most important to him, in the creation of a safe and secure space in which we became joined together in a mutual task, was his sense of autonomy in creating elements of the therapeutic work. For instance, Mr K always arrived early for his weekly appointment, often by as much as twenty-five to thirty minutes. This was never challenged. Staff came to expect that he would arrive early and he simply waited comfortably and patiently in the waiting room. When I arrived to collect him for our appointment he often seemed to be in an almost trance-like state, a state I came to understand as a necessary preparation for the imminent session.

It also became apparent that sessions would evolve rhythmically in different ways. These included at times a manner that allowed him to express violent impulses—now given vent vocally—though previously directed inwards through recourse to a range of addictions which he had developed. At such times, I found that for both of us to metabolise psychologically these intense feelings, there seemed to be an unspoken though shared and recognised sense of witnessing the emergence of raw visceral emotions, based on the reversal of splitting and Mr K's consequent emergence from the psychic retreats he had so long relied upon. At one point, Mr K, facing deep feelings of inner disgust and shame, broke down and began to sob, confused about his own sexual identity and his desires.

Gradually over a period of three months the dreadful anxieties that had so plagued Mr K initially in our work together began to subside. More resistant to change, however, was the sense in which a depersonalised and robotic "It"-like part of the self continued to be relied upon. This It-like part of the self appeared to function as a retreat, which could offer protection from links that would underpin thinking and contact with deeper emotions. This It-like self was manifest in a range of psychosomatic symptoms that ebbed and flowed in intensity, week after week. The early phases of sessions were often taken up with repeated complaints related to these various pains and symptoms. Mr K would begin for instance by saying: "It's my bloody head and I've got such a feeling in it! I don't know what it is! It's constant!" After a short period he might turn to pains in his lower legs or ankles, before returning again at some point to the headache.

It should be noted at this stage that we have absolutely no doubt that Mr K was, at such times, experiencing genuine and considerable physical discomfort and pain. However, the entrenched nature of the symptoms appeared to fundamentally reflect the sense in which inchoate proto-thoughts were dispelled, after links were resisted, resulting in the emergence of a physical-bodily repository of fragmented and split off elements of the ego. This comes close perhaps to more fully developing both Joseph's notion of chuntering and the addictive quality it evinces, and to approaching the work of reversing the split that has occurred, through the process of therapeutic joining together, in a dedicated task—much of which must by definition remain unspoken and unelucidated during long periods of the work together between patient and therapist. It should be noted, however, that somatic conversion and the chuntering that accompanies it means that the therapist really feels the strain with such patients in maintaining both an analytic space and, underpinning this, an analytic frame of mind. By this we allude to the capacity to retain an interpretive and constructive attitude in work with the patient, principally in conceptualising the division between internal and external realities and the vicissitudes and conflicts so engendered.

With Mr K as we approached, in greater detail, the subject of the sadistic and acute sexual abuse he had suffered as a young boy, his mobilisation of protective defences in the form of somatic conversion, mental chuntering, and the risk of substance-induced self-anaesthesia increased markedly. This, we would contend, is to be expected and anticipated in work that seeks to reverse splitting processes, and in turn further highlights the ambivalence experienced by patients during periods of movement, within the broader global compass of d.

During such phases of therapeutic work, if the patient projects aspects of the fragile and needy self into the analyst, ostensibly as a holding function for safe keeping, this process in and of itself may provoke therapeutic impasse and drop-out, precisely because the patient fears his own envious aggressivity, now directed towards the fragile good object as deposited in the analyst. The survival of one aspect of the self may now only be possible if distance from it is ensured, thus actually promoting premature drop-out from therapy. Paradoxically, those analysts more skilled, in a receptive sense, at listening intently and receiving deep psychological communications from their patients may promote distancing and therapeutic drop-out with their patients, particularly if they move to time-limited, less regular (for instance once or twice weekly) interventions.

We now offer a second clinical example to further illuminate some of the difficulties and challenges in day-to-day therapeutic work between analyst and patient, when considering recovery of aspects of the self, long shielded by cover under the psychic retreat and the dynamics that emerge as a consequence of the reversal of splitting.

Clinical case 2: Marek

Our second clinical example (IM) is a forty-four-year-old man named Marek, a research scientist who maintained a painful interpersonal relationship with a woman who treated him in a subordinating and humiliating manner. On initial presentation in twice weekly therapy, Marek was less concerned about this relationship, shrugged off as an "inconvenience" that nevertheless indicated he was capable of human relatedness, than of the assorted manifestations of hysterical conversion symptoms for which no general practitioner or consultant could find cause. Rather matter-of-factly in the first session, which Marek attended on crutches, appearing like a wounded casualty of his personal wars, I questioned the context in which his injury occurred. Ensuing discussion revealed that his shooting leg pain might be causally linked to an overly long hiking trip in which he hurt his leg while wearing footwear inadequate to the mountainous task. "I never thought of that," said Marek.

"Do you mean that it is possible that these pains might have multiple and non-linear causes?" Within several sessions, Marek discarded his crutches; but other disturbing symptoms related to breathing, paralysis, and stomach distress would emerge. It would be over a year before Marek, in a casual aside, related that his family of origin regarded him only in relation to physical pain; and that indeed, he had been the subject of several unnecessary childhood surgeries for problems imagined by his parents "and remedied by foreign quacks".

While Marek's description of his rather full and prominent activities as a scientific researcher seemed cogent and purposive, allowing him a focal sphere of activity akin to Steiner's "psychic retreat", it was a retreat wherein the therapist perceived the patient's competence and health. Increasingly over the three years of our work together, Marek would hint at the depth of his traumatic childhood in Eastern Europe. His parents, both significantly affected by the events of the Second World War and their country's post-war engagement with communism, perpetuated a warlike situation in peacetime. Marek described a childhood in which he never had a bedroom, "lived from a valise" which contained his possessions, and used within the circle of family relations a language different from the language of his host country.

Indeed, given the degree of psychotic dysfunction both of the parents and of his three siblings, coupled with the horrors of childhood which Marek described calmly and without apparent hurt or anger, home life presented a chaotic, confusing atmosphere of catastrophe, narrated in one language which contrasted with the authoritarian but structured world of childhood schooling and education, conducted in another language.

Marek's confusing conversion symptoms contrasted with the dependent, childlike relation to the therapist which began to evolve, evoking in me a protectiveness and forthrightness of expression, as if I were explaining a confusing world to a young child rather than to a middle-aged, savvy, and accomplished research scientist.

What began as an intuitive hypothesis in my mind was the sense of a split within Marek's internal world, demarcated by a linguistic border. This first became apparent when he described growing frustrated by a work colleague and using a non-English word that signified both simple meaning as "enough" and conveyed through gestural movement, internal frustration. Marek explained to me that this was the language of his school-days; and seemed initially stymied about how uncharacteristically assertive he had been in this episode.

In time, together, we posited the transitory hypothesis that Marek was able to contain different aspects of his experience within different languages. Along with an increasingly differentiated willingness to narrate childhood and developmental history, Marek seemed intrigued by this idea. He also linked the different languages to his own experience of somatic symptoms; and hypothesised, like some latter-day Freud, that his idiosyncratic physical symptoms probably represent something deeply felt, "but in another language". Marek displayed great enthusiasm and pride in this quick psychological insight, fairly "drinking up" or "gobbling up" the experience of collaborative thirdness, akin in my mind at this stage to Winnicott's notion of a unit between therapist and patient, engaged in the patient's going on being.

An opportunity brought by Marek occasioned a new stage in treatment. He remarked that he had been invited to a scientific conference in the city where he'd spent his childhood; and indeed, had been contacted by a one-time schoolmate, now on the conference committee. We discussed his ambivalence about returning to this linguistic setting; and he began to feel deeply anxious about what he took to be an abandonment of English, "which at least felt safe", for the uncertainties of the language spoken by him at school, and which had increasingly punctuated his negotiation both of daily life and within our work, where its emergence, together with animated hand gesturing, presented a marked contrast with his general look of defeat and depletion. Marek was physically ill for two weeks before his scheduled trip; but in dutifully attending his sessions, pointing out to me his endurance of pain "like a good boy", against his certainty that I did not know the torment I was putting him through—like his current interpretation of his war-damaged parents—that we discussed his self-care in the context both of daily life and the upcoming conference in his former homeland.

Two weeks later, returning from the conference, he declared himself "a new man". He had "found" himself, a voice that was only beginning to be heard in irruption within the English of our therapy sessions; as he recounted brilliant meetings with childhood acquaintances, all sides catching themselves up on their ensuing lives as his native land emerged from communism. He was thrilled, he said, to be remembered by schoolmates, who furthered our own therapeutic hunches about the "strange" behaviours of his family, cocooned in a second language, different than the one spoken in school.

Marek's return to therapy came too, with his newfound sadness about several issues. The first was that he endured a live-in relationship that caused him continuing tension and grief; and he resolved to focus upon this relationship in continuing therapy. The second, articulated for the first time in our work, was that he could perceive a horizon where life was worth living: of potential fullness. He attributed this to his return to the formerly split-off world of his school-age language, now integrated in his clinical work in therapy, especially as he came to recognise that in moments formerly marked by ambivalence and uncertainty, his linguistic expression in that once-distanced language suggested an inner sense of self that saw things clearly, "just like when I was a boy, in school".

Marek's presentation, oscillating from somatic complaint to wordless, choked confusions, suggests to us the idea of Betty Joseph's "chuntering" as analogous to a traffic roundabout without exits or ramps. Location, first of d elements, jointly affirmed in the clinical encounter, and next, through the development of reverse splitting, seems to establish thinking-points of exit and arrival. Indeed, Marek's reconnection to aspects of self appeared to be aligned with a split-off and jettisoned former language that gave meaningful resonance to previously inchoate expressions represented in somatic pain. In addition, behavioural reconnection with now-older, real witnesses of his childhood experiences, cemented in the extra-therapeutic context, the plausibility of conceptions generated within session, through formulations of d. The authors, in further considering this presentation, also recognise its similarity to Ferenczi's "active technique", especially in the therapist's intuition and encouragement of his patient's inhibited behaviour within the context of the therapeutic relationship (Ferenczi, 1920; Miller, 1991).

Our final clinical case is offered in order to explore reverse splitting and aspects of its relationship to narcissism. We hope the case material also provides an opportunity to consider the countertransferential responses of the analyst and how these assist further understanding of a challenging patient.

Clinical case 3: Professor R

I (IM) had heard of Professor R within academic circles; and when he contacted me, I'd mentioned a paper for which he was acclaimed. Despite his intention to request therapy, he immediately remarked,

"That is only one of my twenty papers and four books," chilling that moment of attempted, polite cordiality.

Working with Professor R for two years, I learned of severe work difficulties, the painful dissolution of two marriages, his children's continuing disdain for him, coupled with grandiose claims regarding the effectiveness of an earlier psychoanalysis in another country, with an internationally renowned analyst, head and shoulders better than anyone else practising, and of his long periods, currently in remission, of alcoholic bingeing.

Within our sessions, his contemptuous disdain for others would sharply alternate with longing idealisation; and the split would rarely be acknowledged. He was conscious of viewing me as a "tool", an inanimate object rising to humanity only to the degree that I seemed similar to his actively hated second wife, who had discarded him and now seemed in her narcissistic self-contentment to get along very well without him. At the same time, while intellectually familiar with the conceptual structure of psychoanalysis, he aggressively denied that there was any transference at all. Indeed, while claiming that he was a successful "product" of an earlier psychoanalysis, he could not say what psychoanalysis or psychoanalytic therapy might be, except that whatever I claimed it to be, it was not helping him much.

A pervasive preoccupation was the injustice of life coupled with envy—especially that he continued in a state of anguish, pain, and misery while his former wives seemed to act as if they were thriving. No, it was not exactly as if they were thriving. Rather, the professor believed that they were "happy": as if "happy" were a continuous and non-fluctuating steady state of idealised bliss. They had reached it. He demanded it too. And he hated me because I refused to give it to him.

His only wonderment at this was at the level of "fairness", given that both of these women had been entirely at fault in the dissolution of his two marriages. He had been twice victimised, yet now their lives were perfect: happy; prosperous; well respected by their friends and children, who hated him and showed him no respect. How was this possible?

Twice, Professor R terminated therapy in a rage at my insistence upon telling him how I saw things. "How dare you," he thundered; and each time, requesting return, he informed me that the therapy was to be "new", having nothing to do with our prior work. Each time, I informed him that I reserved the right to my own belief that the therapy was, indeed, a continuation of what had been, and how I had known him.

I told him that I maintained this view, while respecting his own construction of events, but would also feel free to refer to how I knew him, without necessarily honouring his habit of bracketing, fragmenting, and discarding our continuous joint experience. Dismissively, Professor R agreed; and several times in our work, I would assert my construction, consciously noting that I was aware that this bridging of "one period of therapy with me" to "another differing period of therapy with me" was not to his liking. In effect, I was setting the pattern for reverse splitting in my use of potentially communicative language. He negated it; but following Freud (1925h), in his negation, Professor R accepted its elements for his own later consideration.

Within my countertransference, I often felt abused and violated by Professor R's fierce and disclaimed hatreds. Worry about his self-destructiveness would invade my dreams; and consultation with colleagues about this case, among others, was imperative, as it continually hovered between a tense ongoing sense of continuity and the possibility of sudden rupture as had happened twice before; and even suicide. A pervasive substrate of my appreciative identification with this patient was of feeling shameful and woefully inadequate; and it was in this domain that the action of projective identification felt acidic. My extension of psychic containment to the professor felt like the offering of a landfill, to be used and contaminated by toxic accumulation; but one, despite ruptures and pain inflicted on both sides, that was believed by Professor R to be eternally available in its sadomasochistic capacity, without either his own reflective awareness and therapeutic attempt at self-discovery or my own self-protectiveness against internalisation of his miseries, gleefully registered by him (gesturally, but not in verbalisation) of my accumulating inadequacy to change anything.

One colleague, empathising with the suffering necessary to endure the painful work with such patients, commented that "Sometimes, patients come to us with a 'Do Not Resuscitate' order on their foreheads." He tersely and pointedly affirmed the kind of willed deadness that I felt in Professor R's presence.

During the second year of our work and prior to a rescheduled session, made necessary by my attendance at a professional conference, Professor R took great offence at something I had said concerning his self-endangering behaviour. It was as if years of our work suddenly solidified in his thinking and he had become outraged. "How dare you", he bellowed, "see me like that," referring to my demonstration to him of the diametrical opposition between two split positions which he fiercely maintained. "You hate me! You see me as mad!" His fury was palpable; and on leaving the session, I had real doubt whether he would return.

These concerns infiltrated my thinking over the next several days; and I came to see them as an envious attack upon his intuition of my stability, never spoken. He arrived early for the next scheduled session; and I was surprised that, together with his venomous attack upon my behaviour, he was able to integrate both his idealisations and denigrations of others with whom he'd had contact over the last weekend. "Frankly," he told me, "I was glad of that extra day forced by our rescheduled week, when I didn't have to look at your face. It was a great relief not to have to come here." This was contrasted immediately with his recognition, in looking "in the eyes" of a former colleague, and locating a deadness which he saw as his own. He looked at me and said, "I fucking hated you when you said that this work was about aliveness rather than deadness." And then he burst into tears. Not looking at himself and his deadness had shifted, at least in that moment, into observation, and so aliveness. He had successfully demonstrated a moment of reverse splitting, claiming both sides of his experience. And he had given language to an expression of d, enacted between us.

Conclusion

While our languaging of reverse splitting is derived from specific texts within the Kleinian perspective, it is also possible to arrive at the same point, this "intimate edge" (Ehrenberg, 1992), from the interpersonal development of clinical psychoanalysis which has often located phenomena observed externally within the workings of the therapeutic dyad. Ferenczi, for example, observes what he calls "dialogues of the unconscious" in the unspoken communication and acquiescence between mother and son, applying it within the therapeutic relationship only after a fifteen-year incubation (Ferenczi, 1915, 1988; Miller, 1991). Similarly, Winnicott imports observation of the unitary relatedness between mother and infant as a model for dyadic relatedness (Miller, 2016b; Winnicott, 1949). This form of recognition and clinical location is fundamental to the enlargement of the therapeutic enterprise.

From its beginnings with Breuer and Freud, Bleuler, and forward into the twentieth and twenty-first century, analysts have sought to wrest non-psychotic functioning from a sea of psychotic functioning, reclaiming islands of normality and building upon them in life-affirmative growth (Bion, 1957; Katan, 1954; Sweet & Miller, 2016; Waelder, 1951). Recognising the phenomenon of splitting, together with the fine-grain workings of d, really an elaboration of the verbalisation and receptivity understood by Strachey more than eighty years ago to be "mutative" (1934), we have recognised both splitting and the synthesis of parts, not as bizarre objects but rather as consensually plausible and verbalisable constructions, which through the therapist's intuitive transmutation of his own particular countertransferential experience, allow the struggling patient a purchase on the development of psychic growth from within the nurturing and empathic frame of the psychoanalytic third.

What we have further highlighted in this chapter is the sense in which the non-metabolisation of thoughts, Bion's beta elements and Joseph's mental chuntering, lead invariably to more severe and complex mental health problems, including a range of psychosomatic conversion symptoms that are indicative of either a lack of symbolisation proper or the progressive denudation of the capacity for mentalization of thoughts, feelings, and emotions. In tandem, we have described some of the dynamic subtleties that are inherent clinically, in the re-emergence of and further integration of deeply split-off aspects of the self.

Against this, the process of arrivals in d, which we describe as reverse splitting, are fundamental in the recovery of projected aspects of the self, whether the object of projection has been external to the self or internal (intrapsychic or by the process of somatised conversion).

Much remains to be explored and further elaborated in relation to the concept of reverse splitting. We have not here explored more fully the implications of the concept as they relate to a metapsychological presentation of development, whether one utilises an object relations model (Balint, 1968; Fairbairn, 1952; Winnicott, 1958), a Kleinian schema (Klein, 1946; Segal, 1957; Spillius et al., 2011), or indeed draws on more recent research in the attachment field (Beebe, Rustin, Sorter, & Knoblauch, 2003; Fonagy, Gergely, Jurist, & Target, 2003).

Nor have we, in this chapter, sought to develop more fully the related area of projective counter-identification (Grinberg, 1962) which is often, in work with patients who evince severe psychopathology, accompanied by somatic conversion symptoms in the analyst. The dynamics of such a process and the sense in which we as practitioners also deploy reverse splitting in a self-preservative sense, is perhaps a subject to be developed and elaborated at a further stage.

Finally, we are aware that within the dynamics of reverse splitting, articulations and namings in d are both generated and lost across the temporal course of therapy. We are also aware that the therapist must fashion herself both as an agent of Freudian reminiscence, re-vivifying amnesias as well as in exhumation of the oblivions noted by Bion. We will have more to say about this in Chapter 8, "Meeting Heine in the Bronx".

CHAPTER SIX

On the essay: disclosing emboldened d (**d**)

This chapter illustrates the articulation of **d** elements through the presentational forms of the psychoanalytic essay. We have demonstrated an understanding of psychodynamic process that highlights the complex clinical emergence of momentary d experiences at the level of the clinical dyad, informed by the therapist's conceptual notions of psychodynamic practice, themselves a personalised matrix of meaningfully applicable **d** concepts.

The mutating and changing forms of **d** concepts is historically documented by Sandler and Dreher (1996) in the shifting emphases of psychoanalytic practitioners within different historical generations: from Freud's Habsburg and the traumatic post-Enlightenment experience of World War I; to the social ferment of Weimar; to the catastrophic destruction of World War II; to post-war social belief in the promise of psychoanalytic cure; to the moderating aims of psychoanalysis in line with clinical observations, leading to our own times.

This emergence is anything but trivial not only within each social generation of psychoanalysis but also within the individual psychoanalyst's developing maturity as inclusions and exclusions, where extensions, modifications, and conceptual heresies marked for oblivion determine the range of the therapist's interest, flexibility, clinical courage, and capability (Bergmann, 1999; Govrin, 2016). These begin with our initial determinations within the early years of our clinical trainings, of therapeutic task and scope. They are next elaborated across the years of work-life; and amplified in the main through several realms of experience.

The first, and most primary, is the therapist's own clinical experience. And, as amply commented upon, therapeutic experience is itself a complex business. Individuals are capable of sustaining their own attendance in intensive psychotherapy under resistant conditions in which very little is learned but the gross, temporal fact of having sustained a period of dyadic encounter. At this minimal level, the combative, defensive postures first noted in the 1920s (Landauer, 1924; Reich, 1972; Symington, 1986) and amplified by Winnicott and Bion as resonating with countertransferential hatred (Winnicott, 1949) and "attacks on linking" (Bion, 1957) hold sway relative to subjectively growth-enhancing utilisations of psychotherapy.

More productively, psychotherapy is conceived as having three significant periods: an incubation period of psychological distress predating therapy; the period of passionate engagement in the therapeutic thirdness of dynamic encounter with the therapist-other; and a third period of consolidation, in which the multiple strands of therapeutic experience (or d formations) emergent in therapy are applied productively in the subjective domain of one's ongoing experiences (Symington, 1986). An illustration of such productive use of this extended therapeutic process is reflected in the literary work of Samuel Beckett as well as the mutuality of patient-therapist interactions, mirrored in the therapeutic concepts of W. R. Bion (Miller, 2015; Miller with Souter, 2013).

Critical in such advance, as in all moments of psychotherapy, is the patient's openness to the plausibility of therapeutic intuition. Freud, like his philosophical precursor, Spinoza, would begin explanation of the free association technique with the sceptical instruction that nothing should be taken on belief without its becoming plausible in direct experience. Spinoza urges readers as analysts remind patients, to "continue on with me slowly, step by step, and to make no judgment on these matters until they have read through them all" (1677, p. 39).

Added to personal therapeutic experience (and in the experience of many of our colleagues, multiple courses of psychotherapy at different life stages following Freud's wise recommendations in his "Analysis

Terminable and Interminable" (1937c), are ongoing case discussions with clinical supervisors and peers; as well as contemplation of psychotherapists' writings on the subject of psychotherapy. In every therapeutic generation, as new clinicians learn both the commonplaces and omissions of previous generations as well as advancing beyond them, different matrices of theoretical and practice considerations gain ascendancy. These particularised vernacular expressions of psychodynamic definition underlie the more global naming of therapeutic technique as simply "psychoanalytic" (Miller, 2016a).

We have demonstrated how the insularity of therapeutic vernacular expressions both include and exclude potentially useful clinical concepts. Often, such exclusions are a function of the forms of "heresy" first noted by Freud in 1890 and 1909 relative to the practice of physical medicine, and replicated within psychoanalytic history. In presenting our ideas, we have striven to interweave ideas grounded by the differing and yet complementary experience of two co-authors across differing theoretical, cultural, and clinical domains. In this sense, we are reminded of the demonstrated fact in astronomy that a much more expansive view of the night sky can be gained by an array of telescopes placed across the Earth's surface—for instance in the case of the "Very Large Array" (VLA)—than by singular sightings. By approaching psychodynamic thinking in this way, we both suggest and exemplify a polar opposite view to the narrowly institutionalised perspectives commonly referenced in their respective orthodoxies. By contemplating a full expanse of psychodynamic history and thinking, we are able to appreciate the gaps and negations which each of us amplifies and often blurs through our all too human simplification of what can be explicitly known and accessed at any particular moment, the transitory ds and **d**s of our professional lives.

What follows is necessarily a subjective reading on differences in the expression of psychoanalytic elements as well as the analytic attitude from which such observations of form are made. Part I presents an array of five essays presented by Sigmund Freud at Clark University, in 1909 (1910a). Part II discusses the **d** elements reflected in this articulation of Freud's psychoanalytic expression in relation to those favoured by contemporary psychoanalytic readers during 2014–2015, combining the work of D. W. Winnicott and W. R. Bion (Miller, 2016a). Part III briefly reviews the conceptual matrix of **d** forms reflected in Freud's first 1909 lecture at Clark University.

I

Freud begins his early twentieth-century Massachusetts lectures in a most particular manner. His first comments register his own anxieties in addressing his American audience, which he typifies through a compressed stereotype of his understanding: that Americans are practical folk and solution-driven. Like a good clinician, he says what he thinks he knows; and anticipates clarification. Also, he admits his own trepidation in taking on his present task. Against Lacan's later (1953) reading of psychoanalysis, which we reference in Chapter 8, Freud's underlying position, offered to the audience at Clark, is as old as the oldest, most commonly read strand of Midrashic interpretation, the Passover Haggadah, as he leads his listeners from the anxious confusions of enslaved thinking, to new psychoanalytic freedom. In framing his lectures, he operates from the particularity of his own experience looking forward towards a universality of thought.

Freud begins his comments with reference to the manner in which we know what we know. And immediately explains that our epistemological certainty is faulty. Instead, he explains that "... wherever there is a symptom there is also an amnesia, a gap in the memory, and filling up this gap implies the removal of the conditions which led to the production of the symptom" (2010a, p. 20).

That is, the symptomatic psychological complaint points to a gap in knowing; and that gap is not empty but rather, signals underlying dynamics that eventuate in the clinically presented symptom. Freud immediately fills the gap he opens in the audience's hearing with the concept of an as-yet unrecognised, vibrant underpinning to the patient's psychological presentation, the fundamental **d** of a dynamic unconscious.

He narrates the theoretical development of psychoanalysis, beginning with the pre-analytic treatment of Anna O by Breuer; and underlines what is both an instructive societal observation and at the same time, an example through analogy of psychological dynamics. Echoing comments written twenty years earlier in his "Psychical (or Mental) Treatment", Freud differentiates psychological treatment from the larger medical field. And in so doing, describes a process of professional negation, in the consigning of psychodynamic understandings to the oblivions of heresy and contemptuous exclusion, resulting from a narcissistic reaction to injured omnipotence, followed by hateful rejection and blame.

These observations reflect professional attitudes as much as they disclose psychodynamic acts; and opposed to them, Freud endorses a humanistic psychoanalytic attitude of sympathetic attunement in listening to the patient's complaint. Here, he recognises that Breuer has perceived a positive presence within the "absences" remedied by what the patient, Anna O, calls the "talking cure", operating in the domain of expressed affects and worded communication. Freud tells his audience: "Never before had anyone removed a hysterical symptom by such a method or had thus gained such an insight into its causation" (p. 12).

Freud continues, explaining that the general form observed by Breuer and Freud has been tracked through the convergence of several traumas, compressed into symptomatic meaning. Within our present work, Chapter 7 tracks the obduracy of such embedded experience as narrated in the literary work of Samuel Beckett.

The analogy Freud makes to a "mnemic symbol" is to the historical monument such as London's Charing Cross which fully appreciated, discloses repressed memory, a willed amnesia such that

> "Breuer's patient, in almost all her pathogenic situations, was obliged to suppress a powerful emotion instead of allowing its discharge in the appropriate signs of emotion, words, or actions" (p. 17).

Clearly and concisely, Freud discloses a schematic of emotional constriction occurring between differing psychological levels, one more or less conscious and others unrecognised. The constriction, he explains to the audience, is a function of the patient's moralistic sense of social compliance and propriety; yet, he hints that there is much more. Indeed, in the emotional expression he outlines, freeing the patient both from her symptomatic distress and her ignorance as to its cause, emotional violence is generated. And, on the therapist's side, in engagement with the patient, there is a "considerable amount of labour" both in discerning the roots of distress and in empathic registrations with the patient.

Having taken the audience so far, Freud concludes the day's lecture with a cliffhanger, a novelistic literary form reaching back to Cervantes's description of Don Quixote's attack upon a Basque squire on a country road—not so different in combat, perhaps, than the classic confrontation between Oedipus and Laertes in Sophocles's play. He undercuts Breuer's contribution saying,

> Complete theories do not fall ready-made from the sky and you would have even better grounds for suspicion if anyone presented you with a flawless and complete theory at the very beginning of his observations. Such a theory could only be a child of his speculation and could not be the fruit of an unprejudiced examination of the facts. (p. 20)

And in so doing, leaves his reader waiting for more.

The next day's Lecture Two begins with Freud's historical reference to the theories on hysteria forwarded by Charcot and Janet; but what Freud makes memorable through his linkage to Lecture One, is reference to the strong intellectual capabilities of Anna O. Freud provides a trenchant analogy, undercutting definitively the nineteenth-century prejudice that hysterics are physiologically inferior to the rest of us. In so humanising his own dynamic conception of hysteria, Freud operates in the domain of multiple meanings. His use of Anna's refined skills in linguistic translation extend well past humorous analogy; while it mobilises within rhetorical argument the very dynamic of humour explained by Freud in his earlier work on wit (Freud, 1905b). Freud's thick multiplicity of meaning, similar to the unconsciously embedded truth that makes a joke "funny", also strikes at the heart of the mid–nineteenth-century anti-Semitic characterisation of the Jew as physiologically inferior to gentile "normality" (Boyarin, 1997; Makari, 2008).

As if chuckling with his audience in an affable display of Viennese humour, Freud pointedly suggests that not only is the hysteric more human than otherwise, but perhaps also more gifted in certain regards. His analogy pits the hysteric as a harried shopper struggling with multiple, cumbersome parcels with her skill as extraordinary linguist, deftly demonstrating a capacity for simultaneous translation between multiple languages.

And so, Freud's sharp contrast of a clumsy shopper juggling parcels with the adept linguistic translation of one set of language signs into multiple transformations is not only reflective of the transformative conceptual series he endorses—such as the psychological transformations between symptom, dream, parapraxis, joke, and transference—but also obliquely, of Jewish accommodation from ethnically particular tongues of Yiddish and Hebrew into the more universally spoken languages of Western Europe, as modelled by Anna O in the presence of Josef Breuer (see Chapter 9). Freud's polysemic analogy addresses both mental and Jewish suffering as particular aspects of the universal challenges facing all people as we judge ourselves and others from positions ranging between affirmation and destructive negation, as reflected later in Chapter 8.

Returning to a theme originally signalled in the example of medical science's fragmentation of knowledge between what is certain and what is uncertain to the practising physician, Freud again underlines the idea of hysterical dissociation as a "splitting of consciousness", elaborated by us in the previous chapter. And as if in segue, Freud immediately shifts from this significant underlining of **d** as a conceptual discovery in psychoanalysis to the particulars of his personal experience. This is no segue at all, but **d** at a completely different level of consideration. He admits his personal imperative in finding another technique for approaching hysteria as a "practical necessity" in that he could not himself effectively conduct hypnotic treatments. Today's contemporary reader is immediately reminded of Winnicott's (1949) comments to therapists to be cognisant of their own life experiences, their own special strengths and capacities, as Freud writes that "I was set the task of learning from the patient something I did not know and that he did not know himself" (1910a, p. 22).

Here, another form of **d** emerges in Freud's disclosure, an attitudinal orientation operative at a level interactive with the discernment in **d** of motivated, split-off states of consciousness. The imperative of flexible practice in the face of clinical obstacles (with this example indicative of the clinician's inability) both satisfies an American audience's orientation to the utilitarian and practical as it also affirms scientific rigour in differentiating what we know from what we do not know.

Beginning with the hypnotic technique he neither enjoyed nor mastered, Freud describes an imperative clinical position that illuminates all subsequent psychoanalytic inquiry: an initial starting point between two fields of uncertainty, one within the therapist and the other within the patient.

By this point in the second Clark lecture, Freud has already demonstrated to his listeners and readers, the psychoanalytic generation of a thinking-matrix composed of differing elements relating theory and practice at intersecting levels of conceptual orientation. Not only does he set out the desideratum of exploring the forms by which unconscious and split-off motivations eventuate in symptoms and their relief, but also the attitudinal positions necessarily adopted by therapists in pursuit of such inquiries.

Freud's thinking next concerns the therapist's elicitation of the symptom's underlying components. How is one to elicit what one does not know? He tells the audience that he originally utilised Bernheim's physical laying on of hands, pressing upon the patient's forehead and insisting upon the patient's remembering. This forceful technique was both "laborious" and "exhausting"; and also, in a dramatic expression of what Hanna Segal would one day term "symbolic equation", physically models the notion of repression as a force preventing emergence except when countered by the therapist's strong counter-force! Freud's clinical illustration, predating the focus of the second generation of psychoanalytic thinkers upon clinical resistance, nevertheless illustrates the precedence of resistance to transference within categories of practical clinical significance. Resistance emerges in relation to the very task of learning what neither knows, together with the patient; and is depicted by Freud at Clark as psychic defence.

At this point, close reading becomes critical. Freud explains resistance as the force causing repression, the force that disallows emergence of the wishful impulse. Such wishfulness emerges, according to Freud, as sharply contrasting with the main aggregations of the patient's character or personality. As such, clashing, affect-laden thoughts become "incompatible" with morality, ethics, and aesthetic values. And in this moment of nascent registration, after a brief conflict, Freud writes that "the idea which had appeared before consciousness as the vehicle of this irreconcilable wish fell a victim to repression" (p. 24).

What appears from our historical vantage point as Freud's modest introduction at Clark, illustrating the pushing-out from consciousness of thoughts and feelings antagonistic to ethical standards, is intellectually significant from multiple vertices. Certainly, we recognise within this description, the **d** of dynamic conflict, as two psychic groupings struggle against one another.

And too, we recognise the relativity of strength between these groupings—a suggestion of an economics within psychic life, the phenomenological calculus of internal life, of pleasures and unpleasures, recognised in modern psychology since its articulation within Spinoza's *Ethics* (1677).

For Freud as for Spinoza before him, these relative forces are not simply passive and active, but ragingly alive, passionately violent in their combat. Here, Freud takes a step beyond Spinoza's articulation of three psychic forces operative within all psychology: pleasure, unpleasure, and "desire" (Spinoza, ibid.). Freud operationalises the Spinozan meaning of "desire" as that which has achieved momentary consciousness and so achieves a nascent fusion with the subject's appetitive capacity for action. Spinoza's "desire" is otherwise confusing, operating at a dynamic psychic level conceptually more sophisticated than his pleasure and unpleasure—the operations of which are also entailed within Freudian metapsychology. Instead, Spinozan desire is imbued with a history of having achieved momentary consciousness, from which the fantasy of enactment upon the external world becomes fused within a configuration of internal image or representation and affect (see Chapter 3 on symbolisation).

Freud's second lecture at Clark assumes Spinoza's psychology as a given in the clinical intuition that repression "victimises" in its censorship, the Spinozan idea of desire momentarily appearing before subjective consciousness! Without attribution, Freud's comment supercharges Spinoza's self-observations into a formal dynamic tool, an observation in **d**, useful within the clinical dyadic field. Having implicitly extended psychology from its eighteenth-century Spinozan roots into the twentieth century, Freud now differentiates his own understandings from the contributions of his teacher, Josef Breuer.

And for the first time in this presentation, Freud's reasoning wobbles a bit. Having come so far in establishing the **d** concepts suggested to his audience, he forwards a weak if clever argument, that "… the Anna O case history is not suited to this purpose, because its findings were reached with the help of hypnotic influence. It is only if you exclude hypnosis that you can observe resistances and repressions" (1910a, p. 26).

While correct conceptually that hypnosis may conceal resistance and make its tracings inaccessible, it is clear by the significance in **d** of what Freud has already spent two lectures conveying, that he is ambivalent in his differentiation from Breuer, upon whose work he comments, as if cauterising the gap left by his own departure from his mentor:

> Our most valuable lesson from Breuer's observation was that what it proved concerning the relation between symptoms and pathogenic experiences or psychical traumas, and we must not omit now to consider these discoveries from the standpoint of the theory of repression. (p. 26)

From this point, Freud is immediately back on his rhetorical feet, thrilling the audience with another analogy—his second after the example of Anna O's linguistic accomplishments—this time, engaging not only the context in which he appears at Clark, but what later psychology will call "thirdness" (Ogden, 1994)—the very field in which Freud is operating as a clinician. Engagingly, Freud extends the analogy of a heckler in his own presentation; and addresses the interruption not only of himself as speaker but also of the audience and of his host, Professor Stanley Hall. His analogy requires the understanding that in thinking-through what Freud is describing as repression, all participants within the clinical act of thinking are engaged together!

Of course, while he is brilliantly illustrating the operations of repression, nothing Freud says contradicts anything in Breuer's method; but never mind, he is attempting to move forward into his own discoveries and to illustrate repression as another concept in **d**, even if it requires what seems at first hearing, the imposition of a willed amnesia about the very contexts in which other forms of **d** emerged earlier: exactly along the same line of "reminiscence" represented by Freud's earlier citing of the Charing Cross. That is, while departing conceptually from Breuer, he has not really consigned Breuer to oblivion: his observations stand as foundational to what emerges beyond them; and the memory of this work endures. Nothing is obliterated, but rather, remains memorialised, if not in gratitude then in original attribution.

Freud's Lecture Three begins with a movement familiar to clinicians. He tells the audience that he has been thinking about what has gone on between them; and himself forwards a second opinion, an extension of his own thinking within the context of the present relational moment. Freud is mindful that each encounter at Clark is linked; and that while the present moment is significant, memory and desire of prior experience is continuously evoked within the clinical process.

Freud's revised statement further describes his modification of technique. He again reminds the audience that he is fallible; and that psychoanalysis is a technique in continuous change. He also credits the observations of other clinical workers, those of the Zurich school—including Bleuler, Jung, and Abraham—for discovering the useful clinical form of the symptom complex, another **d** element.

Freud quickly reiterates the centrality of repression, explained in Lecture Two, which is now linked to other dimensions within an unconscious constellation of symptomatic indications, both direct and represented indirectly. His illustration is by another analogy, this time an example of wit. And, recognising that his audience is in gentile Massachusetts, he does not provide a Viennese Jewish joke in the manner of Heine (see Chapter 8), but rather a joke about Jesus among thieves, all to be crucified at the same time. Here, the universality of the idea—both in wit and in the concept of repression—is clothed in the particularity of an example meant to be understood by the audience. The conceptual **d** represented by Freud's direct speech not only addresses the audience clearly in clinical communication, but also utilises concepts and language as recognisable to the audience as to the patient. Echoing Spinoza's recommendation that while sceptical, one must refrain from judgement in the context of mining the "ore" of clinical associations, Freud clearly summarises what at this moment are the three technical domains of psychoanalytic disclosure: clinical free association, the interpretation of dreams, and the understanding of "slips", parapraxes, and jokes.

Tacitly, Freud reminds his audience that they must remain sceptical of what he tells them until arriving at a sense of its plausibility, by drawing attention to himself as engaged on a seemingly ridiculous task through introducing psychoanalysis to the United States, where "It seemed to me almost indecent in a country which is devoted to practical aims to make my appearance as a 'dream interpreter'" (p. 33).

At another level, Freud operates here not only as the butt of his own joke, but also as a thinker who capably puts himself in the other's shoes, anticipating George Herbert Mead's (1934) taking on of the other's perspective, in attempting to demonstrate that he is capable of considering what the audience may have in its collective mind.

And so, Freud continues Lecture Three with a discussion of dreams, arriving at the dream as analogous to hysterical symptoms in the relation between a dream's manifest content and its unconscious dream work. Dramatically, he illustrates how sleep allows a "veil of disguise" against which "… the dreamer can no more understand the meaning of his dreams than the hysteric can understand the connection and significance of his symptoms" (1910a, p. 35).

In rapid succession, Freud expands upon a number of linked **d** elements including: the general technique of dream interpretation; the idea of dream work together with the analyst's synthetic act of understanding dreams, transmitted to the patient; as well as the nature of symbolism, especially in relation to sexual complexes. Additionally, he addresses anxiety dreams and parapraxes, arriving at the observation that our psychic life betrays our most intimate secrets to those who recognise their forms.

By this point at the end of Lecture Three, the reader is fairly swimming in a sea of **d** concepts; and Freud concludes with psychoanalytic conviction in strict psychic determination as the human faces an "arrogance of consciousness" in rejecting psychodynamic demonstration of unconscious complexes—a general statement of the paranoid/schizoid position later developed by Klein, relative to a universally plausible dynamic of the depressive position's difficult arrival as the individual's compromise with reality.

Lecture Four begins with Freud's tracing backward pathogenic complexes to sexual life; and with his now characteristic encouragement of scepticism, he encourages his audience to adopt a similar incredulity. He says,

> People are in general not candid over sexual matters. They do not show their sexuality freely, but to conceal it they wear a heavy overcoat woven of a tissue of lies as though the weather were bad in the world of sexuality. Nor are they mistaken. It is a fact that sun and wind are not favourable to sexual activity in this civilized world of ours; none of us can reveal his eroticism freely to others. (p. 41)

Freud's declaration is revolutionary; and conceptually, also suggests in its impact, a departure from his earlier **d** of cumulative traumatic onsets; but his generation of **d** concepts is expansive rather than restrictive. He extols the growth of trust by the patient in the therapist, rooted in a new-found psychotherapeutic freedom when: "... patients discover that they can feel quite easy about it while they are under your treatment, they discard this veil of lies and you are in a position to form a judgment on this debatable question" (p. 41).

Freud's language appears to grow thickly poetic as repressions and resistances are transformed into veils of lies and disguise, heavy clothing meant to weather stormy conditions in "the world of sexuality". And yet again, Freud seems to wobble, as he had earlier in consideration of Breuer. Now, he steps back, proposing that sexual fixation must occur prior to traumatic onset in that the

> work of analysis required for the thorough explanation and complete recovery of a case never comes to a stop at events that occurred

> at the time of the onset of the illness, but invariably goes back to the patient's puberty and early childhood; and it is only there that it comes upon the impressions and events which determined the later onset of the illness. It is only in experiences in childhood that explain susceptibility to later traumas and it is only by uncovering these almost invariably forgotten memory-traces and by making them conscious that we acquire the power to get rid of the symptoms. (p. 41)

Almost breathlessly, Freud links symptomatic acts within the complex history of early life; and while such linkages might seem simply constructed, their resolution will require the continuous action of transference with countertransference at the therapeutic surface of the working dyad rather than a compressed therapeutic fantasy of the patient's past. Yet, here Freud's enthusiasm becomes infectious, cheerleading the reader in belief that the sexual and "repressed wishful impulses of childhood have alone provided the power for the construction of symptoms and without them the reaction to later traumas would have taken a normal course" (p. 41).

He buttresses his argument with examples from European as well as American research; and returns to an argument very similar to his initial premise about physicians' splitting off consideration of psychic causation as an insult to their professional omniscience, focused now on the rejection of thinking about infantile sexuality:

> It is only too easy to explain why most people (whether medical observers or others) will hear nothing of the sexual life of children. They have forgotten their own infantile sexual activity under the pressure of their education to a civilized life, and they do not wish to be reminded of what has been repressed. They would arrive at other convictions if they were to begin their enquiry with a self-analysis, a revision and interpretation of their early childhood memories. (p. 43)

Gathering steam, Freud conveys more **d** elements including: oral, anal, and urethral zones of bodily stimulation; the relation to others as "objects" of infantile desire; the oppositional pairing of instincts such as the active-passive; and the nature of early childhood psychosexual fixation, against the internalised morality of societal structures set up "like watchmen" to maintain repressions, often overcome at puberty under the "high tide" of sexual demand, from which the flowing courses of psychic energy are determined and channelled.

The reader, barely containing Freud's excited articulations of **d** contents, becomes aware of a pressure while reading: no longer is there time to think or to reflect; rather, the press of words and concepts seems to overwhelm. Pausing, the reader wonders whether Freud's form of presentation anticipates Bion's self-conscious desire to replicate, within essay form, the experience of psychotherapy? Or rather, does Freud's formal pressure upon the reader's thinking replicate in sympathetic parallel, the psychosexual pressures he wants the audience to recognise?

Freud proceeds at great speed, citing but leaving undeveloped pathological developments in sexual development within the relation of subjects including heterosexuality; homosexuality; perversion; the sexual lives of children; the literary stories of Oedipus and Hamlet in relation to familial incest; and the intellectual curiosity of children in sexuality, the epistemophilic instinct. He concludes by characterising the educational nature of psychotherapy in overcoming the residues of childhood.

Lecture Four leaves the reader reeling. It is difficult to contain the proliferation of **d** concepts and elements, as well as their general patterns of interaction; and the newness and forcefulness of Freud's sexual arguments seem to momentarily crush his earlier arrivals into the foundations of his monumental theory of infantile sexuality. The pressured depiction of the human's sexualised world seems to overwhelm the containment in thinking of **d** elements, achieved in earlier lectures. Minimally, at this point, the reader recognises viscerally that thinking itself can become overwhelmed under the pressures emergent in psychoanalysis—even in its literary form as essay.

Lecture Five continues this theme and pressure, as if all the smaller **d** elements have now achieved fusion under Freud's bigger idea of infantile sexuality. He now describes the tracing backward of neurotic symptoms to erotic and instinctual components, arguing that illness results either from external obstacles to gratification or internal adaptive incapacity.

Freud now amplifies the **d** of resistance; and portrays an ego or self that finds unsatisfying the realities offered by the external world. Instead, humans prefer to remain in phantasy's domain of wish-fulfilment. Freud defines success in each person's human project as the turning of wishful phantasies into reality; and its failure is in breakdown, whether for external or internal cause.

Again, as in Lecture One, Freud returns to the similarity of neurosis and normality, finding no neurotic psychical contents that are not found among the healthy. The question of health, psychosis, or superior sublimatory achievement "depends on quantitative considerations, on the relative strength of the conflicting forces" (p. 50).

Freud's balance of conflicting dynamics might come directly from Spinoza. But for its location within the sexual realm of instinctual drives, Freud again mirrors Spinoza's quantitative psychic economics of pleasure and unpleasure mediated by the individual's mind.

Freud concludes these five essays with consideration of the patient's emotional life in relation to the therapist. What begins conceptually in resistance is extended into transference, emergent through material which the patient "can no longer recall to memory" and which is now "re-experienced" in relation to the therapist. Freud terms this relational response the "clinical heart of psychoanalysis"; and construes it within therapy as a "catalytic ferment which temporarily attracts to itself the affects liberated in the process" (p. 50). And so, it is from within transference that the patient (like Freud's reader or audience) develops conviction in the plausibility of method. Freud concludes his lecture series with comments upon our highest cultural achievements relative to our original, instinctual animal endowments. And, characteristically, he ends with consideration of our sexualised animal nature, in the paradoxical form of a joke—about the horse of "Schilda"—a town of fools like Beckum or Chelm, signalling the simplicity of its residents. Freud's joke is a final plea within these lectures to tolerate consideration of the instinctual unconscious and to allow some gratification of the human desire for sexuality, lest the strength of the human project and civilisation's need for the fruits of sexual sublimations die of starvation.

II

Freud's Five Lectures at Clark are a tour de force. They illustrate **d** elements both as conceptual contents and as attitudes of psychoanalytic presentation. Quite dramatically, Freud's demonstrations of **d**, whether as specific elements in psychodynamic theory or as attitudes of therapeutic expression, shift as he seeks to convince the audience on days four and five. It is presumed that by this time, the audience has grown in trust towards Freud, warming to his delivery on days one, two, and three. And the reader begins to experience physically the urgency of Freud's message as the cumulative power of words and concepts itself acts to obliterate thinking!

From Bion's later psychoanalytic perspective, we might suggest that the intensity of language itself derails thinking, causing an attack on linking. But the context of these lectures must also be considered; and a recognition that the passionately radical final days of Freud's lectures require the slower, more painstaking development of earlier thought discernible in Lectures One, Two, and Three. Under either scenario, Freud demonstrates that within the **d** of psychoanalytic conveyance, in literary description as in clinical enactment, there exists a broad range of capacity for thinking and anti-thinking, for the registration against the uncertainties of emergence of knowledge (K) as of anti-thinking (–K) and the destructive negation of thought's contents. More prosaically, the pressures and emotional tones of different psychotherapeutic sessions may vary greatly.

The cumulative impact of Freud's lectures begins to be discerned in Lectures Four and Five. This aggregating force feels obliterating of the carefully discerned **d** elements emergent in earlier lectures; and perhaps less carefully in argument but more passionately in affective charge, Freud succeeds brilliantly in arguing for what certainly remains the revolutionary big idea of psychoanalysis, transformative of twentieth century thinking and morality, in relation to human sexuality.

His presentation of infantile sexuality and reshaping of the theory of repression, originally described as traumatogenic in origins, back in the days of Breuer's hypnosis, recast earlier **d**s into newer, more brightly exciting forms. And it is with this triumphant arrival rather than with the more plodding step of analogy and slow explanation of days one, two, and three, that Freud concludes his work.

Freud's purpose is to convey a certainty of arrival in psychoanalytic theory; and by contrast, the five essays by Winnicott and Bion, reflective of today's most popular choices in the 650,000 pages of our psychoanalytic library, reflect exactly those uncertainties, apparent too within Freud's earlier statement of **d** at Clark, that remain with us—even as we continue to practise in modern cultures radically transformed by Freud's big idea. Psychotherapists must continue to set themselves the task of learning both from self and other "something I did not know and that he did not know himself" (p. 22).

We accomplish this by paying attention to what we do together within the clinical session. Freud (1910a) as much as Bion and Winnicott, focuses on the interpersonal relations within the discrete session; but his mission in a consolidated series of five essays, constructed to convert the already-interested in the compelling work of psychoanalysis, differs from theirs—selected from a historical point, fifty years after their writing and a century after Freud's, signalling useful concepts in **d**, for integration within each therapist's respective, personally attuned matrix of **d** expressions.

Winnicott and Bion leave the reader with the impression of wide gaps still to be explored, against the more enthusiastic, initial certainties of Freud. These are the uncertainties and certain forms of clinical emergence faced in the daily work of psychotherapy; and so, this vernacular expression of psychoanalysis reflects less a polemical introduction to the field then a manual for approaching the necessary challenges confronted by its dedicated workers (Miller, 2016).

Before turning from Freud (1910a) it might be helpful to reiterate the knotted skein of **d** concepts, generated en route to his big idea. These include the **d**s: of the therapist's necessary humility in taking on the work of continuously facing the unknown; the necessity to continually assess and reassess the efficacy of one's working method; the discrete capabilities and blockages of each individual therapist; the building of **d** forms themselves, as variations upon the thinking received from others; the variations of tone and passion from one clinical session to another; and the difficulty of balance, in elucidating one dimension of emergent knowing, of threatening destructive negation of something else. Freud models as **d**: the necessity of saying what one thinks one knows; the awareness of the therapist's own anxiety in doing the work of therapy; hope in therapeutic movement from anxiety to the possibilities of freedom; illustrations of the relation between particularity and universality; the faultiness of our certainty as we confront resistances that are instinctual, social, ethical, and aesthetic; the economics of internal affective experience; and the wisdom of linguistic expression between one person and another in facilitating trust towards the freeing of that which was emotionally constrained.

Reading and rereading these five lectures, we discover more: that the symptom is indicative of a gap, motivated by conflict; that through observation of what people do within the consultation room, we discern their forms of action and intuit motivation; that these include the dividing or splitting of their objects of action and thought as well as the actions of projecting, blaming, and disowning; and that actions may eventuate both in what may be recovered and in what was intended to be obliterated.

Freud's expository manner informs our clinical range of attitude, at times: humorous, balanced, passionate, explanatory, deeply receptive; and continuously mindful of the fine detail of causality within the interactions between one person and another. While Freud arrives at a theory of psychosexual fixation, he also generates a theory of cumulative psychic trauma and symbolisation. Scepticism, argument, demonstration, analogy, are all part of his engaged literary demonstration; as is the confrontation of fixed, prejudicial thinking. All of this is folded into the humanistic notion that what is shared by us all, pathologically and in health, is common to all humans. And that against our obdurate resistance to containing the act of thinking, we all face uncertainty both in relation to what is external to us, and internal within us.

III

This chapter concludes with a suggestion of the matrix of **d** conceptions generated within Freud's First Lecture at Clark University. We suggest that this aggregation of multi-level concepts exhibits a pattern for every psychoanalyst's generation of his own, personalised, and utilitarian vernacular expression, looking backward in psychoanalytic history as Oedipal affirmation and difference; and forward, both to the local conditions of his own practice and to the post-Freudian developments over six generations of psychoanalytic evolution.

Freud's First Clark Lecture describes a matrix of **d** recognitions. These include the following points:

1. Recognition and articulation of the therapist's anxiety in light of preconceptions about the other, whether the therapeutic patient, reader, or audience. This is a demonstration of **d** as an emotional position residing in the therapist.
2. That the therapeutic project is potentially hopeful in its transition from constrained experience to a personal freedom in knowing oneself. This is a demonstration of **d** as orientation to therapeutic task.
3. Additionally, Freud articulates a **d** in the psychotherapist's operational attitude or manner of receptivity and response. Freud depicts

this attitude as humanistic in the sympathetic attunement within listening, hearing, and making meaning of the patient's complaint.

4. The recognition of the symptom as revealing an amnesia, a motivated gap that hints at the original conditions for its generation. This is a descriptively metapsychological **d**, reflecting depth and dynamics. It is also a descriptively epistemological form of **d** , illustrating that the symptom and its mysteries are indicative of not knowing, of what Bion would later term both (O) and (–K).
5. Freud's **d** conviction that the amnesia's gap can be filled: as by effective reminiscence in the example of Anna O. This Freudian certainty is challenged by mid-twentieth-century psychoanalysts such as Winnicott and Bion, towards an indeterminacy in psychoanalytic inquiry, mediated by therapeutic intuition and patient plausibility (Miller, 2015, 2016).

   As we suggest in Chapter 5, through the **d** of reverse splitting, a partial and transitory filling of Freud's gap is continuously worked in the ongoing process of psychoanalysis. We term this a "white hole" in Chapter 4; and it is a structure that often emerges through a process of reverse splitting and verbal articulation.

   Describing this routine, interpersonally dyadic filling, Freud's Lecture One explanation of the unconscious dynamic itself effectively enacts a filling of the gap or anxiety induced by Freud upon his audience. He gives an answer to the question he puts: this is the **d** of the therapist's action with the Other.
6. Freud challenges the audience with analogies in a **d** of psycho-educational persuasion. This is multiply demonstrated. For example, this dynamic **d** (with specific analogous reference to the contemporary medical community) includes observations of separable action elements including: narcissistic injury; splitting; projection; blame; and destruction of the object.
7. Freud's observations in **d** include both: 1) the symptomatic convergence, through the patient's disclosures, of several traumata; and 2) psychosexual fixation.
8. Cumulatively narrated in his Clark Lectures, **d** is depicted in multiplicity and non-linear focus. Its changing dimensions ultimately converge within the therapist's intuition in relation to an object—which is the clinical situation energised by the patient's complaint; paralleling the convergent form of convergent traumata.

9. Freud also introduces the mnemic symbol as a **d** element. The symbol exists on its own as a concept and is implicated in non-linear form, within the dynamics of symptom emergence.
10. Observation of symptomatic emergence becomes the foundation of an evidence-based hypothesis, rooted in observable forms within the consultation room. Reciprocal action upon this recognition by the therapist allows its emotional discharge (against hypothesised suppression) "in appropriate signs of emotion, words, or action".
11. Freud demonstrates interaction between multiple working models as **d** in the recognition of conflict between different levels of conscious and unconscious psychological functioning.
12. Freud ventures another hypothetical **d**, subject to revision in Lecture Three, that the patient's emotional suppression is a function of her internalisation of societal compliance and propriety.
13. An observation in **d** that the encounter between patient and therapist necessitates a considerable amount of labour as well as the generation of emotional violence en route to understanding distress; and in ongoing empathic relatedness to the patient.
14. Finally, before concluding for that day, analogous to a therapeutic session's end, Freud addresses the **d** of uncertainty. He writes that theoretical developments are always partial. And so, both for its practitioners and critics as for the patient, require (in the later language of W. R. Bion) a capacity to contain one's unknowing in light of future uncertainties.

CHAPTER SEVEN

Temporal arrivals in d: Beckett from time (n) to (n+1), (n+2), (n+3), and (n+4)

I

It is helpful to think of arrivals in d as progressive realisations across time. Each is a present formulation expressing the particularities of the patient's "how it is", mediated from within the intuitive resonance of the psychoanalyst. To illustrate such temporal successions of d(n), d(n+1), d(n+2), d(n+3), and d(n+4), this chapter presents a set of literary recognitions which in their repetition and rhythm, parallels the emergence of d expressions in clinical process. For specific detail about the contents of this series, it might be helpful if the reader were to reference its original (n+1) articulation. It appears in Chapter 5 of a previous publication of one of the authors, "How it is across time: The road from Connolly's store" in *On Minding and Being Minded* (Miller, 2015).

Within this illustration and related to the same stimulus array, successive recognitions of d emerge over time. The entire literary sequence is centred on a single reader's appreciative identification of four narrative vignettes published over a period of thirty-three years, by Samuel Beckett (Miller, 2015). While this Beckett "series" assumes special significance in the context of the present chapter, each of its literary elements operates independently of one another in four separate works:

"The End" (2006b, p. 277); *Malone Dies* (2006a, p. 261); "From an Abandoned Work" (2006b, p. 342); and *Company* (2006b, p. 428). Yet, with the recognition of these independent narratives as a unitary series between time (n) and time (n+1) (Miller, 2015), this new composite d consolidation achieves catalytic generativity within the reader's progressive realisation of meaning, further facilitating new d recognitions at successive moments in time. Noting this, we observe that from time (n) onward, each formulation of d, while still centred in these four Beckett narrative vignettes, also partakes of thinking generated through the reader's unique and changing contexts of discovery. Reading, under this recognition, parallels the incremental development of psychodynamic understanding across multiple sessions, each differing in content, questions, and response. Here, in the absence of an individual's capability to remember (Freud, 1914g), reading replicates the therapeutic force of "repeating" in allowing for new and shifting forms of recognition in d, within the task-focused context of the therapeutic relationship (Ferenczi & Rank, 1923).

Yet, with the application of the reader's intuition, as with the therapeutic application of the therapist's intuition, a transformational dynamic emerges between two entities. Therapeutically, this in-between capability is referenced by contemporary psychoanalysis as the "third" (Ogden, 1994); and corresponds to the fusions and defusions of experience within the therapeutic couple, necessitating the analyst's metabolisation of the particularities of patient experience through 1) intuition and 2) linkage with more universalised dynamic concepts, or what we term **d**, before 3) "re-clothing" the resultant interpretive verbalisation in preconceptual language familiar—because it has already been heard or witnessed within the therapeutic third—to the patient. The generalised form of this utterance is in the declaration that, "What you call X, I call Y", with the linkage between X and Y facilitated by the therapist's direct experience of the patient's own naming of X within their joint history of therapeutic meetings. By necessity, the creation of such progressive linkage and elaboration of experience between therapist and patient requires that each must endure challenging periods of not-knowing, uncertainty, anxiety, and at times, anguish.

Within and through this action, Bion's negation of memory and desire in the immediacy of the therapeutic session is reversed as therapeutic containment is mobilised intuitively in thinking and verbalised interpersonal communication. Above, in Chapter 4, we reference this action as the building of a scaffolding between the dreadful experience of the annihilative black hole, itself illustrated by Beckett in "The End" (2006b) as the first member of his narrative series.

The analyst functions as a joint repository of "unitary" (see Winnicott, 1953) memory related to interpersonal experience undergone within what Ferenczi and Rank characterise as the "artificially induced" libidinal relationship that is the therapeutic transference (1923, p. 6).

Similarly, because my own discernment of multiple d expressions across time emerges from private experience of the Beckett series' textual silence, the reader's experience of intuition, like the therapist's and the writer's in his narration, straddles a boundary between one- and two-person psychologies (Mitchell & Aron, 1999; Rickman, 1951) with the reader, like the therapist in psychotherapy, participating actively as witness. These two forms of psychology differ in that one-person psychology focuses upon "what goes on inside one person taken in isolation" (Rickman, 1951, p. 110), while two-person psychology enters the "psychological region of reciprocal relationships" existent "when two persons are in a more or less closed region and are tied to one another by simultaneously acting aims, tasks, or needs" (ibid.).

Twenty years prior to Rickman's differentiated **d** of two psychological forms, Freud had described the same conceptual territory in his elaboration upon his 1905 *Jokes and Their Relation to the Unconscious*. In "Humour" (1927d), Freud distinguishes 1) between the single individual's gratifying reflection upon the world, disclosing a painfully pleasurable irony—as in the example of a condemned man's reflection en route to the scaffold that, "Well, the week's beginning nicely"; and 2) the interpersonal or two-person operation of humour, when the second person is made "the object of humorous contemplation by the other", to which Freud links the situation obtaining between a writer and his characters. Each mode may be appreciated by the reflective consideration of an audience, such as a listener or reader (p. 161).

The process of discerning d at a specific time (n) within the dyadic therapeutic relationship is one of the therapist's necessary tasks. It originates in the therapist's sensuous apprehension of the patient's experience within his own, subjective realm of particular emotional and cognitive resonance. This evocative intersubjective recognition is worked towards mutuality by the therapist in two movements. The first attempts linkage of what is particular to the therapist's experience with what is more psychologically universal to us all. The second further transforms this universality, translating it into the experiential language of the patient in a verbalised gesture towards the mutuality of shared meanings (see Chapter 8).

The following section describes the subjective emergence of my d recognitions over time, and ultimately, recognition of d emergence itself as a universal **d** element in psychoanalysis, as understood from within progressive readings of the Beckett series.

II

My first discernment that these narrative segments might be understood as a linked series began within the more general context of research concerning the relationship between Beckett and his psychoanalytic psychotherapist, W. R. Bion (Miller with Souter, 2013). It was not until my interests shifted to the mutually twinned literary and psychological expressions of Bion and Beckett (Miller, 2015), that the narrative series began to assume greater significance in my thinking. At this (n+1) point in time, the historical and affective links between the four Beckett vignettes in "The End", *Malone Dies*, "From an Abandoned Work", and *Company*, caused me to recognise time itself as a slow-motion connective membrane extending across several literary strands, akin to consolidations of therapeutic motifs across many sessions and years of psychotherapy.

Later, at time (n+2), I considered the series as a literary prototype of the clinical process of working through trauma across long periods of time (Miller, 2016b). However, this articulation in d was itself aided by the context in which I had presented the series at time (n+1). In that earlier context, I had linked Beckett's description in parallel with the life history of a patient seen in my own Dublin practice. This association caused me to consider the parallelism between Beckett's working through of trauma and the working through process observed in clinical psychoanalysis.

Each of these arrivals in d had been accompanied by the equivalent of therapeutic consensual validation, the witnessing and antiphonal response in clinical practice between patient and therapist. Articulations at times (n) and (n+1) were made public in the form of psychoanalytic books (Miller, 2015; Miller with Souter, 2013). Articulation at time (n+2) was in the form of a paper presented at a professional conference, occasioning lively and affirmative collegial discussion (Miller, 2016b).

My revisiting the series at time (n+3) resulted from the receptive encouragement that its articulation had received at time (n+2). My own expression of d seemed at this point to assume a bolder, **d** form as other clinicians enthusiastically affirmed the parallel of literary and clinical links as useful to them in illustration of clinical process. Their resonance with my presentation directed my interest back to my own original recognitions within the Beckett material at time (n) and (n+1). Provisionally, I had hypothesised that these initial recognitions had been conditioned (as had theirs) by the underlying similarities of our clinical training; but I hadn't yet given much conscious thought to the actual conditions of thinking that had influenced my selections from Beckett.

At roughly the same time, my curiosity was further energised by another contextual event, the announcement by the *British Journal of Psychotherapy*, of its 2016 Roszika Parker competition for an essay on the relation of psychoanalysis and art. These external, contextual convergences at time (n+3), related in my mind to a progressive set of d articulations, themselves now tethered in diverse ways not only to Beckett's literary narratives, but also to my own experiences and thinking in reading Beckett and Bion, created the perfect model of what Spinoza (1677) terms "desire"! That is, I was conscious of having achieved the epistemophilic pleasure of discovery in recognitions of d at multiple times (n), (n+1), and (n+2). And, I was also conscious of my appetitive capacity—that I could, by continuing to "work" my thinking in expansion of d conceptions, learn something more; and even better, that an encouraging social venue existed both for creative play and recognition through this very activity, a professional, academic competition. I was conscious of my own quantum of pleasure both in past and future arrivals in d at this delightfully seductive moment as well as of the possibility that through independent judges' consideration of the idea, later "commended" under competition, that I was again subjecting it to another degree of professional, consensual validation.

And so, adding to recognition of the Beckett series' capacity to generate my progressive thinking about formulations in d, here, at the temporal gap between times (n+2) and (n+3), I also experienced a private registration of indebtedness to the Beckett series for the joys of thinking stimulated in me through this undertaking. And yet, this registration of joy would remain inchoate, if preconsciously accessible, until now re-contextualising my new task in discernment of d at time (n+4). In this same moment, I realise that like Freud's original interpretive arrivals in the meaning of dreams, the interactions between my thinking and its linked associative relatedness to progressive expressions in d seemed open-ended and generative, limited only by my own alternation of focal attention.

Yet again at time (n+3), as throughout the timeline beginning with (n), I had recognised my "use" of Beckett's literary series for my own purposes. As Beckett writes in *How It Is*, that which was once without had now been taken within: and so, I would focus on the reverberations or resonances evoked by Beckett's writing (Miller, 2017; Minkowski, 1999) for my own subjective purposes in thinking. I was mindful too, that this is exactly the kind of phenomenological experience Beckett writes about in his monograph on Proust (1931), a bending or deformation of what had emerged at an earlier, lost, time, under the press of present temporal imperatives. At time (n+3) I had observed that:

> Like Freud's investigation into the form of jokes, I find myself becoming aware of a qualitative contrast, having immediate force that destabilizes the reader's immediate sense of coherence. While uncertain of what this means, I intuitively "mark" the destabilizing event, which becomes further marked in its future repetition. This requires emergence over time; and occurs for me only months later, when reading another Beckett work. Here, it establishes itself as possibly consequential in understanding the story, yet still remains evocative, but at the periphery of thought. Again, its resonant textual presence similarly fades in process to the next paragraph in its new context, but begins to register vaguely as I become aware of it at the margins of thinking. That is, its significance emerges in personal reverberation like the "red thread" Freud references as sewn into the rope-lines used by the Royal Navy, a connecting proprietary marker through multiple and differing forms of narrative presentation (Freud, 1905a). (Miller, 2017)

Now, finally, the Beckett series and I, together with you as reader, arrive at the present time (n+4) where the contextual setting is tinctured with the tasks of the present book, *On the Daily Work of Psychodynamic Psychotherapy*. Here, we orient the emergence of multiple d expressions to the temporal domain of W. R. Bion's algorithm and royal road to the practice of psychotherapy, PS $\leftrightarrow$ D PS (n+1) $\leftrightarrow$ D (n+1) (♀♂).

Our observation of d forms is directed to two aims at time (n+4). The first is to illustrate changes in d across different points in time, as d expressions themselves becomes amplified and achieve saturated maturity. For example, relative to the Beckett series, I suggested a therapeutic parallel at time (n+1) between Beckett's original depiction of childhood trauma in "The End" (2006b), and the narrator's mature and final, if still painful memory, having worked through destabilising emotion, in *Company* (2006b). Reflecting upon this Beckettian arrival in d, at time (n+2), I commented:

> Finally, this is the triumph of arrival; but as Leonard Cohen sings, "It is a cold and it's a very lonely Hallelujah" (1984 version) after vast stretches of time, an active and time-intensive period during which small bits of reality-based clarification are painfully fitted into a fabric of understanding, facilitated by the narrator's externalization of intense emotion and piercing recognitions about the mind of the Other as well as his own actions.
>
> Such working through requires time, both subjectively experienced and chronologically elapsed, in clarification of events and their contingencies; together with the capacity to access and to link ideas. Beyond terrified withdrawal, past persecutory dread of annihilation, the capability both to represent oneself and to mind the other are illustrated by Beckett as requirements of what becomes a final step in scarification. The wound remains; but the capacity to fold through thinking what had been unthinkable into the events that characterize one's own life passages, are paramount; and provide a fine approximation to therapeutic success.
>
> *The final statement points to the faint scar, continuing, always present*: "She shook off your little hand and made you a cutting retort you have never forgotten" (Beckett, 2006b) but with self affirmed, agency and causality regained, and emotion contained rather than projected externally.
>
> *Which of course, leaves us facing the challenge of the next chapter, the next session*. (Miller, 2016b)

This example, observed of the Beckett series at time (n+2), parallels the idea of self-development epitomised as therapeutic realisation (Federn, 1940; Sullivan, 1954), itself illustrating the benefit expected by the patient in the therapeutic dyad.

Yet, en route to this observation, I discerned other moments as well. The invitation to discuss the psychoanalytic treatment of trauma together with literature returned my interest to my earlier observations, which I had used as a baseline for observing the "how" and "what" employed literarily by Beckett in this sequence.

Again, as at time (n+1), I observed the narrative depictions of shock, emotional projection "into" physical objects including sky and house, and what seemed to be resolution of the traumatic experience as a function of this individually borne working through. It was a small step to infer the invasive and intrusive effect of the traumatic stimulus, affecting the narrator at a physical level (Money-Kyrle, 1968). Contextually within "The End", the memory of this moment causes the narrator to lose his immediate task focus, suggesting that the pain still endures. This raises into high relief the moderated reflection of the same incident thirty-three years later; and I sought clues in two intermediate vignettes.

The narrator's extrusion of the emotional experiences relating both to the explosive shock of his mother's words and, in later repetition, to the person of his mother (Beckett, 2006b, p. 342) appeared to shift his capacity to represent his experience symbolically to himself. Whereas the trauma itself had been experienced physically, obliterating symbolic capacity (Bonomi, 2003), successive reminiscence together with vivid projection, akin to projective identification in clinical practice, allowed a progressively wider internal capability for thinking in clarifying events and claiming personal agency differentiated from traumatic fusion with mother.

Finally, though mindful of an unfortunate circumstance, never adequately explained, the narrator understands enough of its circumstances to be free of its destructive claim on emotional experience and thinking. I saw this as analogous to therapeutic benefit in a realisation about and through lived experience, both freeing emotionally and contributory to self-development.

The second aim, now at time (n+4), provides the current reader of *On the Daily Work of Psychodynamic Psychotherapy* with a concretised example of shifting versions or clarifications in d across time, through reference both to clinical case material and to literary narrative. This aim presses the d forms of the Beckett series into utilitarian service as a segue into the exploration of the unmarked emotional territory described in Chapter 8, "Meeting Heine in the Bronx". In Chapter 8, d

expressions along the n timeline vary from the present example in that they must be individually and privately noted, lest they disappear into oblivion—similar to the markings by a writer in his narrative depiction or, less enduringly, as the patient marks her experience in vocalisation addressed to the therapist's hearing. Here, the writer has an advantage relative to the patient: written words stand as a more enduring marker than oral and gestural communication.

Yet, each of these active forms contributes to a continuum of landmarks. The author's is more concretised than the patient's. Like a cairn of stones on a mountainside, the author's narrative is concretised and visible. The patient's words, by contrast, may disappear—both because her action in therapy is intended to rid her of the emotion underlying her expression (and so, her attendant lack of attention to the words' communicative force and meaning), and also because the cumulative impact of this projection upon the therapist may obliterate the discrete nature of each vocalised communication. Together with this, the patient's vocalisations require the therapist's acts of containment and memory in order that they may be referred to in their developing forms, and so achieve the mutuality of consensual experience (Miller, 1993).

The analyst's containing function necessarily aids the patient's orientation within the unitary social pairing of the therapeutic dyad. This dyadic participation facilitates both participants' marking of the particular and the universal within private and shared experience. Here, as Bion states, when the patient fully understands the rhythm and work of dyadic psychotherapeutic activity within the reciprocal action of containing and being contained in two-person psychological process, he is able to continue analysis without the benefit of the therapist, a one-person dynamic similar to the working through illustrated by Beckett in this illustrative series. Bion writes of this process, both of the essential dyad and the patient's post-therapeutic journey that:

> It certainly is a collaboration between the two, and there is something fascinating about the analytic intercourse; between the two of them, they do seem to give birth to an idea, and possibly, if you are used to it, you can turn it into an interpretation or a verbal construction of some sort. Patients get better and better at it until, if the pair are fortunate, the analysis becomes redundant, unnecessary, and they can part and go their own ways. (2005, p. 22)

However—and this is a benefit of our having arrived at time (n+4), because we now have the resource of d developments unthinkable at earlier moments, before emergent iterations of d had progressed—the lonely one-person working through of ideas can be more wildly creative than productions within the dyadic therapeutic process. The reason is that therapy always involves the stabilising force of another's minding presence as conception is wrestled from its parataxic form into consensuality (Mead, 1904; Moore, 1921; Sullivan, 1954), if particular expression is to have a more universalised tang and feel in its utility beyond its individual expression in therapeutic projection.

III

Having demonstrated a clinical series in Beckett's writing that facilitates recognition of therapeutic emergence in d, at times beginning at (n) and proceeding forward, this recognition in itself may seem enough! Certainly, the discrete d expressions at discrete times are relevant towards achieving this emboldened understanding in d, its transition—validated by the "other", consensually through multiple forms of publication, oral presentations, and academic competitions—to **d**.

Against the durable and somewhat universalised sense of **d**, the particular arrivals—always in the context of specific direct experiences, including the successive moment (n+1) as influenced not only by the expressed d at time (n) but by the full context-rich experience of d emergence at time (n)—the real conceptual yield is that Bion's algorithm can be approached both in terms of incremental realisations, which we term d and correspond to discrete moments in time "n", and that also build onward, progressively, in time: d(n); d(n+1); d(n+2), etc.

From our temporal perspective at time (n+4) we can appreciate that the very observation of arrivals in d represents a significant **d** element in psychoanalytic psychotherapy. Each of these d formations stand as therapeutic accomplishments useful as scaffolding within the therapeutic task of addressing psychotic states of mind. Especially against negating claims that therapy achieves nothing, or that the patient's momentary state of mind is destructively bleak, therapist containment and memory of simple d-arrivals in n affirm incontestably a momentarily forgotten fact in direct experience: of consistent minding by another in an enduring dyadic unity composed of two individual, sometimes joint and sometimes resistantly destructive intentionalities.

Here, memory and the retrieval of formerly productive arrivals within the therapeutic pair, at momentary expression of consensually agreed-upon d, address the dread of destructive negation (see Chapter 8), and the seemingly bottomless pit of the black hole.

Recognition of d emergence also addresses the phenomenon termed the "third ear" by Reik (1948) as the elaboration of sensuous states of ego-feeling (Federn, 1926) registered by the analyst through daily practice of psychotherapy. Located sensuously within the basic domains of hearing, seeing, tasting, touching, and smelling, are registrations of re-formed experience, gained in practice recognitions through shifting moments of therapeutic surprise (Reik, 1937; Stern, 1990) in awareness of clinically emergent forms at the edge of conscious experience (Ehrenberg, 1992). These become articulated in time, both in the particular utterances of the patient and through the universalised reflective understandings of the therapist.

Finally, the linkage of d to n establishes the working of time, both within the fine grain of momentary experience in a discrete session, and across session, in the consolidation towards clear articulation of emotional experience. Working here, in the sensuous field of emotional resonance, expanding the perceptual recognition of ego-feeling with apperceptive meaning, such expansions become trusted, over time, by the therapist as consensualised by our patients in validation of our d intuitions as plausible.

The joint rumble of therapeutic battle between self and other, observed and probed on a field of life experience mediated in an hour by the felt forces of hearing, seeing, tasting, touching, smelling, and that other more composite sense, of the Reikian third ear, are our preparatory fields for the recognition of clinical forms through surprise and uncertainty.

As with Minkowski's (1999) account of reverberation, we have suggested forms such as fusion, automatism, and mimicry (Sweet, 2010, 2011, 2013) as well as emergence in d itself—beginning in the symbolically inchoate experience, rising through the vividly pictorial experience, and achieving vocalisation initially parataxic until met in its particularity with the shared, consensualised articulation of the other. Offered reciprocally, the patient is presented with an often under-appreciated formation, a springboard if taken within, back into the privacy of one-person psychology, through enacted recognition of our shared, human porosity, a plausible step in self-recognition. Sometimes, it is accompanied with a joyous movement forward. Sometimes, with an unpleasant, and regressive movement until again stabilising. Beckett struggles in *The Unnamable* (2006a) to clarify whose voice it is within that was once external? Bion (1967), presenting his invisible twin not so long after, begins with the therapist's intuitive question that finds resonance with the patient. Here, articulated in one voice, received in another's ear, is a temporary and compelling recognition in d of a moment of twinned mutuality (Ferenczi, 1988; Miller, 1993).

d emerges from the actions and emergences of earlier symbolisations: physically pre-symbolic, idiographic, vocalised, and verbalised. These are claimed by the two members of the group as temporary, but are the focally imminent work products in time of n, n+1, n+2, n+3, and as now, n+4.

Proust, interpreted by Beckett (1931), observed that time is the presiding arbiter of life history within our latest shaping of historical moment in its temporally situated "now". Time forces a distortion in contemplation of today's d en route to tomorrow's d: a unique product from time n to time n+1 and forward. Clinically, recognition of d represents a shaping of the analyst s task-related ego feeling (Federn, 1926) across the multiple moments of preparation and training in life and practice, in meeting and re-meeting the patient.

IV

I am aware that the exercise just described occurs primarily in my own one-person psychology, however based in perceptive identification (Bollas, 2006) with the writing of Beckett. The ideas emergent from time to time, similar to our emboldened d forms include: the similarity of written narrative to clinical inquiry as a parallel form which may be further unpacked for locating the phenomenological arc of experience from traumatic onset to working though; consideration of how the therapist selects what becomes significant fact; the interactive forms of one- and two-person psychology; the therapist's intuitive resonance with the patient's production; and the changing forms of d expression themselves across a timeline from n to other moments.

Therapy continuously oscillates between one-person psychological emergence in the continuous presence of two individuals. However, even "one-person" psychology is continuously peopled with internalised significant others, as Beckett reflects narratively with his Malones and Murphys (Miller with Souter, 2015; Sullivan, 1954). The continuous presence of the minding other, the containing therapist, performs an ongoing function of affirming for the patient (however resistant) that therapy's action involves a unitary dyad. Transit between one-person privacy and two-person articulation involves not only arrivals in content, but maturations of communicative understanding across time, n and forward.

Recognitions in d across a timeline of (n) function as important d concepts, enlarging the therapist's functional toolbox. Therapy is an anxious business, with the suffering of anxiety necessary in its daily plunge into the unknown. There, yesterday's habits, fused and robotic, inadequate to today's uses and unpliable, meet the containing function of the therapist. What has been learned and codified as defending against anxiety achieves pliability through narcissistic wounding (Ferenczi & Rank, 1923), by audacious inquiry and exploratory question, as well as by attentiveness in loving care (Schafer, 1960). d is marked as creative elaboration, permitting articulation as always tentative, without certain knowing except that deformation is certain. Therapeutic containment, appreciation of d and n, operationalise Bion's abstract algorithm and demonstrate therapeutic gaps in understanding. These allow self-reflection and clarification, appearing as discontinuous progressions in time because of therapy's lurching battles, interpersonal and intrapersonal—between the individual and her multiple cultures: regional, national, historical, professional, familial—which form the conflictual battle lines of personal identity. The therapist's toleration of flux versus defensive foreclosure, within the temporal subset of a process ending only at the close of each unique life history in its historical moment, allows recognition of d in n: itself bounded by the sociobiological challenges and limits of our epigenetic developments.

CHAPTER EIGHT

Meeting Heine in the Bronx: negation, the particular and the universal

The present essay

The present chapter describes a process of discovery: 1) beginning in the thick particulars of individual experience; and 2) thickening further through the generation of more contributory particulars useful as contents or resources; towards 3) a generalised intuition applicable within the clinical practice of psychotherapy. In going forward, we are guided by the sentiment of Descartes's Method, in which he expresses that:

> This tract is put forth merely as a history, or if you will, as a tale, in which, amid some examples worthy of imitation, there will be found, perhaps, as many more which it were advisable not to follow. I hope it will prove useful to some without being hurtful to any, and that my openness will find some favour with all. (1637, p. 5)

In this way, not only do we suggest the form in which personal history and meaning become transformed within psychodynamic therapy, but also demonstrate the writers' manner of thinking in broader application to clinical practice, specifically in reference to the emergence and use of **d** forms, described above in Chapters 1, 4, 5, and 6. In this chapter, we demonstrate a stream of transitional and more substantial arrivals evoking affect, memory, and thinking within an individual psychotherapist (IM) engaged in the psychoanalytic transmission of inter-textual commentary. It corresponds at the clinical level to a humanistic practice through which the patient comes to appreciate and enjoy her transitory experiences as the therapist acknowledges and utilises his own "corresponding intermediate areas, and are pleased to find overlapping, that is to say, common experience" (Winnicott, 1953, p. 95).

In describing this process, we note a parallel recognition in the work of Sandler and Dreher (1996), who document a certain lurching form of disconnection as they describe their object of inquiry, the historical discernment of psychoanalytic aims. Like the disconnected clash within the presentational essay forms of the Winnicott and Bion papers most frequently read in psychoanalysis (Miller, 2016a), we suggest that the very discontinuous moments of discovery, emotional and ideational resonance, articulation, recognition, and registration, illustrate multiple, convergent strands of thinking, necessarily contained by the thinker despite confusion, and interactive one with the other en route to arrival, over indeterminate timelines, as newly experienced products of thought, new recognitions both in d and **d**.

Like all essays, the present example leads to a conclusion, a port of arrival differing from that of departure. This essay docks in an awareness of uncertainty tinged with hope: that the humanistic core of psychoanalysis is continuously imperilled by the deadening forces of negation and exclusion in ideation, not only active internally and externally within individuals and groups, but also represented concretely within the textual documents that reflect the vibrant dialogue of psychoanalytic development itself. Conceptually, this challenge unfolds along a constricted **d** continuum of orthodoxy<>heresy (Bergmann, 1999) which contained within the development of psychoanalysis, was suggested by Freud in his "Five Lectures" at Clark University in 1909 (see Chapter 6).

In examining our own very human tendencies, we recognise the ubiquity of negation in the processes of change. Negation operates destructively to foreclose continued thinking. Its destructiveness hugs tight to distinctions such as orthodoxy/heresy, excluding the possibilities of multiple middle positions. In this form, negation generates within individuals the psychological void of oblivion, of senselessness and absence without guideposts or handholds. Alternatively, psychological negation may operate productively. While its initial utterance of "no" directly confronts what is before us, our toleration of multiple possibilities concerning reality in the unsteady containment of what is asserted at time (n) together with what is negated at time (n+1) functions as a bridge for individual achievement of new understanding and discovery (Freud, 1925h).

At Clark, Freud alludes to a "heresy" which he will term "negation" some sixteen years later (ibid.). At its surface, this is a casual reference employed as preface to his presentation of Breuer's early work in hysteria. Freud jokes with the Clark University audience, saying that medical knowledge will not be necessary to understand the psychoanalytic perspective, because medicine and psychological treatment, while both beginning in the patient's presentations of distress, soon part ways. Indeed, the contemporary reader, mindful of the historical internal battles within psychoanalysis over medical and non-medical qualification, might read this retrospectively as Freud's endorsement of "lay psychoanalysis".

But there is something else too. Freud emphasises here, partially for rhetorical effect and partially in dead seriousness, the emotional condition of the physician in the face of the neurotic presentation. Despite considerable knowledge of physical medicine, the physician is reduced, Freud tells us, to the status of a layman when facing neurosis. And in this humiliating diminution of his supposed omniscience, a succession of emotional operations occurs. Freud writes:

> This is not a pleasant situation for anyone who as a rule sets so much store by his knowledge. So it comes about that hysterical patients forfeit his sympathy. He regards them as people who are transgressing the laws of his science—like heretics in the eyes of the orthodox. He attributes every kind of wickedness to them, accuses them of exaggeration, of deliberate deceit, of malingering. And he punishes them by withdrawing his interest from them. (1910a, p. 12)

Freud outlines a series of successive actions describing a behavioural trajectory, much like the reflex arcs studied in the academic psychology known to his audience at Clark University (Dewey, 1896). But unlike the reflex arc, confined to the singular individual's neurological functioning, Freud's description concerns: 1) the internal and private operations of the individual; 2) the resultant thoughts of the individual, preparatory to acting upon the external world; 3) actions upon the world; and 4) subsequent internal processes marking interpersonal relations to the others upon whom one has acted.

Freud's sequence begins in defensive awareness of narcissistic injury to the physician's presumed store of knowledge. Continuing in reaction, the physician withdraws his sympathy from the patient who has threatened his sense of certainty. Next, in a paranoid projection, he vilifies and negates these patients, "like heretics in the eyes of the orthodox" (ibid.). In this destructive (if narcissistically defensive) action, Freud portrays a continuing dynamism threatening toleration of the unknown, necessary within a therapy based in "the task of learning from the patient something that I did not know and that he did not know" (ibid., p. 22).

The reader, who like the therapist, remains attuned to the immediacy of the here and now while allowing historical evocation to shape her associations, becomes immediately aware of Freud's growth in assurance since his first, similar confrontation with contemporary Viennese medicine in the 1890 essay, "Psychical Treatment" where he wrote that faced with neurotic presentations, "physicians came to restrict their interest to the physical side of things and were glad to leave the mental field to be dealt with by the philosophers whom they despised (1890a, p. 284).

In contrast to the 1909 statement, this aside seems underdeveloped. Yet it contains unmistakable markers of later psychoanalytic elaboration including: 1) narcissistic injury; 2) defensive reaction; 3) projection outward; 4) external displacement; together with 5) a negative affect, which in 1890 is disdain or contempt, growing descriptively to heresy or more simply, negation of the other, by 1909. These descriptive words of opprobrium, the end points in an emotional arc described by Freud en route to a more major essay topic, cauterise the physician's emotional response to this patient population, allowing the physician to return confidently to his sorely tried omniscience. For Freud, this action of negation is also the creative birthplace of psychoanalysis because it is within the uncertainty of contemporary medical knowledge that Freud discerns psychological functioning, the influences of mind upon mind (1890a). Freud's own 1925 essay "Negation" later affirms the necessary "no" within disconfirmation of one's present belief in the certainty of his convictions, as a creative window opening upon the potential for changing, evolving thought.

For the moment, let us continue with Freud's first Clark lecture of 1909. The beauty of Freud's skill as essayist is that his compelling argument upon negation leads seamlessly to his next point, the introduction to his New World auditors of the particular nature of psychoanalysis. And in Freud's fluidly compelling presentation, the dynamically noted **d** of destructive negation is contextually abandoned in his differentiation between unsympathetic receptivity to the hysteric and her sympathetic reception within the emergent psychoanalytic attitude.

Freud introduces himself as a student of Josef Breuer; and extols his master, linking Breuer's exquisite observational skill and compassionate attitude to the basic tools of analytic inquiry. If physicians have jettisoned the treatment of the hysteric into the despised realm of philosophy, Freud embraces this realm and elaborates its particulars. Respectfully, he describes Breuer's sympathetic treatment of Anna O as a marker not only of cumulative traumatic causation of symptoms, but also of symptomatic relief through expression of emotion, verbal articulation, and/or action. The interpersonally humanistic tools of sympathetic attunement and attentive response to the other who is the patient, underlie Breuer's address to his patient. Together with all her conscious awareness, symptomatic relief is aimed at the fundamental marker of a presence in hysteria, which Freud terms "absence".

Freud's symbolic illustration of the living presence of absence is the historical monument. His examples are London's Monument to the Great Fire and the Charing Cross. Arguing that hysterics suffer from "reminiscences" presently operative, if unseen, within the fantasies concealed by symptomatic absence, such reminiscence becomes evoked within the difficult and exacting work of psychotherapy. That is, by following the patient's narrative, the therapist intuits the presence of absence, bringing it to the patient's attention. As an evocative object of inquiry, the patient's resonance with the therapist's intuition may have the effect of aiding her expression in words, emotional discharge, or action, freeing her from conflict. Freud illustrates with the famous example of Anna O's phobic reaction to drinking water, and its dissolution in relation to her disgust at her governess's dog, which she calls a "horrid creature" (see Chapter 9).

Within his first comments at Clark University, Freud presents contemporary psychoanalysis with the elements, if not the articulated question, of significant challenge. His deep observation of narcissistic insult, reaction, and negation of the other describes a form of negation very different from the optimistic absences located within the reminiscences of neurotics and historical monuments. It describes a negation that challenges the humanistic grounding of psychoanalysis itself (Fromm, 1964); and yet, as a product of human construction, such negation is itself also documented within the 650,000 pages of psychoanalytic text that are our contemporary psychoanalytic legacy. Looking backwards, the present essay locates these negations as a turning point along another path illuminated by Freud, from the particulars of individual experience towards the universality of human symbolisation and action, which through psychoanalytic operationalisation strives towards recognition of the Kantian categorical imperative (1912–13, p. xv).

On psychoanalytic humanism

Negation contemplates an absence. Freud's symbolic example of the Charing Cross is capable of stirring the stillness of absence and evoking reminiscence in the subject. Yet the absence alluded to as the end point of Freud's emotional arc, beginning in narcissistic injury and continuing through negation of the other in order to address defensively, injured omniscience, operates far differently. Destructive negation succeeds in the oblation of emotional evocation in the subject. If Freud's Charing Cross example signals recoverable amnesia, destructive negation aims at a state of oblivion, a reduction of emotional response to no-thing in the foreclosure and exclusion of evocations resulting in further thinking.

I (IM) first became attuned to this problem of negation in a foreclosed definition of psychoanalysis. Just as within clinical development, my first intuition of the problem emerged from a thickly particular challenge: a clinical supervisee asserted that psychoanalysis could not be considered a humanistic discipline.

My initial response was to clarify meanings. I began with the general idea that humanism suggested a particular orientation to living, an orientation to the immanent rather than the transcendent, affirming the individual imperative to imbue life with meaning. More broadly, I suggested that humanism embraces what is common to all of us, what Harry Stack Sullivan termed the "one genus principle" in that each of us is "simply more human than otherwise" (Levenson, 1992; Sullivan, 1955), resonant with Descartes's (1637) observation that the forms of thought and behaviour we observe are commonly shared within our species. Indeed, while humanism today focuses on that which is intrinsically human as distinct from theological constructions and directives for human action, its classical derivation also includes the idea of being "learned", or a seeker of learning for its own sake (Giustiniani, 1985).

I referenced such readings as Buber (1951, 1957) and Freud's early works including the *Interpretation of Dreams* and *Jokes and Their Relation to the Unconscious*, to trace the Enlightenment's humanistic thought forward into its current psychotherapeutic forms.

Also thinking of Fromm (1964), I considered his alignment of threats facing mankind, half a century ago. While we might describe them differently today, they remain. His "bureaucratisation" of man we might term the robotic automatisms we observe in daily life as in the clinic, reflected above in Chapter 2—as well as in the tragic forms of escape from them abundantly apparent; and his attunement to the threat of nuclear holocaust, the ultimate scientific weaponisation of human rationality in the service of destruction, is chief among today's subsidiary cruelties while nuclear destruction itself remains potential. To Fromm's warning of nuclear threat we must now also add planetary warming as an example of another looming but very human threat to humanity; as well as the denial of its science by elected leaders. However, it was not Fromm but Bion who warned of systematic evasions and destructions of thinking in defensive flight from what is before us as well as what is between us as humans. These inhere within our refined capacities both to attack and to negate our own thinking. Such anti-thinking is noted by Bion as (–K); and through it, we retreat in oblivion from the sorrowful awareness of what we are capable of doing destructively to and with others, defending against awareness of narcissistic injury in acknowledging our own limitations and disappointments along the paths of grandiose belief in enacting our terrifying destructiveness and boundless greed. Here, I demonstrated the psychoanalytic application of humanistic thinking to problems immediately before us, socially, politically, and clinically.

My supervisee's response was an emphatic "No". Her understanding of the psychotherapeutic stream she had begun to study had defined psychoanalysis as outside the borders of humanism, which she claimed derived from Carl Rogers's therapeutic technique. There was to be no discussion, the verdict was final.

Thinking about this, it occurred to me that her certainty matched that of Freud's 1909 physicians. She was just starting out on her professional journey; and all of us who have taken a similar route know our anxious strivings for certainty as well as the relief offered by the crisp inclusions and exclusions provided within the boundaries of our teachers' received wisdom. Our educational paths not only prescribe the content resources with which we reckon, but also choose beyond our knowing, what is to be left out in the past's transmission into the present. In contrast, I also reflected that at the dawn of humanistic thinking, Rene Descartes had commented upon the psychologically broadening virtues of reading and travel. In his introductory essay "Psychical Treatment", Freud himself had relied upon such Cartesian wisdom in arguing against prevailing medical customs by summoning the thinking of the ancients (1890a). Descartes wrote:

> For to hold converse with those of older ages and to travel, are almost the same thing. It is useful to know something of the manners of different nations, that we may be enabled to form a more correct judgment regarding our own, and be prevented from thinking that everything contrary to our own customs is ridiculous and irrational—a conclusion usually come to by those whose experience has been limited to their own country. (1637, p. 7)

My own hard experience of such foreclosed belief and blinkered negation of thinking was considerably relieved both by Descartes and my rereading of Martin Buber's writings on psychotherapy, beginning with his "Elements of the Interhuman" (1957a), presented at the Washington School of Psychiatry, the day before his famous dialogue with psychologist Carl Rogers on the nature of humanistic practice in psychotherapy, at the University of Michigan (Buber, 1957b).

Buber teaches that we cannot exclude, but must integrate all forms of human experience within our uniquely individual, so pluralistic and personally undergone models of psychotherapy. Buber's commentary, written seventy years ago, addresses exactly the kind of negation represented by premature foreclosure, which itself may be a product of our anxieties and transferences to our models of training as it may be too a product of our genuine ignorance. He writes of the therapist that:

> What is demanded of him is that he draw the particular case out of the correct methodological objectification and himself step forth out of the role of professional superiority, achieved and guaranteed by

> long training and practice, into the elementary situation between one who calls and one who is called. The abyss does not call to his confidently functioning security of action, but to the abyss, what is to the self of the doctor, that selfhood that is hidden under the structures erected through training and practice, that is itself encompassed by chaos, itself familiar with demons, but is graced with the humble power of wrestling and overcoming, and is thus ready to wrestle and overcome ever anew. (1951, pp. 18–19)

Buber extends Freud's optimistic "no" of negation in opening the door of potential thinking to the therapist's own, necessary plunge into uncertainty, what Bion calls "O" (1970). Some 40 forty years after Freud at Clark University, Buber addresses the therapist's own dread of confronting what he does not know, beyond the borders of received and acquired knowledge.

From this, Buber recognises that our dynamic task in addressing the human condition is in learning from the crises we personally endure and overcome. That:

> … the psychotherapist, just when and because he is a doctor, will return from the crisis to his habitual method, but as a changed person in a changed situation. He returns to it as one to whom the necessity of genuine personal meetings in the abyss of human existence between the one in need of help and the helper has been revealed. He returns to a modified method in which, on the basis of the experiences gained in such meetings, the unexpected, which contradicts the prevailing theories and demands his ever-renewed personal involvement, also finds its place. (1951, p. 19)

From within such endurance of private experience from which one returns changed, the therapist reinvigorates her incrementally gathered form of "habitual" therapeutic method, built both on abstract principles and learning from experience. Buber recognises its dreadful alternative in negation: the abject arrival at finitude, limited and limiting claims on knowledge, certainty, including the idealised notion that humanism itself is reductively positive, the enacted equivalent of a smiley face emoticon. Rather, the human condition, expressed through knowing and being known in the therapeutic dyad, is always expressive of compromise and the therapeutic horizon of prizing aliveness over psychic deadness, and of recognising human commonality both in its affirmations and negations, within the particularities of human experience.

Buber's aliveness fits wholly with how psychoanalysts engage in discernment of meaningful thinking from the unique experience of the psychoanalytic pair, as stated by Wilhelm Reich, that:

> The analyst must endeavor to wrest the special technique of the case and the individual situation from each individual case and from each individual situation without, while so doing, losing the general continuity in the development of the analytic process. (1972, p. 7)

Pharisees and shopkeepers

At roughly the same time, another particular set of events furthered my inquiries into negation. When I first arrived in Dublin, I enquired locally about how psychoanalytic culture had begun in Ireland. I was informed that two streams had evolved, beginning in the 1940s. One hailed from London, where war-resisting, British-trained therapists had decamped to politically neutral Ireland during World War II. The other hailed from Paris, where an Irish Jesuit priest had attended lectures given by Jacques Lacan during the 1950s (Skelton, 2006, p. 255).

Curious, I enquired about the readings that might best acquaint me with the culture of Irish psychodynamic psychotherapy. Perhaps with some irony, two such were recommended. The first was a polemic, written to convince a sceptical archdiocese in the early 1960s that psychoanalytic thinking was congruent with Catholic theological doctrine (Hanaghan, 1966). The second was Lacan's 1953 paper, "The Function and Field of Speech and Language in Psychoanalysis".

Reading both, I grasped the embeddedness of local psychodynamic understanding within the complex matrices of cultural identity, deeply geographic, political, and religious. This fusion most prominently featured a sharply dichotomous fissure that had shaped local psychoanalytic practices along the lines of a significant and binding split in viewing the world: the centuries-old tension between two Christian worldviews, Catholic and Protestant.

This locally significant binary opposition that had occasioned so much national heartbreak, death, and the continuing division of the island into two countries (see Kapur & Campbell, 2004), also appeared to correspond to two foundational streams of Irish psychoanalytic psychotherapy, one identified with Catholic France and the other with Protestant Great Britain.

What became evident as I read, thought, and reflected on daily experience was a dynamic of exclusion compounded of two movements. It began in a reduction of the psychoanalytic conceptual world along the lines of this geographic-theological-political fault line. It continued in different courses of psychotherapeutic studies along one or the other side of this misrecognised binary division, together with the negation of the unchosen side, which was split off together with any remaining bits and preconceptions in order to accommodate the original reduction. These had become unthinkable: fragmented and dissociated, so proscribed under the allowable categories of local culture that had accurately resonated with the sharp political splits within psychoanalytic institutional organisations.

Indeed, psychoanalytic institutional splitting had been deftly recruited under Irish cultural categories, resulting in two opposing blocs of psychoanalytic definition, each presenting a saturated form of psychoanalytic truth without the possibilities that psychoanalysis had evolved as a singular if divisive movement, both across time and place in its roughly 150 years of development, and that it was developing still (Miller, 2016a; Sandler & Dreher, 1996).

Under such splitting (see Chapter 5), the forms of practice and theory which I had once taken for granted, in which I had studied and worked, seemed suddenly reduced to no-thing, as if they had never existed, in this time and place. Yet, all I had to do was turn in another direction, confirming through a Skype connection or an aeroplane flight to New York to meet with former American colleagues (or to colleagues in Athens and Munich, Melbourne and London), that the same "disappeared" concepts, assumptions, histories, and practice methods remained ongoing and bog-standard, if in another location. The recognition in my continuous shuttle between physical spatial settings of psychodynamic practice and between conceptual affirmations and negations, alerted me to deep and unacknowledged, localised contemporary splits in psychoanalysis, operating under explicit awareness within what was within popular belief, an increasingly "networked" and "globalised" world of international meetings and affirmations of unified fields of understanding.

So, despairing in having learned from one of my recommended Irish readings that Freud the godless Jew was the modern incarnation of

Jesus's social mission (Hanaghan, 1966), I turned my attentions to Jacques Lacan. I paced my reading in order, through attention to the arrangement of Lacan's essay, to gain some understanding about his form of psychoanalytic thinking. And my first encounter was traumatic.

It felt to me, in 2012, like a glancing blow from across time: from that liquid, wartime, ambivalently collaborationist France written about in the novels of Nobel laureate Patrick Modiano (2015), with knowledge dissociated of terrible crimes perpetrated, unmourned, and unaddressed explicitly. I would later resonate with this socio-historical, intergenerational visitation of trauma in the psychoanalytic work of Francoise Davoine and Jean-Max Gaudillière (2004). I could not believe what I was reading: written less than a decade after the Holocaust, and from a Paris recently liberated from "Occupation", Lacan was condemning refugee Jewish analysts in America as "Pharisees" and "shopkeepers", the same stridently hateful language both employed by the Nazis and also signalling two millennia of anti-Jewish negation (Nirenberg, 2013). Lacan observes that: "Pharisees and shopkeepers interest us only because of their common essence, which is the source of the difficulties both have with speech, particularly when it comes to 'talking shop'" (1953, p. 246).

This surely was Thanatos present within psychoanalysis, however spurted in "jouissance". Lacan had followed the model of Freud's 1909 physicians in generating a binary split between his own particular concept of psychoanalytic orthodoxy and heresy. Yet Lacan's fiercely negating language also necessarily condemned the original Pharisee-shopkeepers, Breuer and Freud, in his purification of psychoanalytic particularity, as it did too, their successor generations before World War II, who in free clinics and private practice, would develop such clinical dimensions as surprise, resistance analysis, and the complexity of the ego within psychoanalytic development (for examples see Danto, 2005; Reich, 1972; Waelder, 1936). Instead, Lacan had slashed psychoanalytic history with a sharp razor of language, not only negating history itself in his self-assignment to the role of Freud's successor, but also effacing its traces and demeaning its still-productive survivors!

I wondered about my own traumatic experience of this reading. Was it because in my own insularity within psychoanalysis itself, I had not been confronted with direct expression of hatred against Jews (Frosh, 2009)? Or was it influenced by my relocation to Ireland where a colleague had wryly reconstructed my American Jewish identity, compressing it to a local witticism, "Are you a Catholic Jew or a Protestant Jew?"

Perhaps Lacan's acidic comments sharpened my experience, sixty years later, that an aspect of my own multicultural identity had been cunningly circumcised, cut off by the Occam's razor of a still-operative and negating theological binary within which psychoanalysis endured somewhere between Freud's dreaded "Jewish national affair" and Jesus's social mission for the Catholic Church. I found myself oddly cast in a doubled role of apologist: first for myself, for my own identity, aliveness and affirmation as psychoanalyst, and next for psychoanalysis itself.

While my Irish Lacanian colleagues were not sensitive to Lacan's very clear meaning of "Pharisee" and "shopkeeper", I was. There was no coded meaning, no dissimulation or duality here. Understanding required only historical resonance; and awareness too, of Freud's very active concern that the humanistic orientation of psychoanalysis not be reduced to anti-Semitic negation. Yet it occurred to me that local obliviousness to such meaning was not dissimilar from local political and language practice. World War II is sometimes still referred to as "the Emergency" in Ireland, accenting the particularity of national political imperatives shaping the early nation state.

I was also aware that the psychoanalytic movement had not organisationally protested Nazi persecution and genocide; and that in the early days of Hitler's rise had acted in conciliatory form to ensure the continuation within Germany of psychoanalytic practice (Frosh, 2009; Kuriloff, 2014; Yerushalmi, 1991). Particular Jewish survival was marked institutionally by ambivalence. Ernest Jones, for example, brilliantly coordinated the refuge of European Jewish analysts while at the same time characterising Jewish refugees from Nazi Europe as unpatriotic draft-dodgers. Institutionally, Jones endorsed the continuity of the Judenrein Goring Institute as well as the post-war reintegration of many of its members into the International Psychoanalytic Association (Frosh, 2009).

Six years after Freud's death, Jones's own 1945 statements concerning Jews included an envious negation of their intellectual "superiority complex" as well as their physical deformity of the "Hittite nose", while urging Jewish disappearance into Gentile societies by means of intermarriage and assimilation, which was his prescriptive route for solution of the "Jewish Question" (1951).

But oddly, despite my knowledge of such historical information together with a personal lack of directly significant anti-Semitic experience, it was only in that Irish moment, reading Lacan in anticipation of better understanding local practice, that I was brought face-to-face with another's wish for my own annihilation; and this from within an aging (if locally significant, so contemporarily living) psychoanalytic text! Oddly, I confronted silent malevolence. There was no live, human interlocutor to engage in protest or clarification. I had reached the event horizon of study: these were my thoughts evoked without a living, responsive thinking other. Text had resonated with my thoughts and in the absence of a human respondent, the agglomeration of my thoughts, following Bion's 1962 model, had eventuated in thinking.

My recognition of difficulty went further as I contemplated contemporary local obliviousness to this originating, deep hatred and negation. In fact, annihilation as recognition had already occurred, in that the meaning of these words went unrealised. As language symbols, these words would endure in plain sight. Yet their significance was denied, shrugged off or attributed instead, as a Dublin colleague indicated, to "Lacan's jouissance".

Within this extraordinary moment of hideous negation, I was left alone to contemplate a deeply destructive oblivion within my own field of professional pursuit.

That my Irish colleagues, whether Catholic or Protestant, did not, could not, resonate with this experience seemed to me to be a function of differences in our particularities of identity. No matter how "American" I might be, it was not Lacan's anti-Americanism that got my attention. Rather, it was in the linguistic ferocity of Lacan's own words, still resonant from the recent destruction of European Jewry; and however comprehensive the magnitude of this butchery, still insufficient for some.

These evocations then, were particular in relation to my own complex identity. I felt strangely alone in Dublin where Klein could be read as if she were a British Protestant and Freud as Jesus's Catholic social mission. These were radically different psychoanalytic identifications and condensations than those with which I was familiar; and faced different domains of negation and oblivion. I reeled at the recognition of this destructiveness within our own psychoanalytic inheritance.

It also occurred to me that while Lacan had attempted his own linguistic Final Solution, that he was wildly out of step with his own time. He had completely missed a broader, universalising acceptance of psychoanalysis as a humanistic, therapeutic discipline under the vernacular expression of its non-Jewish British representatives W. R. Bion and D. W. Winnicott (Miller, 2016a). Still, stunned, and rather like a patient stumbling away from an impactful session (or like a therapist's countertransferentially repetitive chuntering, attempting to communicate aliveness and hope in the face of a patient's addiction to near-death, against the obdurate resistance and annihilating defences of the patient), I pondered this situation for a great while; and quite consciously, employed early writings in psychoanalysis, including the Clark Lectures of 1909 and the 1890 "Psychical Treatment", to provide a container for my thinking. Here, I was first able to clarify the Freudian domain of absence in its relation to productive and destructive forms of negations.

Après-coup

I felt myself, over time, faced with a terrible conflict; and one familiar, I think, to readers of Freud's essays. On the one hand, I could credit what I knew as destructive negation, operative still within the inter-textual legacy of psychoanalysis; and marking my territory, I could dig in to the hard Freudian/Cartesian task of rational analysis.

On the other hand, I could gloss over my momentary arrivals in thinking, as if they did not exist, preferring another array of juicy **d** concepts, more conveniently pleasant for myself, at least, to ameliorate the discomforts I felt. But my suppression of what I knew would remain incomplete. How was I to wrestle in reconciliation with the psychoanalytic expression of its own self-directed hatred?

At Clark, Freud comes to the rescue in directing therapeutic attention to choice between such paths. He writes in relation to psychoanalytic exploration and the exhuming of unpleasant unconscious residues that a

> … final outcome that is so much dreaded—the destruction of the patient's cultural character by the instincts which have been set free from repression—is totally impossible. For alarm on this score takes no account of what our experiences have taught us with certainty—namely that the mental and somatic power of a wishful impulse, when once its repression has failed, is far stronger if it is unconscious than if it is conscious; so that to make it conscious can only be to weaken it. An unconscious wish cannot be influenced and it is independent of any contrary tendencies, whereas a conscious one is inhibited by whatever else is conscious and opposed to it. Thus the work of psycho-analysis puts itself at the orders of precisely the highest and most valuable cultural trends, as a better substitute for the unsuccessful repression. (1910a, p. 53)

My own conviction, then, is that psychoanalysis itself must be capable of acknowledging containment of its own unconscious hatred, at least within the articulation of its own professed adherents. That is, that psychoanalysis must be able to account for itself in its containment of destructive negation.

Lacan (1953), like Jones (1951) and like Jung (1936) in his proposal for a uniquely Aryan psychology in contrast to his characterisation of Freud's "Jewish" psychology and in attunement with the tenets of National Socialism (Frosh, 2009), commits a categorical error. Each mistakes the particular, from which all individual experiences arise, for the universal, which is at the heart of therapeutic intuition. Freud's experiential particulars were rooted in the aspirations of his time, place, and community, the secularising Jews lampooned by a writer frequently referenced by early Freud, Heinrich Heine.

I discovered Heine's presence within Freud's particularities by a roundabout route; and in this discovery, came face to face with my own willed foreclosures and exclusions of thinking, my own negations. I discovered these by admission to myself, of not adequately understanding what Freud was writing as I progressed through *Jokes and Their Relation to the Unconscious*. Certainly, I had read *Jokes* before; but never before in the ponderously slow way I approached it now. And in this new reading, I felt deeply ignorant.

My first admission of ignorance came through contemplation of the translation, "jokes", itself. Freud's term is "Witz" or "wit" in English; but this didn't help me much. Like a joke itself, which had gone "over my head", there was something I could not understand, something which I suspected was immediately evocative to Freud's original audience. Only in reading an essay on the history of psychiatry and the nineteenth-century categorisation of psychology by the "Scottish school" of philosophy, which tradition Freud knew (Moore, 1945), did I realise that "wit" was an important component category within a psychological hierarchy which posits five internal "senses" of mind (sensation, perception, association, reasoning, volition) that in combination create the foundational domains of consciousness, attention, reflection, contemplation, and wit. Not only had I not known (or remembered from graduate school) the Scottish school and its formulations, but also the translation of the German "Witze" into the English "jokes" would have precluded any linkage with the psychological category of "wit", analogous to consciousness. Unlike Anna O, my capacity to move between European languages is woefully deficient. On several counts therefore, including basic ignorance and forgetting, my own education contained the seeds of my current awareness, my unwitting and deep obliviousness of something immediately evocative to Freud's original auditors. By fathoming wit, Freud was approaching a discernment of all of psychology's dynamisms; and his audience knew it!

Freud's first example of a joke, borrowed from Heinrich Heine, is of a Hamburg lottery agent named Hirsch-Hyacinth. Freud's comments on the joke's exegesis both by authoritative writers on wit and by Freud himself are especially passionate. He writes:

> What Heine has put into Hirsch-Hyacinth's mouth is a correct and acute observation, an observation of unmistakable bitterness, which is understandable in a poor man faced by such great wealth; but we should not venture to describe it as in the nature of a joke. If anyone is unable in considering the translation to get away from his recollection of the shape given to the thought by the poet, and thus feels that nevertheless the thought itself is also in the nature of a joke, we can point to a sure criterion of the joking character having been lost in the translation. Hirsch-Hyacinth's remark makes us laugh aloud, whereas its accurate translation by Lipps or our own version of it, though it may please us and make us reflect, cannot possibly raise a laugh. (1905b, p. 17)

Freud observes that what determines wit in this case is exactly the contradiction that discloses Jewish suffering. Arrival at the universal is by way of the particular.

Admitting to myself that I had always glossed over such examples in previous readings, desirous of arriving at the main points of Freud's writing, I realised too that I had consigned Heine to my own pool of ignorant oblivion. I was shocked when reading his *Travel Pictures* (1826), the book Freud references in the Hirsch-Hyacinth example, to find a narrative description of projection and displacement into an external object, very similar to Freud's own 1890 and 1909 descriptions of physicians' extrusion and projection of psychological causation. Describing an old woman in the German mountains, Heine links such projections not to the negation of emotional foreclosure but to the intergenerational interiorisations of identity formation. He writes:

> The old woman seated between the old cupboard and the warm oven had on a flowery skirt of outmoded pattern, the wedding

> gown of her late beloved mother. Her great-grandson, a blond, twinkly-eyed little boy dressed up as a miner, sat at her feet, counting the flowers on her skirt. She must already have told him many a story of this skirt, many serious, enchanting stories that surely the boy will not soon forget, stories that will waft back into memory, when, soon enough, as a grown man, he will have to entertain himself while working alone in the dark night of the Karolina mine, stories which he will perhaps recount when his beloved grandmother is long since dead and he himself, a silver-haired, weary ancient, will sit in the circle of his grandchildren, in the cozy nook between the big cupboard and the warm oven. (p. 26)

Immediately, I was able to construe the receptivity of Freud's original audiences to the qualities of Freud's thinking; they themselves, like Freud, were well acquainted with Heine, a Jew who very loudly and discontentedly converted to Protestantism in furtherance of his career. Freud would encounter the same religious block to career progression at the University of Vienna, a generation later.

Freud's audience was richly prepared by Heine to resonate with the evocative particularities of Freud's own original essays and later with the generalisations and clarifications of the dynamics clearly suggested, at least in hindsight, by Heine himself!

But reading further, in the Heine chapter called "The Baths of Lucca" from which Freud extracts the Hirsch-Hyacinth passage, I encountered a passage reminding me of Freud's famous "Signorelli Dream", a narrative of two Jews meeting on a train and discussing Italian church art (1901b). These were, in Heine's fiercely sarcastic words, individuals "I'd sooner expected to meet on Mount Sinai than on the Apennines" (1826, p. 103); and indeed, at the baths of Lucca, one such character prides himself (as does the Freud of "Signorelli") in his aesthetic acuity. Heine writes: "You can bind my eyes and take me to the art gallery in Florence and every painting you put me in front of I can tell you the painter who painted it or at least the school he belonged to" (ibid., p. 106).

Later, in the city of Lucca itself, Heine's narrator describes an artistic excursion through a cathedral predating Freud's reminiscence of Orvieto.

Laughing, I thought of Freud's urbane Jews on an Austro-Hungarian train attempting the same thing as Heine's Lucca characters—as if out of a nineteenth-century German-Jewish caricature or as a familiar form of Yiddish literature (Wisse, 2013); and then I recalled Signorelli's first name. It was Luca, sounding just like Heine's narrative location of painfully imperfect Jewish mimicry in the attempt to assimilate within Gentile society, the title of the chapter where Freud locates his Hirsch-Hyacinth joke. I chuckled, considering that Freud himself had neglected this association in relation to Signorelli.

Given Lacan's close readings of Freud's Signorelli Dream (Lacan, 1957–58), it seemed impossible to me that Freud's (as Heine's) particular field of personal conflict in the social definition of Jews within a Gentile world had gone missing for him. Rather, the situation was quite the opposite. Lacan was well aware of Freud's therapeutic genius in deploying the magic of words, of language (Freud, 1890a) to translate the particularities of individual subjective experience into a universal structure of anxiety and defence, expressing emotional disruption and conflict.

Like Heine's, Freud's expressions are reflective of the secularising Jewish society in which he was raised and lived. In Freud's own life, the position of the Jew relative to the Austrian state changed radically, as reflected in his famous dream of his father's Sabbath hat. Powerless to act against the Gentile bully, Freud's father would have been a member of a "tolerated" minority; and aggressive retaliation would result in punishment of the larger Jewish community (Boyarin, 1997). This situation would change legally when Freud himself was eleven years old in 1867, and Austrian citizenship was extended to Jews. Only with this shift might a realistic state of mind emerge wherein the necessary submission against unprovoked aggression be countered with a new and plausible possibility, extended through law and potentiating Freud's famous identification with Hannibal; rather than a frustrated and necessarily suppressed fantasy (Freud, 1900a). In this sense, Freud's dream is a statement of increased Jewish political equality and hope under Austrian citizenship, with a state of mind reflective of personal self-defence guaranteed by the state. This personalized, Freudian fantasy of identification with Hannibal, anticipated in illustration by Heine, was itself a common fantasy of Jewish schoolboys in the ghettos of Germany (Heine, 1840, p. 16). Prior to citizenship, such articulation itself would have been seen as politically seditious.

It is not difficult to extend the particularities of unique cultural experience to the level of the universal. Shakespeare imagined such a move in writing:

> Hath not a Jew hands, organs, dimensions, senses, affections, passions; fed with the same food, hurt with the same weapons, subject

> to the same diseases, healed by the same means, warmed and cooled by the same winter and summer as a Christian is? (*The Merchant of Venice*, 1596–99)

Yet how different are such expressions from Lacan's own French, Catholic particularities and his own vile characterisation of Jewish ego psychologists as "Pharisee" and "shopkeeper". Indeed, one of Lacan's own particularistic contributions to psychoanalysis derives directly from Catholic liturgical expression, "In the name of the Father"—who of course, is entwined with the "Son" and "Holy Ghost" (Kohon, 1999).

Only as I read Heine was I able to recognise the widely known particularities of Jewish experience presented by Freud. Immediately, it seemed conceivable to me that Lacan's reductive characterisation of the particularised Jewish expression to the hateful "Pharisee and shopkeeper" resulted from his own personal foreclosure from such experience, itself so densely formative within Freud's early discernment of psychoanalysis (ibid.).

Could it be from within this confusion of particular tongues that Lacan voices his outrage at Jewish experience that is forever foreign to him; yet, at Sullivan's level of the one genus principle, of human similarity, might something otherwise be intuited? Here, Lacan turns in outraged foreclosure as if to segregate his own psychoanalysis from the toxic variety of Pharisees and shopkeepers, thereby fragmenting and condensing the fractious movement in which he participates to the measure of his own particularity.

Lacan seems snared in passion, particularised within his own subjectively Catholic and French experiences. Together with an ongoing French-German rivalry for an illusively imagined fantasy of superiority in European thought (ibid.), especially after recent German defeat in World War II, Lacan's unfortunate condemnation of refugee psychoanalysts sheltering in the United States reads as an assertion of French pride which must also negate the humiliating influence of American intervention in accomplishing such victory. Lévi-Strauss (1952) narrates a similarly destructive story from the same post-war period, of a French town that burns Santa Claus in effigy because of that fictive character's strong identification with the United States!

At the same time, Lacan's particularist challenge is to reorient the once German-languaged psychoanalysis (however, derivative historically from the reflections of Descartes), now developing in English, to his particularised, French linguistic expression. Together with this is his legitimate claim to the particularity of any and all analysts' originating and continuing particularities of experience. However, in blurted outrage, similar in form to Jung's (1936) triumphalist heralding of an "Aryan" psychoanalysis in contrast to the "Jewish", some fifteen years earlier, Lacan mistakes the psychoanalytic universal for the particular. That is, by substituting a metapsychology redolent of Christian theology, itself based in French linguistic theory relating backward in time to the opening sentence of John 1:1, with the absented "third" of the Christian *Logos* continuously present (as absence) in the referential relation of "signifier" and "signified" according to Foucault (1966, pp. 70–71), Lacan theologises psychoanalysis against the secularisation of its godless Jew, Freud. This regressive movement redirects time's arrow in the history of ideas, clothing psychoanalytic secularism in the language of theology rather than in the opposite, secularist direction established by Descartes and Spinoza!

Effectively, Lacan's Oedipal move, converting psychoanalysis "in the name of the Father", must also have implications for those Pharisaic shopkeepers with their obdurate ego psychological refusal to acknowledge Lacan's own expression of his new psychoanalytic testament.

Lacan's signifiers, "Pharisees" and "shopkeepers" reveal Lacan's psychoanalytic error; and that error is in his mistaking what is and must always be particular in psychoanalytic origin for its refinement as universalised selected fact, destined to be extended to another, for reintegration into newly expanded particularities.

I considered how the presence of the other signals the difference between two minds, as narcissistic insult to one's demanding singularity; and recognised how intolerable such an experiential gap between Gentile and Jew must have been to Lacan's felt omniscience. Such Lacanian behaviour fits the pattern described by Freud at Clark relative to the outraged defensiveness of humiliated physicians, with omniscience reduced to lay knowledge.

Like Freud's physicians, claiming that the hysterical patient heretically challenges their orthodoxy, Lacan insists that a destructive negation must occur within psychoanalysis itself. Expressed as "Pharisees" or "ego psychologists", the action defensively elevates Lacan's particularity to orthodoxy; and in his inquisition, all else is consigned to heresy requiring the purifying purge. And by impugning the practicality of American psychoanalysis, Lacan may also read early Freud literally, the

Freud of the Clark lectures who reductively defines the United States as a "country which is devoted to practical aims" (1910a, p. 33); as if Lacan were a self-imagined son cleverly enlisting his own hatreds intertextually, together with Freud's, in the name of the Father.

Lacan's implicit recapitulation of Freud's 1909 description of negation forecloses further thinking, leading beyond to a lack of awareness, curiosity, and the proscription of extending human feeling into the abyss of one's own uncertainty. The success of Lacan's negation is in the obliviousness to some close readers of Lacan, psychoanalytic colleagues unable to recognise, even when confronted with the Lacanian language itself, that destructive negation has even occurred!

This is oblivion, with its fevered culture of anti-thinking; and the negation of Freud's and Buber's humanism.

Heine in the Bronx

Heading east, up the hill from Yankee Stadium, past the tatty souvenir stands and the fast food restaurants, the walker arrives at the Grand Concourse. And directly to the north of the Bronx County Courthouse, surrounded by a low iron fence and unsigned, he spies an aging, somewhat Rococo statue representative of that Rheinish spirit, the Lorelei. Looking closely, the observer discerns a depiction of a man's face and a name, close to the base: it is Heinrich Heine in the Bronx. The Heine monument, once destined for placement in his native Dusseldorf, has endured a long diasporic history to arrive at its now forgotten place of residence. Once beloved by German-Jewish readers in New York, who recognised in the precision of Heine's prose a kindred relation to his successors in the poignantly humorous writing of Yiddish literature (Wisse, 2013), Heine is relatively unknown in today's Bronx. The neighbourhood's German and Yiddish readers have all vanished over time; and their American children, grandchildren, and great-grandchildren have both moved away and long been educated in classics of an English language literary canon. What remains is a marble gesture to literary creativity, abandoned in time.

The Heine monument is typical of its kind: a material example of commemoration, a momentary notation in the relentless evolution of peoples' memories. In this sense, like Freud's Charing Cross, it is a concretised example of d, a representative statement of human desire and feeling, transitory in time. Here, in full operational form, the monument as object is created by human desire and meant reciprocally to evoke appreciative meaning. If the Charing Cross is a symbolic monument that evokes reminiscence, then the Bronx Heine monument is the end point of memorialisation: a monument having no evocative resonance, an object without subjects' reminiscence.

Freud's Clark lectures describe two forms of absence. The first, which he formally calls absence, is the structure of neurotic negation, from which memory, desire, and meaning may be evoked. The second, which he describes in an act of foreclosed thinking, serves the injured pride of misrecognised omniscience. In its destructive, projective violence, it extrudes that which disturbs the internal world, seeking to locate it externally, where it may be demeaned or rendered as nothing.

The therapeutic journey involves the continuous transit between particular experiences—the experiences and narratives of the patient as well as the evocative, particularised resonances of the therapist in transition, via the "significant fact", the universalised intuitive therapeutic leap, for presentation again to the patient in the service of revaluation within particularised experience.

Returning to his *Travel Pictures*, Heine's scope of psychological causation is broader than Freud's at Clark University. Freud's neurotics, like his Charing Cross example, follow the same resonant path as the wedding dress of Heine's old German woman. Recovery of meaning is possible.

Heine, though, presents another situation that is hinted at by Freud in consideration of physicians' insulted omniscience, but left inexplicit. Heine references the situation of modern urbanites, who are so consumed with the magnitude of their own affairs that they pay no attention to yesterday's clothing; or even today's (1826, p. 26). For them, the evocative object evokes no resonance. He writes,

> Even our clothes remain strange to us, and we hardly know how many buttons are attached to the jacket we are wearing this very minute. We do, after all, change clothes with such frequency that no single garment maintains any lasting connection with our private and public persona. Why, we can hardly still remember what that brown waistcoat looked like, the one that used to draw so much laughter and on whose broad stripes the dear hand of an old flame so sweetly lay! (p. 26)

This is the situation we all face in light of our own requisite pools of oblivion. We may choose to foreclose, to negate that which disturbs us.

Alternatively, we may screw up the courage to endure what is uncertain (and even consigned to oblivion), generating in this containment both new resources for our thinking in our discoveries and the recognition that just as we bear the capacity for aliveness, we also bear the capacity for deadness, for destructive negation in narcissistic retreat. Through this action, we risk losing our humanity in gaining what is general to us all, through insistence on a sameness for all rather than acknowledgement of what is particular.

Heine's approach, like his successor Freud's, was just the opposite. Each begins in toleration of the particulars of experience; and continues towards the intuition of a generalisation potentially evocative to us all. Only by tolerating "the task of learning something from the patient, something that I did not know and something he did not know himself" (Freud, 1910a, p. 22), by facing into the abyss of the unknown, does our method develop and deepen. To turn away in omniscient foreclosure is to destroy the possibility of learning from experience.

Coda

Reading psychoanalysis from its beginnings, we might recognise that Freud's thinking begins with a fundamental split. In this, Freud also follows Reason's formal methodology, as described by Rene Descartes (1637). He takes an object described as a whole, for example Viennese medical science in his 1890 paper, and splits it into parts such that medical science is understood as physical and psychological. Next, he proceeds by focusing on one dimension rather than another. This is analysis, the continuous bearing-down on an increasingly fractionated dimension of experience; and it is congruent with Descartes's rationalist method of inquiry. In their classic papers on hysteria, Breuer and Freud in this manner illustrate many overlapping episodes of traumatic causation eventuating in symptomatic distress.

Our present question remains: what happens with the discarded aspects of these conceptual splits? Are they forgotten, later to be remembered and reintegrated? Or are they to be abandoned, consigned to oblivion? If so, will their destruction be final or will their absence be traceable through hard analytic effort?

Freud's conduct as leader of the psychoanalytic movement reflects similar negating action. Famously, the heretical or deviant thinkers were expelled, exemplified by Jung, once the heir-designate. And within the broader organisational movement, politically driven purification would also take place as in the Nazi renaming of the Berlin psychoanalytic clinic the "Goering Institute" together with the extrusion of its Jewish members. Furthering this split post-war, former members of the Goering with identified Freudian rather than social-psychological leanings, were readmitted to the International Psychoanalytic Association (Frosh, 2009).

So it is that splits and extrusions at multiple, particular levels characterise psychoanalytic history and thinking. But too, it has not gone unnoticed that orthodoxies of earlier periods, such as Freud's insistence on very specific understandings of psychosexuality and neo-Lamarckianism, have become generalised and rounded in conceptual understanding many years later, revised and clarified by clinical observation in the course of time (Miller, 2016a; Sandler & Dreher, 1996). So it is too, that aspects and forms of particularistic observation become useful in generating new particularities and universals. Andre Green's concept of the "dead mother" for example, secularised and related to Meltzer's claustrum in its clinical recognition, was in part derived from Lacan's thematically Catholic **d** articulation, "in the name of the Father" (Kohon, 1999).

What counts in the present is the idea (**d**) in thinking as it becomes elaborated, formed, and deformed, from time (n) to time (n+1) to time (n+2) and forward. Here, the shift from particular to particular as well as from particular to universal must withstand the tensions of ongoing negation: with its poles of destructive negation and creative potential. As Freud said in his Clark lectures,

> There is a dictum in general pathology, Gentlemen, which asserts that every developmental process carries with it the seed of a pathological disposition, in so far as that process may be inhibited, delayed or run its course. (1910a, p. 45)

Like our hopeful rediscovery of Heine in the Bronx, reminding us of destructive negation and oblivion at one end of a continuum, facing Freud's Charing Cross of neurotic reminiscence at the other end, the clinical enterprise is always entwined with the actions of negation, both potentially destructive and productive.

CHAPTER NINE

Origins of the dyadic **d** in the talking cure of Breuer and Anna O

I

The original statements of **d**, of the clinical search for direct links between body and mind through "psychical treatment", are at the heart of two clinical reports that are perhaps, our most important introductory essays in psychoanalysis. Both illustrate Freud's statement that psychotherapy rests upon the influence of one mind upon another (Breuer, 1893; Freud, 1890a, 1893).

Chapters nine and ten circle back to the beginnings of psychoanalytic history to address these cases in the same way we have approached our own clinical vignettes. Necessarily, we do so mindful of operating from a palette of **d** conceptions today that were unthinkable yesterday, as their recognition has emerged only through clinical experience within psychoanalysis.

The radical **d** idea of two mutually influencing minds is illustrated within the interpersonal dynamics of Breuer and Anna O in one case (Breuer, 1893); and of Freud and Frau Emmy von N in the second (Freud, 1893). Each focuses upon two fundamental principles. The first is that the pairing of therapist and patient is the foundational context of psychoanalytic method. The second is that the joint task of psychotherapeutic inquiry is in wresting that which is unknown from within the clinical interaction.

With the cases of Anna O and Frau Emmy von N, an evolved idea of psychoanalytic definition is as yet unrefined. It might be said to be "unsaturated" in the language of Bion; or, alternatively, located within its early developmental stage relative to later developments; but immediately recognisable to us within its rhythms and vernacular elements.

Relative to the complexity of contemporary landmarks in psychoanalytic psychotherapy, this "pre-psychoanalytic" clinical work is partial. That is, each narrative stands as an expression of a broader idea that is as yet "confused" or deformed as a symbolic representation relative to what psychotherapy "will be", using the terms articulated by Benedictus Spinoza in the first formally structured statement of psychology (Fromm, 1964; Spinoza, 1677). Perhaps more to the point is that Breuer's and Freud's early method is fused with what therapeutic method itself seeks to discern; and along an unexplored frontier without clinical landmarks to mark the way.

The subsequent development of psychoanalysis allows our return to these now literary landmarks of psychotherapy's initial **d** statements. These provide us with the opportunity to inquire into clinical interaction between therapeutic participants. This is exactly the shift in psychoanalytic understanding expressed in the contemporary vernacular by reference to Bion and Winnicott (Miller, 2016a) or by others in notation of differing periods in psychoanalytic history, each anchored in a matrix of changing **d** constellations at the centre of the psychoanalytic project (Green, 1975; Sandler & Dreher, 1996).

Linking back to our reading of Freud's Clark lectures, we remember that Freud's rhetorical argument wobbled for an instant in his declaration about the case of Anna O in that the "case history is not suited to our purpose" (1910a, p. 26). According to Freud, this was because hypnosis distorted a clear view of emergent, repressed material. But also, more fundamentally, it is because Freud did not like hypnotic technique and because he was not very good at it. Hypnosis, as we shall see, with Freud and Frau Emmy von N, also provided a distorting screen for the social operation of a tragicomedy of manners, unfathomable without a conceptual baseline from what would later be termed psychoanalytic "neutrality", or at least a perspective from which the analyst might view his co-participations with his patient.

At Clark, Freud does not repudiate Breuer as he shifts to the significant **d** of infantile sexuality as the foundational substrate of repression. Rather, he writes:

> Our most valuable lesson from Breuer's observation was what it proved concerning the relation between symptoms and pathogenic experiences or psychic traumas, and we must not omit now to consider these discoveries from the theory of repression. (ibid., p. 26)

Instead of excluding Breuer from membership in his psychoanalytic project through splitting and consigning the work of this era to oblivion by destructive negation, Freud moves a complex phenomenon in **d** observed at time (n) to a new formulation in **d** observed at time (n+1); and maintains Breuer's place as a foundational psychodynamic researcher. Here, while negation occurs in the necessary process of change, it is a productive negation en route from time (n) to time (n+1), inclusive of Breuer's contributions, rather than a destructive negation, leading to oblivion.

While the dynamic nature of two individuals' psychologies has been a continuous presence within psychoanalytic history, the actual limitation of technical categories descriptive of this pure psychology is remarkable. These have operated under the larger categories of transference and countertransference, as well as resistance and counter-resistance (Miller, 2000). More recently, this categorical range has expanded to differing understandings of the psychotherapeutic "third" (Benjamin, 2004; Bolognini, 2011; Ogden, 1994).

Because of its own formal development, the therapeutic relationship's centrality to the conduct of psychoanalytic inquiry has been hotly contested since its recognition in the era following the First World War, when it was underlined by Ferenczi and Rank (1923). Today, our "consciousness" of the interpersonal relationship within the **d** categories of vernacular expression rests upon our generalised consensus of psychoanalytic elements, largely expressed in the writings of Winnicott and Bion (Miller, 2016a).

Despite workers' attentions to the fine-grained movements of process between therapist and patient (see for example: Boston Change Process Study Group, 2007; Gray, 1994; Joseph, 1982; Levenson, 1992; Nahum, 2002), psychoanalysis itself has suffered from an impoverishment of language concepts concerning therapy's relational basis, not unlike that of the patients we treat; however, "beneath" this impoverishment, there is a wealth of knowable, if inchoate experience.

While conceptually nestled under such broad umbrellas as transference, countertransference, and therapeutic third, the transient and shifting levels of attentional focus and impact experienced both by the patient and by the therapist continue to operate outside formal psychoanalytic categories. Our range of process-related **d** concepts risks qualitative loss in clinicians' understanding through their saturated conceptual landmark categories, subjectivised in individual use.

Yet it is this qualitative dimension of psychoanalytic experience that continuously surfaces two fields of psychic interest, each broadly described by Karen Horney (1991) as moving towards, against, and away from others within the relational interest or the desire of individuals in minding the experience of the other (Miller, 2015). This is the humanistic form of desire discerned by Buber (see Chapter 8), of knowing or yearning for inter-human relatedness; and corresponds conceptually to the Winnicottian notion of the unitary relation, with its original psychoanalytic prototype in the relation of mother and child (Winnicott, 1949, 1953).

Therapy cannot go forward without psychic interest, often first manifesting as worry or concern on the part of the patient, in shifting qualities related to the therapist's determination to attempt understanding through listening, response, and conviction of efficacy in "psychical" therapy (Freud, 1890a). In this, at least at certain junctures, the desires of patient and therapist are aligned. Such psychic attunement is not a structure of mind but operates both as a transitory and relatively enduring convergence of two individuals' focus. It is how, characteristically, one is "interested" or "uninterested" in the individuality and similarity of the other. It is how one's sense of coherence or fragmentation is presented to others in the external world of daily conduct. In this sense, just as such qualities are discernible to the other with whom one engages, they are discernible to oneself through the act of self-reflection, itself a skill encouraged through the clinical action of dynamic psychotherapy.

William James portrays such psychic interest as corresponding to shifts in levels of social and self-interested, private relatedness within the continuous oscillations of an individual's attentional stream (James, 1890; Miller, 1987). Ernest Schachtel (1959) elaborates the concept in his description of individual perception. Psychic interests are represented both in the pervasive and unique patterns that constitute the individual's characterological viewpoint and in the discrete perceptual experiences of uniquely particular moments. Field theory extends psychic interest beyond the borders of individual psychology, examining the harmony and disharmony of psychoanalytic participants within an interpersonal field (Baranger & Baranger, 2008; Colm, 1955). The convergence and divergence of individuals' interests, their attunements and misattunements, are the primary experiential data of the therapeutic relationship.

Psychic interests always point in a direction. Each is a complete perspective, an interest in something determined by the immediacy of a self whose whole interest (in the moment) it is. Psychic interest reflects the individual's experience of himself in relation to self and others. That is, extended both to one's own self-related actions and externally, to the world of others, it is a projection of one's internal world. Interests emerge both consciously and without the necessity of consciousness. Within psychotherapy, such emergence may be dissociated from the conscious awareness of one or the other within inquiry.

Freud acknowledges the therapist's conscious revelation to the patient of his psychic interest with the "active step" (1916–17). The analyst's activity is in the presentation of his interpretation, theoretically linked to the patient's conflictual difficulty. The active step accomplishes much more. With the analyst's revelation of his interpretive awareness, he alerts the patient to something particular. That is, from his own particularity, he demonstrates in general terms how he sees the emergent clinical situation in which both he and the patient are embedded. More comprehensively, each of the analyst's participations in the presence of the patient, consciously considered or spontaneously lived and reflective in gestural communication (D. N. Stern et al., 1998), reflects the analyst's shifting psychic interests in self and other.

Similarly, each of the patient's participations in the presence of the analyst becomes knowable to each psychoanalytic participant. Both the analyst's and patient's conscious and unconscious interests contribute to the process with no definitive rule to determine the correctness of meaning in what transpires. The fluidity of this situation, and its plausibility to participants in light of the dyadic context of therapy, contributes to momentary emergence of consensualised d experience.

Each participant contributes constructively and equally to the degree that he is focused and attentive—whether to self or other. Similarly, each may unlock an unrecognised quality of psychic interest in articulating what is momentarily meaningful. The patient's personal interpretation within transference may illuminate his own struggle with himself and others more brightly than the analyst's interpretation. The analyst's interpretation of events from within his receptive countertransference may accurately penetrate a defensiveness steadfastly denied by the patient.

The analyst's work is to respond to the patient's struggle emergent in the immediacy of each therapeutic session. The range and fluctuation of the analyst's psychic interests originate in the analyst's experiences. In this sense, while ultimately collaborative with the patient, they are psychically independent from the patient.

Psychic interests may be elusive. They are the momentary affirmations, elaborated in utterances of d, of how it is, immediately, for the individual. They are markers of meaning in a skein of living experience. Though ultimately private, their cognitive-emotional subtleties are communicated publicly within the inter-human relationship of the therapeutic dyad. The emergence of psychic interest, consciously and unconsciously affirmed by one individual in the presence of the other, is the radical **d** contribution of psychoanalytic inquiry, first documented by Joseph Breuer. Characteristic of Breuer is his generous attribution of this discovery, this "talking cure", to "Anna O", his patient, Bertha Pappenheim.

II

Breuer's treatment of Anna O provides a rich perspective on the interaction of psychic interests and the suggestion of multiple arrivals in d and **d**. However, with this first psychodynamic case, the explicit differentiation and inquiry into the nature of psychic interests does not occur. The case is formally an inquiry into the meaning of symptoms; yet, in the therapist's demonstration to the patient of symptomatic meaning by word and action in a manner meant to convey complex causality, it is a prototype of our own arrivals in d across therapeutic time from its dyadic baseline at time (n) and onward.

We recall that Anna enters treatment following a long period of caring for her terminally ill father. Her symptomatic complaints include: headache; visual problems; difficulties in moving her head, arm, and leg; as well as periods of hallucinatory "absences". During treatment, Anna's symptoms extend to: an inability to speak her native language; a refusal to eat; several suicide attempts; and a long period of hydrophobia.

Our discussion focuses upon the integration of Breuer and Anna at different points of the two year treatment. The case material presented by Breuer reflects both the spoken and unspoken psychic interests of therapist and patient as they weave the joint fabric of thirdness in clinical inquiry. It illustrates the unconscious willingness of individuals to listen intently beyond the manifest contents of words, to what the other is actively struggling to convey.

Throughout, Breuer conveys his respect for Anna's personality. He is impressed by her strong will, and notes that Anna is convinced only by cogent argument. Yet what may be taken as her tough, intellectual "obstinacy", a defensive oppositionalism, dissolves frequently into what Breuer recognises as a genuinely reciprocal kindness and regard.

Breuer relates Anna's distress to hypnoid states of dissociated consciousness. He explains their effect on Anna as causing "two selves, a real one and an evil one which forced her to behave badly" (1893, p. 24). Anna's descriptions confirm Breuer's working model of a good person, passively captive to a dark, interior force. Additionally, it is likely that this formulation is also supplied directly, or conveyed through Breuer's gestural attitude, as a precursor of a transitory verbal articulation, d (such as the later declaration by Anna that her former nursemaid's dog was repellent to her, repeated to his Clark audience, more than twenty years after the treatment, by Freud).

The contemporary reader encounters a confusion of interpretive voices in Breuer's careful remembrance of Anna. The apparent correspondence between Breuer's descriptions and later psychoanalytic concepts such as the conflict of instinct with society or the distinction between the truth and falsity of an individual's social presentation of self, vie for the reader's attention with Breuer's vibrant descriptions of their mutually interactive words and actions.

While foreshadowing future conceptual developments, Breuer approaches the case with a particular interpretive outlook. He divides the waking consciousness within which it is assumed that an individual is moral and good from a dissociated, secondary state within which the individual acts with uncharacteristic naughtiness.

Anna, of course, is aware of Breuer's theoretical perspective. Not only does she provide Breuer with explanatory descriptions, but as a woman completely unsuggestible through hypnosis, she accommodates him with her willingness to move from normal discourse into the incomplete if revelatory freedom of autohypnosis. That is, Anna avails herself both of Breuer's psychic interest and his theoretical conception, his own formulation of therapeutic **d**, to allow herself the freedom to articulate emotions and words expressive of her own "secondary" or socially proscribed experience. And, together, they do so in such a way that Anna's proscribed experience may be seriously heard and minded by Breuer in a manner previously inconceivable within Anna's experience. From our contemporary perspective, Breuer provides a hearing containment, including person, setting, and time, for the emergence of dissociated experience.

Yet as understood within the case presentation, there is a mix-up of contributions by patient and therapist that defines the first talking cure. Both Breuer and Anna tacitly agree on the tactfully social conduct of the case (until Anna's pregnant fantasy of carrying Breuer's baby) while operating through their unarticulated psychic interests to address and to avoid what occurs between them.

Anna becomes reticent to speak. When she finally does, she makes it difficult for others to understand. Eschewing her native German, spoken by Breuer and the nurses at the patient's home bedside, Anna translates everything into English. Her translations include German-English, French-English, and Italian-English. In her flamboyant style she even writes employing Elizabethan calligraphy. Anna forcibly demonstrates, through this virtuosity, her polyphony and strong intelligence, reduced to caring in her role as nurse to a dying man, while her younger brother nourished his own intellect in school. It is notable that in his Clark lectures, Freud uses Anna's linguistic strength to counter contemporary medical ideas that hysteria is founded on emotional incapacity and finds in the medical establishment's derogation of psychological causation, its own demonstration of narcissistic insult, splitting, projection, and demonisation of the patient in hatred of the patient's symptomatic and unconscious insult to the physician.

Next, Breuer speaks with Anna about what he suspects may be anger underlying this linguistic wilfulness. How does this suspicion arise? The reader is not told. Nevertheless, following this discussion, this articulation of a transitory d embedded within therapeutic process, Anna's symptomatic movement problem abates. However, she still continues in her refusal to speak German.

It is likely that Anna has recognised Breuer's keen interest as well as his own capability in understanding this concretely "foreign" language, a linguistic screen for her unconscious and unspoken experience.

He next instructs her nursing staff that English alone must be spoken with the patient. Even the monolingual German-speaking nurse must now accommodate the patient in a foreign language!

Yet, while Breuer recognises Anna's anger, he does not construe her behaviour as noxious, but tolerates it. Breuer does not formulate the notion of resistance, that first category of therapeutic relatedness recognised by Freud. Rather, Breuer recognises affect-laden meaning in Anna's symptomatic behaviour; and puts his understanding into words.

Breuer demonstrates peculiar sensitivity to Anna's linguistic demands. He accommodates or gratifies the patient's insistence on English rather than German. This is an implicit acknowledgement of the patient's intellectual range with the explicit willingness of the therapist and his entourage to follow the patient's lead. Anna, the respected and demanding patient, is in control. Her interpersonal demand is acknowledged through behavioural accommodation. It is not discussed but enacted.

A co-participatory accommodation emerges. Who induges whom? Is Breuer on Anna's wavelength when he construes anger underlying her insistence on English? Does Anna resonate with Breuer's understanding when she accommodates her physician—interested in symptom remission—with what he's looking for? Are Breuer's accommodations to English and his directive to his nursing staff his behavioural signals of respect for the power of his patient? None of this is directly articulated according to the case presentation. However, it is through the progressive layering of such inter-human indications of psychic interest that the first analytic case proceeds.

Next, Anna refuses to eat. She allows only Breuer to feed her. Not only does Anna's willing dependency upon Breuer grow, but also Breuer's interested relation to Anna, mirrored in a kindly paternalism. Breuer observes:

> I was the only person whom she always recognized when I came in; so long as I was talking to her she was always in contact with things and lively, except for the sudden interruptions caused by the bane of her hallucinatory absences. (1893, p. 26)

In the midst of this growing relationship, Breuer plans a brief trip away from Vienna. He reports that on the day prior to his leaving, he introduces a substitute consultant to the patient. The introduction is made through the formal demonstration of symptoms common within nineteenth-century psychiatry. Breuer asks Anna to "perform" her symptoms. Anna complies responsively; but with a seductive twist. She demonstrate symptomatic "peculiarities" for Breuer's guest, while coquettishly reminding Breuer that she remains conscious of what is going on, what he is asking her to perform. Still in the presence of the substitute consultant, Anna addresses Breuer in English, now literally a common language between them, developed within their dyadic relational history. She tells him that what is going on is like an examination.

Is Anna delighted in their collusion? Repelled by it? Does Breuer's interested willingness to follow her and also to delight her in her helpless intelligence—the performance by this gifted woman for the appreciation of an observing male physician—an experiential correlate of her interaction with her own delighting father?

The record is silent. However, the patient's interactive enlistment of Breuer signals a moment in directly knowable **d**, but unrecognised consciously by the therapist. It is he who reports it in the case record. Yet with this prototypical first case in psychoanalytic history, the unspoken integration of interests is beyond the therapist's theoretical comprehension. It simply happens. Unarticulated, the convergence of therapist and patient interests propels the treatment forward.

Nonetheless, Breuer's documentation of the treatment suggests that Anna has a sense of what is happening and says so. She tells the doctor in their mutual language that the meanings to be made conscious are within their shared relationship. Anna points to the field of psychic interests as the key to deciphering her distress. After the guest's visit, when Breuer leaves town, Anna attempts suicide. Is this a message that her subtle communication to Breuer is unacknowledged? Indeed, if Anna means her demonstration as a token of togetherness, Breuer's leave-taking signals a terrible rejection. Even so, isn't suicide an extreme and unyielding demand for another's total attention? Perhaps, in the language we have introduced above, Anna's perfect dependent fantasy upon Breuer has exposed the abyss or "black hole" to her. Faced with dread, suicide becomes an enacted blathering of her sense of non-being: as yet, she has no consensualised d elements to weave a supportive emotional scaffolding (Chapter 4).

The immediate outcome of Anna's gesture is that she is moved from Vienna to the country. There, treatment resumes. Anna continues with numerous suicide attempts. Writing of this transfer, Breuer explains that Anna had "without saying so, expected and dreaded" the move from Vienna. Clearly, through the action of suicidal attempts, Anna has assured herself of gaining Breuer's attention.

Yet Breuer's own explanation is unconvincing. He attributes Anna's self-destructive gesture to a fear never articulated by the patient. What more remained unspoken?

Breuer's narrative voice falters. Explaining to the reader that he had never threatened Anna with the move, he suggests a guilty concern that Anna's manipulative and despondent gestures might have had some relation to his own therapeutic participations with the patient.

How could they not? Of course, Breuer knew nothing of what Freud was to discover as transference. Nor was he consciously cognisant that Anna's desperate enactment of non-being related to the physical absence of Breuer, upon whom she depended. Within the narrative of the case but distant from Breuer's explicit attention to the remission of Anna's symptoms, is a rich skein of interests, woven between the two people passionately involved in therapy. Breuer's focal concern in the methodology of abreaction remains theoretically paramount. However, his deeply engaged personality is reflected in a keen responsiveness to Anna.

Breuer explicitly recognises his patient's growing dependency on the therapist; and remains actively interested, if not delighted, in the patient's veiled communication of her "naughty" cleverness—the intellectual acumen esteemed both by her late father and by Breuer. Interestingly, just as Breuer asks Anna to demonstrate what ails her in the presence of a third party consultant, which she does, emphasising her relationship with Breuer, Anna's suicidal gestures act on Breuer to focus his attention upon his own co-participation with Anna.

The therapeutic importance of the relationship between patient and therapist would not be formulated within this treatment. Neither would Breuer formulate the idea of therapeutic process as a vehicle for transferential enactment. These were to come later in analytic history.

Together, Breuer and Anna extend their interests across the great divide that separates the therapist's theory from the experiences of therapist and patient. Breuer would not have embarked on his cathartic therapy without a curiosity about dual states of consciousness. Anna accepted Breuer's authoritative hypothesis about the use of hypnosis; but subtly limited it with her own self-induced secondary state. Breuer accepted that.

Breuer's willingness to listen within his theory of separate states allowed Anna the fiction of autohypnosis from which she could speak what couldn't be spoken directly, given the constraints of Viennese decorum. Yet it was Anna who could interpret the therapist's interactive experience with her from within his protected framework; and Breuer who was unable to acknowledge that the difficulties presented were enacted within each participant's directly felt experience.

Breuer's technical contribution is considerable in the discovery of a bridge between his own theory and Anna's need to be heard. He observes a chance interaction between Anna and her nurse. The nurse repeats a phrase used by Anna during autohypnosis. The patient willingly recognises and elaborates upon it in her waking state. Here is an early indication of d, linking the hearing and articulation of meanings, embedded in therapeutic interaction. Beyond this, the utilisation of this recognition, towards engaging meaningfully with Anna, is a precursor of what we recognise in reverse splitting.

The simplicity of this technique, formally incorporated by Breuer, only seems apparent. The activities both of recognising meaning within dissociation and conveying that recognition explicitly to the patient are prototypical of the therapist's active step. They reveal to the patient the therapist's conscious acknowledgement of interest in minding the patient.

Yet, what of the patient? What of her reciprocating active steps and what they might reveal of her interests? Anna was ready and willing to engage with Breuer. How long had she waited for a curious physician to recognise that the interaction between patient and nurse was significant in articulating psychic meaning impermissible within normal, daily discourse? Without Breuer's willingness to hear the forbidden (or inattended) as meaningful, the patient might have remained unheard.

Breuer listened to Anna's associations and heard in them stories like those of Hans Christian Anderson, "always sad and some of them very charming" (Breuer, 1893, p. 30). Within this listening, Anna found relief in what she called the "talking cure" or "chimney sweeping".

Anna recognised that Breuer paid attention to her. He listened actively as she spoke. Anna's was really a "talking to Breuer" cure—as much about the listening as about the telling. Yet even within the relief of the talking cure, Anna remained demanding. Breuer observed but did not pursue the meaningful particulars of Anna's demands. He accommodated. For example, he noted that if Anna failed to tell a story one night, she required that two be told the next night.

Breuer, consciously the scientist within a scientific treatment limited in its interactional focus, understood Anna's storytelling behaviour as her role in abreaction. His role was in providing Anna with a psychic container capable of relieving "the whole stock of imaginary products she had accumulated since my last visit" (ibid., p. 30).

Anna's behaviour at this point seems tenderly childlike. Breuer listens, unselfconsciously paternalistic in the kindest sense—aware of the patient's interpersonal operation upon him, but not of its therapeutic significance. Both are aware of Anna's conscious conviction that monologue in Breuer's receptive presence lessens her defensiveness.

Yet it wasn't always smooth sailing. Anna fell silent again although her anxiety persisted. Breuer felt an obligation to aid the patient's talking cure. He urged her. He pleaded with her. He attempted to prime the pump by repeating Anna's habitual opening formula for the telling of stories, an attempt at reverse splitting much like the nurse's earlier recognition.

Yet this time, Breuer's plea was met by the patient's silence. Breuer's decisive response was to prescribe medication! A limit to Breuer's containment had been reached. His prescription changed the form of Breuer's genteel accommodation with this difficult patient. It was a reminder that Anna's co-participant was *Doctor* Breuer, the man in charge. Perhaps the anxiety for which Breuer prescribed was his own, disowned but insistent psychic interest on being at all times the effective good doctor. Perhaps, in true patient form, Anna's consistently insistent presentation had abraded his own professional sense of capacity.

For the second time in treatment, Breuer leaves Anna. When he returns a few weeks later, he describes her condition as a "wretched moral state, inert, unamenable, ill-tempered, even malicious" (ibid., p. 32). His response was to indulge. He allowed her to return to Vienna for a week. During this period, he listened to up to five stories each night. Breuer accepted these compensations for his absence as the associational detritus generated during the time he was gone. Yet the punishing force of Anna's demand in her marathon telling of bedtime stories was accepted by Breuer.

How did he decide on this course? Was it an attempt to reverse Anna's transfer away from Vienna following his first absence? Did it reflect guilt about his temporary desertions both of the talking cure through pharmacology and next, of physical absence from his dependent and demanding patient, however temporarily? Were either Breuer or Anna consciously aware of Anna's effect on him through her maliciously inert state? Clearly, the unarticulated relationship developed between them involved abandonment, guilty seduction, angry counter-seduction, and a degree of complicit acquiescence on the part of both participants.

The breakthrough of the case, remembered by all psychology students, concerns Anna's "vexations" of 1881. Following Anna's six-week period of hydrophobia, Breuer recounts that:

> One day during hypnosis she grumbled about her English lady-companion whom she did not care for, and went on to describe, with every sign of disgust, how she had once gone into the lady's room and how her little dog—horrid creature!—had drunk out of the glass there. The patient had said nothing as she had wanted to be polite. (ibid., p. 34)

He recalls that Anna's energised expression of repressed anger in the telling of the story does the trick. The patient asks for a drink of water!

Indeed, Breuer listens; and he listens without judgment. His acceptance of the patient's alleged desire to be polite seems discrepant in today's postmodern culture. After all, what was she doing snooping around another person's room, the room of a person she knew she didn't like? And what was so horrid about the dog, anyway?

Breuer doesn't enquire. While aware of the effect on Anna of a monotonous family life and the absence of adequate intellectual outlets, he does not consider the ways, other than daydreaming, through which the patient achieves some limited fulfilment—for example, by acting on her curiosity, however surreptitiously, when she invades the privacy of the English governess. And might Anna's use of English in the therapy also point the way to the guilty transgression involved in this behaviour? Breuer doesn't ask. Perhaps his countertransferential sense of propriety barred the question.

This well-remembered vignette exemplifies both the conscious and dissociated aspects of this case. Through Breuer's interested explorations, Anna experiences a triumphant liberation from her distress. Left unasked are questions concerning relationships between Anna and significant others, including Breuer.

III

Breuer's therapeutic approach to abreaction is not conceived in terms of convergent and divergent psychic interests. His attention to symptoms and states of consciousness is the metapsychological fulcrum that makes present what both Breuer and Anna tacitly agree are her states of absence.

Yet a century and more later, Breuer's active psychological attunement to Anna appears to be a dominant, if unrecognised **d**, present in the treatment. The intimate human dimension of interrelatedness is so fundamental to Breuer that its consideration as a therapeutic attitude or value concept would seem superfluous. Nevertheless, his unique responsiveness to Anna O and her to Breuer reflect a powerful integration of psychic interests operating together within their careful inquiry into the meaning of hysterical symptoms.

Freud, writing from a later stage in psychoanalytic development, comments on Breuer's sensitive "use of a very intense suggestive rapport" with Anna (Freud, 1914d). Consistent with his own metapsychology, Freud locates Breuer's rejection of neurotic sexual aetiology as proof of his early mentor's countertransferential difficulties in the realm of sexuality and the reason for the treatment's premature termination.

Freud's observation of Breuer's relatedness with Anna and his own dismissively interpretive critique reflect Freud's own ambivalence towards the mentor he'd outgrown. On one side is Freud's recognition of Breuer's gentle humanity, acknowledged as a facet of Breuer's personality rather than as Breuer's locus of therapeutic attention. On the other is Freud's need to establish himself as the father of psychoanalysis, necessarily dismissing Breuer as conventionally opposed to Freud's controversial discoveries.

Breuer's emotional make-up allows him to accommodate what another might feel reactively to be the patient's powerful manipulation. The treatment record documents Anna's continuing tests of Breuer's interest, as well as his unremittingly tolerant and accommodating compliance with her. Breuer does not discuss the meaning of Anna's demands with her. They remain the elephants in the room, unmistakably present.

Anna is a psychodynamic pioneer every bit as much as Breuer. She is the predecessor of analysands who indicate the direction that they must journey in the presence of the therapist, and insist on being heard beyond the simple sense of words. Anna was fortunate in working with Breuer, a dedicated scientist responsive enough to accept Anna's conditions within a "hypnotic" treatment absent of formal hypnosis. Breuer's uncritical acceptance of Anna's conditions together with her critical acceptance of his cemented an alliance through which the central psychodynamic premise of meaningful unconscious determination and articulation would be tested and affirmed.

If a failure in understanding presents itself in this first analytic report, it emerges from the disparity between Anna's expertise at doing what she does and Breuer's relative inexperience as a psychotherapist. He is formally limited in his therapeutic involvement as the passively receptive abreactor of Anna's psychic experience.

Neither participant makes explicit the subject immediately before them. The symptom is the thing for Breuer, as is the talking for Anna. Yet in her talking she puts her willing desire to talk on the table. She says whatever she wishes, albeit encoded. The case report reflects that Breuer's unconscious psychic interests, his attentions and inattentions to Anna, extend farther than his conscious theory of treatment.

Anna demands from her therapist a willingness to accommodate which, two psychoanalytic generations later, would be recognised as technical "elasticity" by a patient of Ferenczi's (Ferenczi, 1928). Certainly, Anna did not have these words for the markers required by her; and Breuer, unlike Ferenczi, would not have been prepared to understand.

Within his own overindulgence, Ferenczi would recognise a reaction to countertransferential hostility, later documented by Winnicott (1949). In this, Ferenczi operated at an advantage relative to Breuer; and Winnicott at an advantage of recognition, relative to Ferenczi. Beyond the benefit of his own brief personal analysis and continuing self-analysis within the treatment of patients, Ferenczi was heir to Freud's theoretical articulation of countertransference. Breuer worked only with his own abreaction theory and his felt, if consciously disowned experience of Anna. Winnicott benefited from two decades of personal psychoanalytic experience with James Strachey and Joan Riviere in recognising hatred within the psychoanalytic encounter.

Throughout Breuer's work with Anna, the patient comports herself in a mischievous way. She is indulged—spoken to in her language of choice without inquiry into the meaning of her demands; and perhaps, frustrating for her, listened to in a selective way—in relation to symptoms rather than in relation to the activities and assumptions that characterise both the treatment and her life.

Breuer maintains a courtly inability to locate the operation of disrespect within the patient he intrinsically respects at a level not only social, but also psychological. Anna's psychic interests partially resonate with Breuer's. However, she cannot accept the incompleteness of Breuer's attention to her. Failing to reach him emotionally through provocation, Anna intensifies her struggle.

Breuer encounters her resistances in an uncritical bear hug, which nevertheless provides plenty of opportunity for Anna to ventilate. Yet Breuer's superordinate psychic interest leaves little room at all for Anna to relieve herself from being a good soul, pliantly autohypnotic, and folded within her therapist's goodly parental toleration.

It is exactly this kind of experience which is questioned throughout the treatment by the patient through her behaviours. Anna struggles in what is later termed the transference, provoking the therapist and receiving real feedback against which her struggle both abates and escalates: linguistic demands; suicide attempts; demands for storytelling time; provocative tales; and finally, denial of there having been a problem at all. Withal, there is improvement. Breuer sticks with her, respectfully and sometimes slavishly; but never questions her provocation.

Breuer's theory contrasts the pathology of Anna's distress with her true goodness of character. He consciously acts, with Anna's interested acquiescence, as an environment for the patient. He provides a caregiving service. Other aspects of his experiential co-participation, including his unconscious receptivity to Anna's demand for more and his own blinding determination to understand the patient, are disowned.

Anna's interactions with Breuer are not polite, however. She demonstrates the steely stuff she is made of, its complexity and range of capacity. She demands to be at the centre of Breuer's psychic interest not as symptoms but as who she is; and demands too that Breuer be alive to her beyond mere toleration.

Nevertheless, Anna both derives partial relief through the articulation of her thoughts and accepts Breuer's recognition of meaning within her actions. Breuer works beyond the limits of his abreaction theory in drawing emotionally near to Anna. She moves him in appreciative identification, in joy, and in pathos. Despite her demands and Breuer's dissociation, Anna recognises Breuer's psychic interests within his offer of therapy. While unacknowledged explicitly either by patient or therapist, Anna reciprocates Breuer's interested participation and willingly speaks her mind with conviction. The rest is commentary and refinement within the development of the psychoanalytic dyad.

CHAPTER TEN

From Freud and Frau Emmy to today

Like Breuer's collaboration with Anna O, Freud's collaboration with Frau Emmy von N (1893) portrays a textured fabric of interpersonal relatedness. Yet, differing from the unspoken, loving accommodation of Breuer and Anna, unattended in the collaboration between Freud and Emmy are the competitive interests of its heavyweight participants. The treatment pivots upon hostile resistance to emergence, both psychic and within the therapeutic dyad.

Freud's case report of his work with Frau Emmy von N acquaints us with the clinical operation or **d**, of resistance. However, long before resistance and its metapsychological sibling, repression, are formally announced, Freud narrates this relentlessly bruising inter-human integration, passionately joined by therapist and patient. With Freud, we recognise how much clearer it is to identify the resistance of others than the resistances of one's self, one's counter-resistance. Treatment continues for seven weeks during the first year and eight weeks during the second year.

The narrative begins as the reader hears Frau Emmy's voice from the hypnotic couch. She breaks off conversation with Freud every few minutes with the shout, "Keep still—don't say anything—don't touch me." Freud tolerates this expression; and does not enquire either about her experience or his own.

In light of Freud's own acuity in discerning the individual's fragmentation of an object in the location of discrete parts as opposed to wholes (1890a), today's reader notes that Freud's engagement with Emmy, from its beginnings, consistently attends to parts of their engagement rather than to its fuller interpersonal picture. Tactically of course, Freud is focused on symptom remission rather than therapeutic process. For example, he is attuned to Frau Emmy's startle response when the consulting room door opens without warning; and he orders that further interruptions be preceded by a knock. As case material, this is presented without explanation as a matter of fact. However, Freud's action suggests an intuition concerning privacy or at least the absence of externally derived surprise, based on his recognition of the patient's startle reaction. And so, his action in management of the clinical setting reflects Freud's responsiveness to certain patient behaviours. But he does not take Frau Emmy at her word, that she desires neither physical touch nor Freud's verbalised observations. While aggressively conveyed by her to Freud, her sentiments are by tacit agreement consigned to the impolite and even violent realm of the unconscious, impossible to fathom within the formulaic allowances of bourgeois social discourse. As we detail in the chapters above, such behaviours within our own contemporary consulting rooms would suggest an assault through destructive negation upon the therapeutic project itself.

Like Freud's description of Anna O at Clark University a decade later, his observations of treatment with Frau Emmy are fused with nineteenth-century social forms, blurring the clarity of how individuals affect one another directly, within a pairing relationship. Employing Freud's own logic from 1909 relative to hypnosis as a veil obscuring clinical process, his own embeddedness in the social formalities of Habsburgian interaction with what appear in the case of Frau Emmy to be complications between therapist and patient of class, wealth, and age, underwrite a tragicomedy of manners clouding a bare-knuckles clinical narrative of interpersonal power relations.

Ignoring Frau Emmy's explicit, if publicly dissociated commands erupting from her unconscious state, Freud orders warm baths for her. His aim is compassionate; yet the attempt at physical relief confounds a therapeutic technique predicated upon the influence of mind upon mind. This confusion is itself heightened as it explicitly negates the patient's dissociated, if strongly stated, demand for her minimal conditions within treatment—which today might be understood as a plea for "optimal distance" (Bouvet, 1958).

Instead, Freud himself undertakes to massage the patient's body twice daily. Doing exactly what she prohibits, he touches her, enacting the forbidden. In this, Freud actively challenges Frau Emmy in a test of wills. Today, we might enlist a **d** concept concerning the mutuality of therapeutic enactments in explanation (Ehrenberg, 1992; Ferenczi, 1988; Levenson, 1991; Stern, 1987). We might observe that, given the nineteenth-century context of combining psychotherapy together with massage, Freud unwittingly finds himself in a situation, unknown to him in relation to this patient, but potentially knowable to the patient herself: a transformation of the therapeutic relationship into a shape and form recognisable to her, and linked by the therapist to her conscious self-reports within therapy (for example, her admission of being a tyrant to her daughter), demonstrable within the multiple participations within the therapeutic third. But as a study model in hysteria, this remains under the radar of explicit notice. It would only be much later in psychoanalytic history that even the very concept of therapeutic meeting between patient and therapist would be construed through the implicit **d** of interpersonal conflict within the very fabric of therapy's dyadic structure (Bion, 1957; Landauer, 1924; Reich, 1972).

While Freud acts the cultural role of considerate physician, he also acts contradictorily. On the one hand, he privileges the spatial privacy of the Freud-Frau Emmy relationship, but on the other hand, he extends his own authority to intrude upon her physical privacy. In applying massage, he provokes Emmy against her directly expressed wishes, however spoken under the veil of dissociated, hypnotic experience, that he not touch her. Consistently, Freud demands a hierarchical one-up position from his patient; and she pushes back.

Freud also relates that although he "put her to sleep" twice daily and together they discussed "every sort of subject", neither patient nor therapist comment explicitly on the thick form of interrelatedness that transpires between them within the authoritative hierarchy of physician and patient. Hypnotic treatment, theoretically allowing a dissociative experience congruent with the patient's hysterical symptoms, provides a velvety screen of dissociated actions relative to the developing interactive fabric between therapist and patient.

Nevertheless, Freud finds the patient's "gruesome stories" entertaining. This is an awareness recognised by Frau Emmy, who clearly sees her effect on her young physician, determined to succeed in his clinical trial, with Frau Emmy his subject.

Early in the therapy, Frau Emmy tells Freud that she is a woman of the last century (1893, p. 52). Is it possible that she is unaware of her not-so-subtle seduction, in derogating herself just so that the therapist might formally respond, "Ah, but no"?

Weeks later, in apparent clarification of this statement, she explains to Freud that she had been thinking of antique furniture when Freud asked her age. This fragment of case narrative suggests a clarifying development over time, and within Freud's observational awareness if not explicit marking, of the dyadic behavioural dynamic we term d. Here, a confusing statement, richly embedded in the relationship between Freud and Emmy, is articulated weeks after its first sighting, seemingly spontaneously, within the context of later therapeutic developments. And with its recognition, Freud might gain potential insight as a young therapist into Emmy's vanity and anxious dread: the passionate young physician has asked a mature woman her age and after some time (and within a different clinical moment), she provides an associational response, suggesting her sense of self as useless and deadened, like the discarded fashions of an earlier time, into the last century's old furniture. In this moment, had Freud remembered his beloved Heine, he would have recognised the warning about modernity's oblivion we reference in Chapter 8—as the enduring habits of the past, once nurtured in memory by the present generation, become discarded in the oblivious hurly-burly of modernity (Heine, 1826, p. 26). Little wonder that Frau Emmy has sought the continuing attentions of physicians and the persistent seeking of "cure" as a device to preserve others' interests in her!

Certainly, this disparity of age between man and woman is on Frau Emmy's mind. She says quite consciously that this is at the root of her troubles. Frau Emmy positions herself as uninteresting to Freud because of her age; yet against this belief, continues to seduce him effectively, palpating the relation between an older woman and a younger man's interest behind the private and closed doors of a hypnotic, massage-intensive "therapeutic" context of social relatedness.

Freud, though, attends to another task, very different than Emmy's explicitly stated interest. Based in his own therapeutic model, he believes what he does to be oriented towards the wiping away of his patient's gruesome mental images.

Freud's conceptual fixity upon the **d** of symptomatic removal facilitates the dissociation of his own physical and psychological enactments with the patient. Freud actively splits off consideration about his own physical touch and the larger question of power relations, from physical touch and verbal seduction to interpersonal authority within the therapeutic relationship, as effecting treatment.

In so doing, Freud limits the meaning of Frau Emmy's stories. These are the very stories that make Emmy feel herself interesting to Freud, her calling card for an entertaining and charged relationship. Emmy's compliance with him is in the provision of animal stories together with images of corpses. The youthful Freud proceeds as ardent healer in service to an experienced older woman, who has told him that her difficulties all began with the death of a man. Does Freud not hear her characterisation of herself as a man killer?

The case begins in conflict initiated by both participants. The patient's conditions for treatment are different from the therapist's. Frau Emmy begins her own study upon hysteria by insisting on her (and with her, Freud's) privacy; and by shouting a single condition: keep away!, which condition is somewhat compromised in her later compliance with sensual massage. Freud hypothesises that Frau Emmy's verbalisation is a defensive formula that keeps the patient's hallucinatory psychic material from emerging. Further, he believes the patient to be unaware of her narrative interruptions in this manner. Rather, Freud construes Frau Emmy's shout as a phenomenon of her internal world. He therefore dissociates his own consideration of Frau Emmy's demand within the inter-human activity of psychotherapy.

From Freud's perspective at this historical moment, Frau Emmy's situation is simply a symptom to be understood according to his reinterpretation of Bernheim's and Breuer's techniques. He assumes that Frau Emmy has read about hypnotism but he does not ask about her preconceptions or experience of hypnosis. Her current understanding goes unquestioned. Rather, Freud assumes the patient to understand that hypnotic treatment may include physical touch. Certainly, Frau Emmy understands that physiotherapy involves massage.

Oddly, given the later development of psychoanalysis, the idea of physical touch as linked with psychological intrusion is not considered. Touch is relegated to the mechanistically concrete dimension of medical treatment and dismissed in its psychological meanings. Its actual presence within the treatment as a confusion between therapist and patient is not considered at this phase of psychoanalytic development. Sexuality itself is construed as the patient's psychological affair without its enacted physical correlate, massage and touch, in the interpersonally objective world shared by therapist and patient.

Yet, the concrete dimension of sexualised touch between the two participants in this early case, a dimension that will become a boundary violation of psychoanalytic method in later years, only complicates the richly textured relationship evolving between them. Having shouted her conditions for treatment at Freud—that he keep away from her, not touching her—Freud himself undertakes to administer a regimen of baths and massages to Emmy, who does not complain! She gratifies him with her symptomatic relief and she is rewarded with his comforting touch. An impasse begins to form in which the older woman entertains the young doctor as the naïve and attentive Freud seems seduced.

This somewhat bucolic course of treatment is interrupted with the entry of Dr Breuer, Freud's older mentor, together with the house physician. The patient immediately displays her symptomatic clacking noises; and the visitors leave. Frau Emmy makes light of Breuer to Freud, who seems to relish this act of ridicule. But subsequently, perhaps guiltily, Frau Emmy reconsiders her flippancy. Freud writes that during her massage, later that day, Frau Emmy admits "that she still felt badly about having given Dr Breuer away today" (1893, p. 55).

Here, the young Freud's response is unusual, given the sceptical Freud we have come to know in retrospect. He tells us, "I pacified her with a white lie." Freud feigns politeness in pacification, assuring Frau Emmy that her comment is not indiscreet. Superficially, he acts the Viennese gentleman; but he has sealed with his words an interpersonal integration of collusion and deception with Emmy that is to intensify throughout the treatment.

Perhaps Freud attempts to silence Frau Emmy in order to pacify his own ambivalence about Breuer. Perhaps the ambitious Freud momentarily relishes the patient's arch aside and feels reactive contrition. This is not unrealistic. Perhaps he is embarrassed at being observed by Breuer in the presence of an unruly, symptomatic patient. Certainly, Frau Emmy's confession makes Freud anxious. Does her upset require pacification? After all, here is a woman who can endure dreadful hallucinations of animals and corpses. Can she not tolerate her own realisation that she's been rude socially? Of course, Freud's feeble assurance does not pacify. Rather, it acts to focus Frau Emmy who, equally politely, refuses to be quieted in the face of Freud's resistance to her own expression of remorseful feeling. Her continued probing appears to be an inquiry into Freud's behaviour.

Frau Emmy, who seems able to live harmoniously with her hostility, presses onward. The next day, Freud reports his patient's distress at having offended Freud during the massage by saying something "which seemed to her to be impolite". That is, she reminds him obliquely both of his behaviour and of her own. The interpersonal dynamic of Emmy's offence and Freud's defence becomes complex. Its focus is no longer the patient's flippant comment about her physician's esteemed senior colleague. It shifts for Emmy to the relational enactment between her and Freud, anchored in the unspoken realisation that even contrition about her hostility has somehow offended her therapist. He will not accept this, her conscious honesty, however socially ugly. Who is uncomfortable with what aspect of what's transpiring between Frau Emmy and Freud?

Chronologically, this case occurs before Freud's discovery of transference and countertransference. Nevertheless, his work with Frau Emmy alerts Freud to the patient's resistance. The psychic origins of resistance will evolve into the psychoanalytic theory of repression and defence. Yet the interpersonal origin of this dynamic within discovery in the clinical context is an integration of: Frau Emmy's resistance; Freud's resistance; and Frau Emmy's determination, both conscious and overtly dissociative, to manipulate Freud's refusal to "hear" her. Frau Emmy does not demand that Freud analyse his resistance in her presence. What she does demand is that concern about what she says, her interests, be at the centre of Freud's professionally directed, psychic interest. She demands that Freud consider how it is for her, the nature of her life's situation.

Frau Emmy presses the point. Freud again attempts to "soothe" through a didactic reassurance that there is "no need to be afraid of what is new, since it also contains what is good". It is difficult for today's reader not to feel compassionately towards Freud at this point. He is a beginning therapist trying to appear confident with a bright, capably seductive, and increasingly angry patient demanding an honest response rather than a defensive reflection of the therapist's lack of understanding. He cannot have felt pleased with this development.

The pressure increases for Freud. Enquiring in hypnosis about asylums, spoken about by the patient in her waking state, Freud rationalises that his "energy seems to have carried me away" as he interrupts Frau Emmy with his own supportive interpretation of her experience. Freud's response in this moment reflects a proprietary interest in his own construction of reality. Freud prefers that Frau Emmy accept his thinking rather than her own explanation of childhood experience. He "appealed to her good sense" as if the resolution of Emmy's anxiety hinges on a competition between his own authority and the patient's psychic relatedness to a childhood nurse. Freud's denigration of Emmy's recollection, as about a "silly girl", obliterates consideration that the patient's difficulties might not result from literal belief in the nurse's lurid tales, but from a more complex skein of experience, including the psychiatric hospitalisation of Emmy's mother. Freud seems to lose the patient as his interest shifts from the plausibility of the patient's psychological narrative to the buttressing of his own interpretive authority.

Frau Emmy responds angrily to Freud although she is polite enough to request his permission to be "released" from the requirement of hypnosis. Freud attributes Frau Emmy's response to her "unruly nature". He understands that she is angry, yet his understanding is not relational. From the perspective of today's psychoanalysis, Freud substitutes a "one-person" psychology for the "two-person psychology that forms the dyadic "thirdness" of this case, as we discuss in Chapter 7. He assumes that Frau Emmy is simply angry as an interactive result of her character and his interruption of her dominating narrative.

Freud's attribution of causality to the patient's nature removes his own participations from consideration within the evolving form of therapy. He does not consider that the patient's insistent prohibition against touching refers too to her sensitivity about others' impositions of their constructions upon her experience. Freud forgets that her injunction at the beginning of treatment includes not only touching, but of Freud's even speaking. From the outset, Frau Emmy has demanded the therapist's silence in her telling of her narrative.

The difficulty is complex. Frau Emmy will tolerate neither the therapist's interpersonal freedom to work with her nor his psychic freedom of participation within the therapy. Her authoritarianism is her chief resistance; and it finds its match in Freud's steely demand to be continuously correct. Freud's press to succeed dominates his psychic interest, allowing the minding of this patient to fade. It clouds his view of an entrance to Frau Emmy's difficulties through acknowledgement of his own interpersonal participations. For his part, Freud is aware of a power struggle. He notices that Frau Emmy keeps a "critical eye" on his work. He assumes that her condescending provision of further narratives without associative thoughts is her reproachful quid pro quo for his interruption of her narrative. It is probably that and more.

Frau Emmy remains compliantly responsive. Her connections seem to fall away only when Freud impatiently understands her according to his own theory and speaks disrespectfully of her psychic reality. While she remains watchful of Freud's performance, Emmy continues to modify her participation, albeit with annoyance, as a hostilely compliant patient.

Freud's attribution of Frau Emmy's compliance is to his own "influence" (1893, p. 56). He notes her adoption of his conversational technique as an uncensored supplement to hypnosis. Freud, like Breuer, notes the willingness of the patient to talk without the fiction of hypnosis. Unlike Breuer, Freud's aggressive impatience is felt by the patient, who savours a defensive battle rather than productive inquiry.

Freud asks Frau Emmy, following massage and hypnosis, why she has gastric pains. His hypothesis is that the patient's bellyache and her animal hallucinations are linked. The patient begrudgingly answers that she doesn't know. Impatient, Freud instructs her to answer by the next day. When the answer to Freud's question is avoided by the patient, Freud, the therapist, becomes authoritarian. Yet Frau Emmy is every bit as tough as her young interlocutor. According to Freud (p. 62), the patient grumbled at him from her hypnotic state and said that he "was not to keep on asking her where this and that came from" but to allow her to say what she had to say!

Frau Emmy proceeds to tell Freud about her resentments, including: her dead husband; her child; her husband's relatives; and her relatives. She is blunt, forthright, and moderately imperious. She speaks freely after successfully countering Freud's theory-bound impetuosity. She enacts her authoritarian resentfulness with Freud as she explains this resentfulness in relation to others. Frau Emmy now refuses to gratify Freud's interest in stomach pain and imaginary animals. Rather callously, she demands her right to tell her story. Will Freud listen?

Frau Emmy says that she was not fond of her daughter. She believes that she has concealed this antipathy. Yet this dissociated relation to another is similar to that which develops between Emmy and Freud in what he would one day term transference. While Emmy speaks freely of her resentfulness and authoritarian intolerance, Freud counters by refusing to locate these issues within the therapeutic field. This confusion of contributory hostilities continues to mount: Emmy's defensive hostility; Freud's defensive counter-resistance; Emmy's redoubled resistance to Freud's resistance.

Breuer visits yet again. Once more, the patient appears startled. Freud writes (p. 65), "She felt so sorry on my account that she should have had to betray this relic of her former nervousness." But in this interpretive gloss, Freud mistakes the unspoken d, too certain about the present origins of Frau Emmy's startle. Does it really relate to the former symptom and its refusal to abate? Or does her sorrow arc backwards to Emmy's sensitivity about their earlier collusion in disrespect of Breuer? Perhaps she is sorry that Breuer's visit evokes anxiety for Freud, with the repetition of an earlier treatment-related faux pas, re-enacted in the present?

Frau Emmy von N joins Anna O as a pioneer in the development of psychoanalysis. Their contributions correspond to the unconscious attunement of patient and therapist within therapy, along the lines of what Ferenczi (1988) termed "dialogues of the unconscious". Anna's contribution is in her compliant autosuggestion coupled with Breuer's receptivity to the utility of her talking cure. Frau Emmy's is in her authoritative insistence upon telling her story her own way, and in its enlistment of Freud's countertransference or counter-resistance. Frau Emmy perseveres. She continually returns to what she never verbalises, but which she wields fiercely beneath the register of words, a resentful and unforgiving critique of Freud. Quite explicitly in her narrative, she approaches her self-characterisation as itself resentful and so completes what will be a later psychoanalytic notion linking the projective domain of the internal object, through transference, with external objects.

Freud does not seem to understand. He lectures Frau Emmy (p. 66) and tells her that she is too self-punitive. She responds, under cover of hypnosis, by manipulatively telling Freud that she suspects the imminent approach of her menstrual period. Again she plays the sexual card. Withdrawing, Freud's approach is to suspend therapeutic massage temporarily. Emmy becomes cheerful, with her glee related to transitory success in the authoritarian tug of war in which she is locked with Freud.

Frau Emmy adapts to the authority of the other by a hostile submission that is also self-preservative. She attempts self-analysis of her collusive disrespect towards Breuer with Freud. She attempts revelation of her own contemptuous attitude to others. She attempts silence and then acts contentiously and resentfully with Freud. Finally, she resorts to the physical idiom of her body, acceptable to Freud as physician. He suspends both hypnosis and massage.

Frau Emmy's achievement at this juncture with Freud must be a practised operation of daily life for her. Her articulation of her own position has been silenced and her vengefully pyrrhic victory must be achieved manipulatively. Her hard-won objective is in the domain of the relational, though reflective of psychic interest. Freud literally takes his hands off of her. Ingeniously subverting social discourse, Frau Emmy achieves a measure of autonomy from Freud's resistance to hearing her.

Given these events, Frau Emmy's somewhat fragmented associations about two suspicious men, a kneeling and harmless lunatic beggar and an intrusive break-in of an isolated country house are understandable as the patient's projective interpretation of clinical process. Her comments, though encoded, seem descriptive and defensive. Frau Emmy alludes to the suspicious intrusions of Dr Breuer and Dr Freud. This opposes Freud's interpretation of a sexually abstinent woman's persecutory anxiety following her husband's death. Certainly, the notion of intrusion into an isolated country house fits the metaphors generated in this therapy. Earlier on, Frau Emmy forwarded a related idea, that of antique furniture, in describing herself to her young hypnotist-masseur. From the beginning of treatment, the patient's shouted demand has been not to intrude upon her, psychically or physically.

The final clinical vignette during the first seven week period of Frau Emmy's two courses of treatment follows Freud's recommendation that the patient substitute cool baths for her customary lukewarm baths. A century later, the dialogue still conveys a terrific charge of demand and hostile compliance. Freud writes, "My advice to her to take cool baths was not delivered in such an authoritative manner as to prevent her from having the courage to give open expression to her hesitations." And Frau Emmy does just that. Given the opportunity to speak directly, she takes full advantage. She tells Freud that cool baths will depress her. However, characteristically, she also indicates that she will comply. As if with a seductive wink she says, "I will try it if you like; you mustn't think I wouldn't do whatever you tell me."

Freud attempts a manipulative ploy. He pretends to rescind his suggestion. However, during the next day's hypnosis, he "suggests" again that the patient should herself propose the taking of cool baths. Yet again, Frau Emmy complies; but she artfully turns the table by becoming depressed—as she'd consciously indicated earlier. Freud, of course, asks her why she is depressed. She reiterates her original statement that cold baths depress her. She again takes the upper hand.

Snared in his inability to concede, Freud attempts his second manipulation. He employs the fiction of hypnosis against Frau Emmy, telling her that cool baths were her idea from within the hypnotic state. Next, he attempts to turn the table by suggesting resumption of lukewarm baths. Finally, he switches gears and enquires, "Was it really the bath that depressed you?" Frau Emmy responds that she was depressed not by the baths, but by the thought of her brother far away in Santo Domingo, a concern earlier dismissed by Freud. So saying, she steps into a cool bath, effectively underlining the correctness of her interpretation, balanced against a well-practised submission to male authority.

Frau Emmy and Freud go at it hammer and tongs in this therapeutic precursor to Edward Albee's *Who's Afraid of Virginia Woolf?* (1962). The therapist's resistance is met by the patient's resistance on a fiercely active relational field. Freud insists on his version of Frau Emmy's experience. This evolves into the therapist's resistance to Frau Emmy's freely associative telling of her narrative. Freud's unanalysed authoritarianism clashes dramatically with the characterological hostility of which the patient is conscious.

Yet Freud cannot recognise what is happening. He has not generated sufficient psychoanalytic **d** elements in his alphabet to make sense of the dyadic interaction. He is fixated upon the extension of Bernheim's theoretical idea of split consciousness and its relation to the patient's symptomatic mistrust. He does, however, reveal a nascent awareness of his own participation in the struggle with Frau Emmy. He writes, "The patient who develops a symptom on a particular day—whether owing to the unrest in Santo Domingo or elsewhere—is always inclined to attribute it to his doctor's latest advice." Nevertheless, he locates the difficulty within Frau Emmy's distortions of the causes for which she alone is to blame. The two-person psychology of later psychoanalysis is suppressed beneath the powerful one-person psychology of Freud's investigative model.

Freud is only partially correct. The resistance-counter-resistance matrix which is developed throughout the treatment would later in psychoanalytic history be addressed by the therapist. Frau Emmy seems ready throughout the treatment to look inward. She awaits Freud's responsive hearing.

The first phase of treatment ends and Frau Emmy returns home. Even at this remove, her hostile dependent transference continues. She accuses Freud of responsibility for her daughter's gynaecological problems. Only through Breuer's intercession does Frau Emmy relent.

However, she declares the impossibility of working therapeutically with Freud.

Following brief sanatorium treatment elsewhere, Frau Emmy returns to Freud one year after their first session. Again the patient complains of her earlier symptoms. Again Freud enquires about the patient's inner visions of animals. Again, he is rebuffed with Frau Emmy's hostile, "Oh keep still" (p. 78).

The treatment continues in its accustomed form. Freud diligently continues the hypnotic technique but seems to harden his position into that of clinical inquisitor. He writes, "I accustomed myself to regarding as incomplete any story that brought no improvement, and I gradually came to be able to read from patients' faces whether they might not be concealing an essential part of their confessions."

Frau Emmy tells Freud that she is angry at another physician's abusive manipulation of hypnosis. During her sanatorium stay, the other doctor had compelled her to spell the word "toad" during hypnosis. Frau Emmy asks Freud to promise never to make her say it. At this point, Freud plays what he calls a "practical joke", doubling what Frau Emmy terms an "abuse of hypnosis". He induces the patient to become confused about the name of the institution at which this event happened. Freud is duly instructed by Breuer to cease this behaviour; and to relieve the patient of this new symptomatic burden.

What is going on here? What dissociated psychic activity is the young doctor acting on? How does the patient unconsciously respond? Soon after, Frau Emmy begins a fast. It is apparent to Freud that Frau Emmy will not heed his recommendations. Trying to induce hypnosis, Freud fails. He writes that the "furious look she cast at me convinced me that she was in open rebellion and that the situation was very grave".

Freud sets a limit. He gives Frau Emmy one day to choose between eating or termination of the treatment. She relents. The patient complies with hypnosis, puts on weight, and leaves treatment.

The following spring, Freud spends several days at Frau Emmy's estate to consult upon the condition of the patient's daughter. During a walk with Frau Emmy, Freud asks the patient about an infestation of toads, not so subtly referencing what Emmy had long before requested he not do. He writes, "By way of reply she threw a reproachful glance at me, though unaccompanied by signs of horror." She amplified this a moment later, "... but the ones here are real", referring both to the incident at the sanatorium and the promise exacted from Freud. Freud tests her yet again and calmly, consciously, she again spars with him in his own metaphor.

Even past the end of treatment, the hostile integration between Freud and Frau Emmy continues. Freud seems not to be able to desist. A footnote later in *Studies* relates that Frau Emmy had continued unsuccessfully with many doctors. Freud locates in her "reward" to hypnotists of her successful recoveries, followed by quarrel and deterioration, a "genuine instance of the compulsion to repeat" (1893, p. 105). Sadly for this hostile and dependent widow, her consciousness of her own hostility was not the focus of serious inquiry; but occasioned only the repetitive form of sanatorium cure to gain the minding of others.

Writing in a footnote to the case, Freud relates that the patient's daughter viewed her as a tyrant, although Emmy had pretended to believe that no one else recognised this tyranny. Had Freud's own insistence not obscured his vision, matching Frau Emmy cruelty for cruelty, her case might have resolved differently.

Freud's interpretation of Frau Emmy's tenacity bequeathed the clinical operation of resistance to psychoanalysis. His felt experience of that tenacity in his counter-resistance, dissociated by Freud, prevented his dispassionate inquiry into Frau Emmy's distress. Freud's conscious theoretical interest in Frau Emmy's treatment, his confident drive to develop his pragmatic clinical enterprise along specific theoretical lines, obscures his recognition of the interplay between two participants' psychic interests.

Frau Emmy, unlike Anna O, does not accommodate her therapist in a positive sense. She does not reward him for his insightful attempts at trying to understand. Breuer and Anna dance the polite steps of dissociated transference-countertransference attunement, avoiding hostility. Freud and Emmy spar in hostile attunement, avoiding concession. Freud's youth and easily provoked authoritarianism prohibits his relaxation in the presence of this seductively demanding older woman. Despite the manifest and conscious interest to treat Frau Emmy, Freud acts to convince her or to tame her. It is unclear what underlies this motivation. Yet it remains a prominent psychic interest of Freud's throughout the treatment. Contrary to Breuer's stance, he refuses to be moved by the pathos of this patient. Defensively, his interest becomes an all-out attempt for her to change; or else, finally, an attempt to manipulate her harshly.

Following treatment, Emmy invites Freud to her estate. They continue their sparring on a wooded path to the sea. Perhaps Emmy relishes Freud's unremitting pursuit of her hostile interests as well as his thrill in her material wealth. Perhaps his own hostility is piqued in his discovery of the obstacles along the royal road to the unconscious.

Frau Emmy, however, takes the step of self-interpretation. At this stage in psychoanalysis, it is a step the analyst will not reciprocate consciously. What is so painfully conscious to the patient must operate outside the analyst's consensual validation. Despite Emmy's direct attempts to alert Freud, his psychic interests are deflected by his psychic and interpersonal engagement with the patient, looking away from Emmy's struggle.

Coda

Freud's own clinical horizon, in his work with Frau Emmy, did not have the benefit of evolving landmarks through a century and more of psychodynamic recognition. However, there is something familiar in the malignancy of the therapeutic enterprise within the Frau Emmy case, especially in relation to her own litany of hatreds and dislikes, which suggests some of our own most difficult patients.

Freud would learn, as each of his clinical successors must in her own practice, from these most difficult of patients. Each of us is grateful (if often weary) for the pressures exerted by such patients upon our learning: and, as in the patients described in Chapters 2 and 5, we have learned about psychotic regression, inchoate violence, destruction of thought-linkages, as well as destructive negation.

Despite our best efforts to surface how it is in relation to the significant facts emergent as d, often teased from within the automatic, the mimetically fused, and repetitive chuntering, we have been brought back, again and again, to the confrontation between the patient's own relation to aliveness as opposed to deadness. That is, the therapist may find himself confronted with an obdurate, shiva-like object, proclaiming the endurance of an intrinsic rootedness in a malignant state of mind. The transformational imperative which now confronts us (often across great periods of chronological time) is one which William James once termed the "slow, dead, heave of the will" (1890), the patient's readiness or refusal to consider destructive negation itself as a meaningful d moment, potentially useful to her in a shift from regressive ideation to thinking; or not.

CHAPTER ELEVEN

d from time (n) to time (n+1)

The present chapter illustrates and extends our thinking about the dyadic, creative accomplishment of a consensually verbalised understanding within the clinical dyad, which we recognise as d.

d operates as a transient emergence, agreed upon by the two parties engaged in "individual" psychotherapy, the therapist and the patient. Its simple articulation is given by the form "What you call X, I call Y"; with recognition and reference possible to either or both therapeutic actors that extends forward from a present point in time (n) in the co-creation of here-and-now understanding within clinical contact; and then backward from a later point in time (n+1), with reference to experience undergone both earlier and together.

Although d seems at first glance to be a singular, emergent element of "content", a tentative partial clarification within analytic practice, as an understanding oriented within a session at a given time and in a given space, the reflective capability of either patient or therapist in relation to d as co-construction entails a broader aim: that d, within the sphere of interpersonal minding of two-person psychology (Mitchell & Aron, 1999; Rickman, 2003), is bound in subjective mutuality which itself forms a basis for thinking about thinking. We also recognise that there is in this idea a resonance with those developmental theorists and attachment therapy practitioners who have described and developed further the earliest processes involved in the evolution of a "social mind" (Fonagy, 2001; Fonagy & Target, 1996b; Morton & Frith, 1995). Here, both the concepts of mentalization and reflective function are apposite, in that a secure attachment bond with the primary caregiver appears to facilitate the child's progressive capacity to interpret and to understand putative mental states, related to behaviours of self and others. We agree with Fonagy (2001), that the evolving capacity to explore the meaning of others' actions, in terms of mentalization and reflective function, may crucially contribute to affect regulation, self-monitoring, impulse control, and, more globally, the evolving sense of one's self-agency.

We would add, however, that productive thinking "about thinking" occurs when the weight of ideas forces the linkages essential to the transformation of mere "ideation" (Rapaport, 1950) into vocalisation and verbalisable thinking (Bion, 1962a). Schematically, this is movement from (Freudian) dream elements, operating as "primary process", to interpretive elaboration of such elements, mobilising them towards utilitarian purpose in action from the individual's internal world, outward to the external world (Bion, 1962a, 1992).

Within this collaborative action, d acts to clarify parataxic distortion (Moore, 1921; Sullivan, 1955) as it does also to facilitate a communicative platform between individuals within therapy. As a unit of demonstrated verbalisation and arrival at transient meaning, it illustrates in its daily if critical and continuous presence, a "learning from experience" (Bibring, 1954; Bion, 1962a; Waelder, 1951), in the sense of the formal activity of analyst with patient contributing something new to the experiential world of the patient, however understood as "after-education" (Bibring, 1954), mutative structural action (Loewald, 1960; Strachey, 1934), or the momentary construction of a therapeutic scaffolding against the patient's plunge into annihilative anxiety (Miller & Sweet, 2017; Sweet & Miller, 2016). Additionally, with comparative observation of d expressions between times (n+1) and (n), event causality is demonstrated repeatedly within the therapeutic pair. Such repeated demonstration of d expressions appears necessary in the daily work of psychodynamic practice, in order to facilitate growth and change for the patient, as it is in the relationship between caregivers and their young, during the formative phases and stages of mentalization and the internalisation of reflective function.

While our original recognition of d emerged in its capability to form a scaffolding or "white hole" against the patient's sense of dread in relation to black hole phenomena (see Chapter 4), the present chapter extends the utility of d recognition by analyst and patient to two other domains. The first clinical example extends the patient's recognition of d as a personally significant takeaway transformed by the intuitive listening of the other, outward to mobilisation in the world external to psychotherapy, of taking on the perspective of the other (Mead, 1934). Here, we observe that the action of the consulting room functions in a second transitional sense, as a potential touchstone for the patient's engagement in the external world beyond the consultation room. Beginning with our Chapter 5 case report of a patient called "Marek", we report on further therapeutic emergences in d as building-blocks in thinking dynamically about what other people feel and think.

Our second clinical report concerns the use of a patient's self-articulation in d to guide himself beyond the formerly dreadful certainty of black hole experience through internalisation and memory of the therapeutic relationship at time (n), validated within an actual therapeutic session at time (n+1).

Case 1: Marek from time (n) to time (n+1)

Our earlier description of Marek's psychotherapy centred on the shared observation of analyst and patient that he was able to contain different aspects of his experience through compartmentalisation within different languages. Through an extra-therapeutic opportunity recognised by Marek, he then tested this idea in the "field" beyond the consulting room; and returned with his exploratory findings.

Among his thoughts, on return, was consideration of his life within a formerly split-off world of school-age linguistic experience, now becoming integrated through therapeutic work. Marek recognised that in present moments marked by ambivalence and uncertainty, his linguistic expression in that once split-off language suggested a confident inner sense of self that saw things clearly, "just like when I was a boy, in school"; but that became engaged in English-language chuntering, as if caught in a traffic roundabout without exit.

Marek at time (n+1)

Approximately a year later, Marek had become preoccupied in therapeutic focus, upon one of his many work projects. He recognised that Roger, a colleague whose competitive presence on the project annoyed him, represented a transformation of his own relationship to his father, exposing a vulnerability to power relationships of submission and dominance; but having recognised this gem of insight, he found himself incapable of productively using it.

Anguished, Marek would recall the events of their twice-monthly meeting, replicating again an impossibly insoluble round of chuntering (Joseph, 1982), leaving him exhausted and "unable to think my way out". Both of us, remembering earlier moments in therapy, recognised this pattern as a characteristic state of mind, imbued with Marek's own sense of crushing self-defeat.

Together with this recognition, I found that Marek increasingly used me therapeutically, in the role of witness—possibly a benign paternal presence (Schafer, 1960) or an evenly hovering presence somewhere between passivity and activity (Benjamin, 2004). Here, I recognised myself as observant of his suffering, if somewhat inept in offering potentially clarifying comments. I was also mindful of the parallelism between Marek's sense of intimidation by Roger and the unspoken issue of submission and dominance in our transference-countertransference relationship.

Marek's insistence on repetitive tellings of this narrative, now well off-track from a direct probing of transferential relations to his colleague (or to me), and deeply disturbed by his own incapacity for thinking in Roger's presence (and mine), I considered Marek's transferential relation and use of me as an external containing of thinking.

In retrospect, I was also aware, if without explicit consciousness, of Marek's earlier d recognition in the boyhood splitting of experience between two forms of language. "What do you suggest I do?" he asked. I replied that he himself had told me that he needed "a strategy for daily use", even as he recognised that he was engaged in working through a deeply historical, transferential relation to another. I noted to myself that my answer represented not so much my own thinking, as my own listening and minding of Marek, and my capacity to remind him of his own thinking. In form, this response simply "contained" the product of Marek's own production.

"I have noticed", Marek told me, as if substituting my answer with his own, "that when I tell my stories, you seem to be one step ahead of me in predicting what my colleague might do. How do you do that?" Almost immediately, I thought of Breuer and Anna O, of stories told and convergent situations occasioning symptomatic emergence. And too,

I realised that Marek was asking me the kind of question a youngster asks a teacher or a parent; and with this Ferenczi's care about a confusion of tongues was also in my thinking, perhaps functioning as a supervisor's (textual) voice in my ear.

At this therapeutic moment, my sense was not that I was "supplying" a thinking outcome, but rather, actively representing the "possibility" of thinking, of productive linkage between thoughts hideously infiltrated with fantasies and feelings of persecutory dread.

I wondered to myself about Marek's own capacity for splitting, demonstrated vividly in his differing uses of language; and considered with him, that perhaps there was also a secreted "part" of him, capable of discerning something helpful in his anguished flailings. Marek had sharply marked a difference between his own form of mental activity and my own; and had asked me to help him develop his. Looking back, I seem to have responded in my witnessing role as a benign parent, reflecting on a difficulty "brought home" by a confused schoolboy—certainly not within Marek's own historical range of experience; and so, therapeutically approximating the kind of genuinely new experience described by Loewald (1960) from within the transference-countertransference matrix.

I told him that I had listened over many sessions to what he had told me; and, while listening to his situation, had also thought about his image of Roger, his colleague, from the vantage point of Marek's narrative. Based on what Marek had told me over the months, I had come to view "his" version of Roger as somewhat predictable; and wondered out loud, for Marek to hear, about how Marek had seemed oblivious to his own characterisation of Roger's actions.

The momentary clarification in d was immediate. Marek laughed and said: "Yes, I have been fixed on me, describing him; but I have never chosen to ask myself how he is, at least from my experience." And then, he chuckled, "That's knowledge I can use!"

My later recognition was that this was the seeking of d, coming as a question from Marek in the form, "how"—how might he think about things? How might I think about things? Like our recognitions together of reverse splitting in the use of language, Marek and I had built upon implicit conviction in arrivals at d, here flexibly exemplified in a very different clinical moment.

This session passed; and the subject of Marek's relation with Roger only emerged again weeks later, with Marek's claim to have negotiated a difficult meeting in a manner which was new and exciting. He was pleased with himself; and announced a newfound sense of capacity. "This is not control," he told me, "but rather an increased capability in thinking-through a situation, by thinking about the way in which I have come to understand Roger." Unknown to Marek, he was discovering what George Herbert Mead long ago characterised as taking "the role of the other", one's own capability of standing in another person's shoes; and indeed, a process that we now understand to be a touchstone of healthy interpersonal relations, namely the capacity to mentalize one's experience in relation to the effects generated between the self and another. Marek's own demonstrated capability in reversible perspective, decentring from his narcissistic focus of being affected by another to thinking about how the other was affected by him. Independent of my therapeutic guidance, Marek had enlisted our now-internalised relationship and his productive "use" of me to break free from anxious chuntering and to discover personal agency and newfound capability.

He continued, saying, "I began to get anxious in the meeting, and then thought about what you and I had discussed in therapy, that it was possible to know 'something', something that I had not focused on in thinking about my own terrors. And that reminded me that I could think about what I knew about Roger. And from there, I could think clearly!"

Conceptually, it seemed that Marek's use of therapy as collaborative "play" in the same sense that Winnicott illustrates with the "Squiggle", allowed him to view social roles in work at the level of a game, with rules of play which might be reflected upon (Mead, 1934). Mead's point is that in taking on roles, the child must also anticipate the reciprocating social role of the other, what the other might do and how he might act.

More profoundly, the taking on of roles relates directly to the collegiality between Marek and me in the therapeutic relationship: to the extent that my participation was descriptive of my own activity in "thinking about" something about which Marek had not yet explicitly conceived as possible, despite all his complicated thinking. And specifically, as I thought "about" Marek and thought "about" the Roger who Marek described, I had inadvertently demonstrated an exit road for chuntering.

Marek had "taken" me along with him into the extra-therapeutic world. He had also taken along with him a way of thinking about things demonstrated within psychotherapy, but belonging to us all.

The analyst demonstrates this in observation: how the destructive work of person X affects the group; or how person Z always seems to make sexual advances; or how the patient herself is prepared to greet people both from a position of naïvety and trust, as if she has never learned anything, and at the same time with a terror that such trust will cause her annihilation. Articulating these anchor-points become testable and malleable propositions in d, from which the individual comes to differentiate her own point of view. Here, in the gap between therapist and patient, parataxic distortion becomes clarified (Moore, 1923; Sullivan, 1955).

And from within such chains of action, the analyst perceives a changing horizon of possibility in expanding growth, within his work with the patient (Loewald, 1978).

Case 2: Paul

I've got a story for you, Paul said. And as I listened, I realised that this was exactly what Paul said: a story requiring acute listening and almost no interpretation, a story which required the therapist's holding or containment as anxiety was transmitted—much as it is transmitted in the telling of a joke, Freud's early contribution to the interpersonal dynamics of human communication. Yet what Freud did not accentuate here was that the occasion of the story prepares a field of expectation in the listener; and I was prepared to receive Paul's effects upon me. The therapist, as much as the patient, operates in space, time, and causality. Within this moment of the therapeutic session, Paul was instructing me that a period of time was to be bracketed by me for close attention to him; and that the expectation on both sides, Paul's and mine, was for some transformation of some kind to happen.

Paul's was a story in the transforming shape of d; and to be fair to context, Paul did state, "I want you to understand that all that I'm telling you is a week later." That is, the telling itself is prefaced with Paul's recognition, his arrival in approximation of the Kleinian "D" (Klein, 1946) in relation to the tale he would tell, of multiple d moments.

Paul's once-weekly sessions were a continuation of three years of twice-weekly therapy; and Paul would be quick to say that his reason for referral was "rage". He was a fiery tempered businessman, who acknowledged that the turning point in therapy seemed to be the long period during which he "forgot" his sessions in deep immersion of work tasks, and came to realise that the forgetting was both a tool for erasing the intrusive presence of the therapist and for securing a conflict-free fantasy of independence, separate from his experience of persecutory, rejecting others.

This moment had resolved in the course of therapy; and Paul's ostensible reason for continuing was "trouble-shooting". Family relations as well as business situations were still occasions of periodic anxiety and destabilisation.

Paul's story began with the importance of his trip to Italy. A very lucrative new deal was at stake and he outlined in great detail the preparations for the trip including seat selection for the outgoing flight and his care in booking a taxi to the airport. In this telling, although laboured, I noted silently Paul's attention to the multiple considerations of d that would build towards his goal. And, anticipating by the form of the telling and the delight with which he stretched his narrative, increasing my pressure in bearing the certain uncertainty of what would come, I also understood that he was well aware of me as listener. Not only had a change occurred in therapy in relation to his unnoted "forgetting" of me as an other (as well as multiple sessions themselves), but he was delighting in playing with me as a peer, trusted and listening. To call it "selfobject" would be to distort the importance of my otherness to him—indeed, the difference between us as participants and my attention to his narrative was critical.

Retelling the story in writing risks losing its dramatic telling. Essentially, it is a story of disappointment transcended in triumph through awareness and mastery of anxiety through linked-up thinking.

> I was at the airport in plenty of time to get through that terrible security line. And, despite my wife's belief that I'm terrible in planning, I had all my gels and liquids in their appropriate plastic bags, my coins in my jacket pocket with my belt and the whole lot folded in one of those dreadful grey trays. I was a symphony of personal administration; but of course, the woman in front of me caused a back-up in the line as she started reassembling her kit on the conveyer belt rather than removing it, which would have been considerate. But fuck it, I thought. That's narcissism and I have plenty of time.
>
> I even bought a paper and a cup of tea: the gate for the flight was due to be posted; and so I had time. I went to the loo, peeked

> around the tax-free shops, and finally saw that the flight was going out at gate 207. That's odd, I thought, and then rechecked the board. Yes, 207. I knew it would involve a long underground walk from terminal 2 to terminal 3, but then, I had plenty of time.
>
> A fellow pushed past me on the moving stairs as I headed out to terminal 3, and it occurred to me, "I'm feeling pretty cool, this is great"; and then I arrived at the terminal, realising that I had to walk past another arcade of shops and still further to get to the gate. It registered upon me that this was becoming bloody inconvenient. I was beginning to sweat—as if I had just hit my regular pace while jogging. But fine, I thought, I'd prepared myself with a bottle of water, so I was cool.
>
> I checked the departure board once again: and the gate now said 407 instead of 207. This threw a spanner into the works, as it would require retracing my steps back to terminal 2. So I walked on until there was another announcement board and checked again. This time it said gate 207. I had a momentary wobble. Time was beginning to pass quickly until the flight and I reckoned that if I had to go back, it could be a twenty minute walk. I began to fume, anxious I suppose, and then caught myself: this is unproductive, I reminded myself. So, I found an official—he was wearing a lanyard and had a shirt with an embroidered airport symbol on it—and asked him to clarify: gate 207 or 407? He took out his walkie-talkie and vanished for a couple of minutes, returning with a smile and an apology, "I'm sorry for your efforts, but you'll have to backtrack and go to 407." I thanked him and hurried off.
>
> By now I was sweating and dropping things—all those items I had neatly packed and organised, cursing inwardly the inconvenience of this kind of thing.

Listening quietly, I was aware of his report from the front lines of modernity: here he was, competent in doing his part to facilitate his global presence—in business, in travel, in application of his learning about the minor and multiple attentions and considerations necessary in performing the task of air travel. Against this competence and capability there was something else, something uncontrolled by Paul: in this case, a directional signboard conveying conflicting information. At root here, despite Paul's obvious competencies, were his dependencies on externalities uncontrollable by him; and more, his expectancy in the airport, where he'd assented to his own compression into an abstraction, a well-packed, instruction-following filler of an expensive aeroplane seat as printed on his boarding pass, that his dependent expectations were not fulfilled. Indeed, operating competently from within an assumption of dependency upon instructions from others, he was experiencing stress: despite doing things properly, his project was going wrong!

So far, what was therapeutically significant in my thinking were two things: 1) his playful, creative use of me as a necessary partner in this relational situation; and 2) the importance to Paul that I understood how he had both accurately parsed and handled himself under normal conditions, almost falling into a well-known sinkhole of anxiety but mastering himself and vaulting himself from disappointed dependency to goal-directed action.

I continued to listen, smiling as I relished where we'd arrived, together. Paul smiled too. He described arriving at gate 407 and deciding that it might be significant to notify staff, for the benefit of other passengers. He was treated rudely, as if he were speaking another language. Finally, a stewardess, doubting him, had him show her the contradictory signage on an electronic board directly opposite the gate. She thought for a moment and then said, "Of course. That's because our airline code-shares with another airline for the same route and sometimes we go from this gate and sometimes from that gate." Paul registered that this answer made no sense; and asked her if she thought that this signage was helpful. She started to giggle. "Let me see your ticket," she said, "and I'll see if I can give you a better seat for your trouble."

Paul said, "These kind of things happen all the time to all of us. It is easy to compress them all into nothing, into the flow of the day. But I am aware of the choices, of the choice-points and the moments of certainty and then anxiety, as they proceed. Giving up something of my own competence in arriving at the airport as a passenger, I expected something more from the airline. Had I gotten to the gate late, after all the jigs and reels, I would've been treated like a rude schoolboy. And in-between, what was required of me was thinking and thinking about where I was in what was really, realistically, what you call a 'transitory' state: my God, I was in transit! Sure, in the end, I got a seat upgrade as the stewardess's response, and she was acting as a good representative of her employer—doing what was in her control to soothe a customer who'd been ruffled. But the real learning is my own, about me: about realising these moments of certainty and then normal anxiety, back and forth, in the simple living of every day."

Paul has articulated the transitional, transitory shift noted by Winnicott (1953), in the phenomenological experience of "between thumb and forefinger", in the momentary awareness of multiple aspects of experience within a single narrative of an arc of action, here restricted to arrival at an airport gate en route to a business meeting. Within this quotidian action are multiple moments of Paul's awareness, both attended and unattended, formulated and unformulated (D. N. Stern et al., 1998). Central to the arc are two dimensions: primary from the perspective of a one-person psychology, is Paul's unitary capacity to recognise the onset of anxiety, to preside over the anxiety, to recover thoughts' linkage en route to productive action; and from the perspective of a two-person, object-related experience, the relishing of his communicative capacity to be attended, to be minded, by a reliable other whether directly in therapeutic experience or as an internalised capability.

Conclusion

Psychoanalytical models of development primarily concern themselves with the individual's evolving capacity to organise primary representations of experience into secondary representations, at both the mental and bodily level. We have, in Chapter 3, outlined and described the ways in which we understand the emergence of d elements to be crucial constituents of evolving symbolising capacities and, in addition, we have further developed our thoughts on the restriction of such capacities and the implications of such restriction, in terms of psychopathology. Our primary aim, throughout the preceding chapters, has been to demonstrate the explanatory utility of the book's underpinning concept, both in the clinical situation and as a method for further hermeneutical understanding and translation of the psychoanalytical method, principally with reference to key developments within the discipline of psychoanalysis and to the application of those ideas within other fields (following the example of Winnicott's essay (1949) in extending psychoanalytic discovery as useful beyond psychoanalysis).

The two cases presented in this chapter are emblematic of the gradual changes which occur with patients over time, as a result of the daily work of psychodynamic psychotherapy. The emergence of a shared reflective capability, between patient and therapist, is hard-won over time, binding (see also Freud's concept of *Bindung*: Freud, 1911b) the patient and therapist together through the experience of subjective mutuality. Such binding eventuates as a shared capacity to think about thinking.

As previously observed, within this collaborative action, d acts to clarify distortions of thinking and facilitates a communicative bridge between individuals within therapy. Discrete d elements coalesce as units of transitory meaning, however precarious and membrane-like they may be, during the earliest and tentative periods of their emergence. In time, and given the tenacity of the therapeutic pair to survive the inevitable resistances and enactments which threaten their relationship, these elements are fundamental in forging a greater capacity to reflect upon experience, learn from it and, in turn, gain a greater awareness of one's self in relation with another.

CHAPTER TWELVE

Conclusion

Descartes famously wrote that

> I have formed a method that gives me the means, as I think, of gradually augmenting my knowledge, and of raising it by little and little to the highest point which the mediocrity of my talents and the brief duration of my life will permit me to reach. (1637, p. 4)

In this sense, beginning with its first principles in the necessity of a dyadic relationship and the engagement of the dynamic unconscious, psychoanalysis follows Descartes's incremental course of learning. Our own starting point is similarly Cartesian: the algorithm of W. R. Bion, who beyond his integration of Klein, Kant, and the Mad Hatter (1962a), links psychoanalytic inquiry with humanism's first applied philosophy of the individual, operating upon the split between embodied self and mind. Psychoanalysis is our contemporary, twenty-first-century development of what Foucault (1988) terms a "technology of self", the intensive study of how life and its vicissitudes are experienced by the individual; and how, through the exercise of reflective practice in the company of another, one comes to think and to act with a greater sense of freedom and ease, than had earlier been possible. In this way, across the time comprising days, weeks, and years of fifty minute sessions, the clinical dyad incrementally strives towards the Cartesian achievement of raising life, "little and little to the highest point which the mediocrity of my talents and the brief duration of my life will permit me to reach".

Our own path is towards appreciation of what we discern as d, the incremental, transient, and dyadic accomplishment of an articulated meaning, which is the cornerstone of the daily work of psychotherapy. Amplifying this therapeutic accomplishment, we recognise it too, in the **d** of incremental changes in the history of psychoanalytic thinking, as expressed in the communicative form of the psychoanalytic essay.

We have traced d and **d** formations in literature and in the clinic; and have located these as conceptual elements within the matrix of every clinician's thoughts—brought forward from time to time from within the therapist's intuitive experience to the patient's as both constructive and interpretive presentation; and so, verbalised, enacted, and co-created within the daily back-and-forth of psychoanalytic psychotherapy.

Both d and **d** shift across time, in the transit from time (n) to time (n+1). In this, they operate within the domain of temporal "transience". This is a concept that becomes the lingua franca of psychoanalytic discourse, following the conceptual leaps of Winnicott and Bion, in the middle of the twentieth century (Miller, 2016a), but that also hearkens backward, in its dyadic, interpersonal resonance, to a term coined by Seneca in "On Tranquility", his articulation of an earlier technology of self (Hadas, 1958). Seneca recognises the **d** of human "permeability", our openness to the experience of being affected by others in the external world, and to our own internal subjective and physical experience. This permeability is what Ernest Schachtel (1959) terms "allocentricity" in our times.

Like permeability, our clinical recognitions of d are a function of **d**. We recognise emergence because we recognise clinical landmarks; and our starting place for such recognition is experiential—within the clinician's own, personal experience of intensive psychoanalytic psychotherapy.

d is ultimately a codification, a temporary ordering and articulation of that which resonates from one's particularities of experience in orientation to a specific task and object. It achieves clarification in such a way that the journey from vaguely apprehended experience to intuition to articulation achieves recognition as a generality, or universal, potentially useful to another.

Reflecting upon the hard-won clinical emergence of d, we recognise, with Bion and Waelder, that productive thinking and its attendant actions involve a battle as consensual reality is wrested from paranoid ideation. And that the forms of behaviour recognised clinically (Chapter 1) together with the symbolic representations (Chapter 2) in our own gesturings, blatherings, and articulations, are multi-levelled and in continuous emergence and regression to and from the depressive position. Always clothed in the particulars of the patient's narrative and expression, they are inscribed within the therapist's experience from which the therapist's action upon their felt, countertransferential particularity must be retranscribed: first into a universal notion and then into the particular language of the patient, such that what one calls "X" is understood as what the other calls "Y". This empirically verifiable action proceeds across the clinical timeline from (n) to (n+1) to (n+2) and beyond, of fusing and defusing formal recognitions.

We demonstrate the utility of such thinking in several domains. First, we recognise it in the clinical form of d emergence we call reverse splitting (Chapter 5). Next, we describe its presence in Freud's presentations of linked essays (Chapter 6). Using literary narrative as our example, we depict the expression of d in affect and clarified thinking, together with the activities through which the clinician (or reader) recognises these developments, in Chapter 7. Chapter 8 proceeds along the path of what contemporary theorists call a "wicked problem", not unlike the knotted and inchoate intimations brought to us by our patients. It proceeds through interlocking sections to arrive at the workings of destructive negation as well as the intuitive dynamic wherein the therapist's subjective and particular experience is refined into a generality, useful in articulation to the patient. Chapters 9 and 10 return to early and foundational case presentations, circling back to Breuer's and Freud's original studies from the perspective of our d and **d** recognitions, so discerning through today's landmarks what was less distinct yesterday.

Following Descartes, we hope that this journey proves productive as a contribution to the reader's practice; and while provocative, that the benefits of thinking outweigh its discomforts.

REFERENCES

Albee, E. (1962). *Who's Afraid of Virginia Woolf?* New York: Dramatists Play Service.

Bakewell, S. (2011). *How to Live. A Life of Montaigne in One Question and Twenty Attempts at an Answer*. London: Vintage.

Balint, M. (1968). *The Basic Fault: Therapeutic Aspects of Regression*. London: Tavistock.

Baranger, M., & Baranger, W. (2008). The analytic situation as a dynamic field. *International Journal of Psychoanalysis, 89*: 795–826.

Bateman, A., & Fonagy, P. (2006). *Mentalization-based Treatment for Borderline Personality Disorder: A Practical Guide*. Oxford: Oxford University Press.

Beckett, S. (1931). *Proust*. New York: Grove Press.

Beckett, S. (2006a). *The Grove Centenary Edition. Volume II. Novels*. New York: Grove Press.

Beckett, S. (2006b). *The Grove Centenary Edition. Volume IV. Poems, Short Fiction, Criticism*. New York: Grove Press.

Beebe, B., Rustin, J., Sorter, D., & Knoblauch, S. (2003). An expanded view of intersubjectivity in infancy and its application to psychoanalysis. *Psychoanalytic Dialogues, 13*(6): 805–841.

Benjamin, J. (2004). Beyond doer and done to: An intersubjective view of thirdness. *Psychoanalytic Quarterly, 73*: 5–46.

Bergmann, M. (1999). The dynamics of the history of psychoanalysis: Anna Freud, Leo Rangell, and André Green. In: Kohon, G. (Ed.), *The Dead Mother. The Work of André Green*. London: Routledge.

Bibring, E. (1954). Psychoanalysis and the dynamic psychotherapies. *Journal of the American Psychoanalytic Association, 2*: 745–770.

Bick, E. (1968). The experience of the skin in early object relations. *The International Journal of Psychoanalysis, 49*: 114–118.

Bion, W. R. (1957). Differentiation of the psychotic from the non-psychotic personalities. *International Journal of Psychoanalysis, 38*: 266–275.

Bion, W. R. (1959). Attacks on linking. *International Journal of Psychoanalysis, 40*: 308–315.

Bion, W. R. (1962a). The psycho-analytic study of thinking. *International Journal of Psychoanalysis, 43*: 306–310.

Bion, W. R. (1962b). *Learning from Experience*. London: William Heinemann Medical Books.

Bion, W. R. (1963). *Elements of Psychoanalysis*. London: Karnac.

Bion, W. R. (1967). *Second Thoughts*. London: Karnac.

Bion, W. R. (1970). *Attention and Interpretation*. London: Karnac.

Bion, W. R. (1987). On arrogance. Paper presented to 20th Congress of the International Psychoanalytical Association, Paris, France, July–August 1957. Reprinted in: *Second Thoughts* (pp. 86–92). London: Karnac.

Bion, W. R. (1992). *Cogitations*. London: Karnac.

Bion, W. R. (1994). On turbulence. In: *Clinical Seminars and Other Works*. London: Karnac.

Bion, W. R. (2005). *The Tavistock Seminars*. F. Bion (Ed.), London: Karnac.

Bleuler, E. (1911). *Dementia praecox oder die Gruppe der Schizoprenien*. In: G. Aschaffenburg (Ed.), *Handbuch der Psychiatrie*. Leipzig, Germany: Breitkopf und Härtel.

Bollas, C. (1987). *The Shadow of the Object: Psychoanalysis of the Unthought Known*. London: Free Association.

Bollas, C. (1992). *Being a Character*. New York: Hill & Wang.

Bollas, C. (1995). *Cracking Up: The Work of Unconscious Experience*. New York: Routledge.

Bollas, C. (2006). Perceptive identification. *Psychoanalytic Review, 93*: 713–717.

Bollas, C. (2008). *The Evocative Object World*. New York: Routledge.

Bolognini, S. (2011). *Secret Passages*. London: Routledge.

Bonomi, C. (2003). Between symbol and antisymbol—the meaning of trauma reconsidered. *International Forum of Psychoanalysis, 12*: 17–21.

Boston Change Process Study Group (BCPSG) (2007). The foundational level of psychodynamic meaning: Implicit process in relation to conflict, defense and the dynamic unconscious. *International Journal of Psychoanalysis, 88*: 843–860.

Bouvet, M. (1958). Technical variation and the concept of distance. *International Journal of Psychoanalysis, 39*: 211–221.

Bower, M., Hale, R., & Wood, H. (2013). *Addictive States of Mind*. London: Karnac.

Breuer, J. (1893). Fräulein Anna O. In: *Studies on Hysteria, Case Histories. S. E., 2*: 19–47. London: Hogarth.

Britton, R. (1998). *Belief and Imagination: Explorations in Psychoanalysis*. New York: Routledge.

Britton, R. (2003). *Sex, Death and the Superego*. London: Routledge.

Buber, M. (1950). Distance and relation. In: J. Buber Agassi (Ed.), *Martin Buber on Psychology and Psychotherapy*. Syracuse, NY: Syracuse University Press, 1999.

Buber, M. (1951). Healing through meeting. In: J. Buber Agassi (Ed.), *Martin Buber on Psychology and Psychotherapy*. Syracuse, NY: Syracuse University Press, 1999.

Buber, M. (1957a). Elements of the interhuman. In: J. Buber Agassi (Ed.), *Martin Buber on Psychology and Psychotherapy*. Syracuse, NY: Syracuse University Press, 1999.

Buber, M. (1957b). Audio transcript. In: R. Anderson & K. N. Cissna (Eds.), *The Martin Buber-Carl Rogers Dialogue*. Albany, NY: SUNY Press, 1997.

Cohen, L. (1984). "Hallelujah". http://www.leonardcohenforum.com/viewtopic.php?t=9866.

Colm, H. (1955). A field-theory approach to transference and its particular application to children. *Psychiatry, 18*: 339–352.

Conci, M. (2009). Bion and Sullivan: An enlightening comparison. *International Forum of Psychoanalysis, 18*: 90–99.

Danto, E. A. (2005). *Freud's Free Clinics. Psychoanalysis & Social Justice, 1918–1938*. New York: Columbia University Press.

Davoine, F., & Gaudillière, J.-M. (2004). *History beyond Trauma*. New York: Other Books.

Descartes, R. (1637). *Discourse on Method and Meditations on First Philosophy*. New York: Barnes & Noble, 2004.

Dewey, J. (1896). The Reflex Arc Concept in psychology. *Psychological Review, 3*: 357–370.

Ehrenberg, D. (1992). *The Intimate Edge. Extending the Reach of Psychoanalytic Inter*action. New York: W. W. Norton.

Eshel, O. (1998). Black holes, deadness and existing analytically. *International Journal of Psychoanalysis, 79*: 1115–1130.

Fairbairn, W. R. D. (1952). *Psychoanalytic Studies of the Personality*. London: Tavistock.

Federn, P. (1926). Some variations in ego-feeling. *International Journal of Psychoanalysis, 7*: 434–444.

Federn, P. (1940). Psychoanalysis as a therapy of society. *American Imago, 5*(1): 65–80.

Felman, S. (1992). Education and crisis, or the vicissitudes of teaching. In: S. Felman & D. Laub (Eds.), *Testimony. Crises of Witnessing in Literature, Psychoanalysis, and History*. Routledge: New York, 1992.

Ferenczi, S. (1913). Stages in the development of the sense of reality. In: *Sex and Psychoanalysis: The Selected Papers of Sandor Ferenczi, M. D.* E. Jones (Trans.). New York: Basic Books, 1950.

Ferenczi, S. (1915). Psychogenic anomalies of voice production. In: J. Rickman (Ed.), *Further Contributions to the Theory and Technique of Psychoanalysis*. London: Maresfield Reprints, 1980.

Ferenczi, S. (1920). The further development of an active technique in psychoanalysis. In: J. Rickman (Ed.), *Further Contributions to the Theory and Technique of Psychoanalysis*. London: Maresfield Reprints, 1980.

Ferenczi, S. (1928). The elasticity of psycho-analytic technique In: M. Balint (Ed.), *Final Contributions to the Problems and Methods of Psycho-Analysis*. New York: Brunner Mazel, 1980.

Ferenczi, S. (1988). *The Clinical Diary of Sandor Ferenczi*. J. Dupont (Ed.). Cambridge, MA: Harvard University Press.

Ferenczi, S., & Rank, O. (1923). *The Development of Psychoanalysis*. Madison, CT: International Universities Press, 1986.

Fonagy, P. (2001). *Attachment Theory and Psychoanalysis*. New York: Other Press.

Fonagy, P., & Target, M. (1996a). Personality and sexual development. In: C. Cordess & M. Cox (Eds.), *Forensic Psychotherapy: Crime, Psychodynamics and the Offender Patient*. London: Jessica Kinsgley.

Fonagy, P., & Target, M. (1996b). Playing with reality: I. Theory of mind and the normal development of psychic reality. *International Journal of Psychoanalysis, 77*: 217–233.

Fonagy, P., Gergely, G., Jurist, E., & Target, M. (2003). *Affect Regulation, Mentalization and the Development of the Self*. London: Karnac.

Foucault, M. (1966). *The Order of Things*. London: Routledge.

Foucault, M. (1988). *Technologies of the Self. A Seminar with Michel Foucault*. L. Martin, H. Gutman, & P. Hutton (Eds.). London: Tavistock.

Foucault, M. (1989). *The Archaeology of Knowledge*. London: Routledge.

Freud, S. (1890a). Psychical (or mental) treatment. *S. E., 7*: 281–302. London: Hogarth.

Freud, S. (1893). Frau Emmy von N. In: *Studies on Hysteria, Case Histories. S. E.,* 2: 48–105. London: Hogarth.

Freud, S., & Breuer, J. (1895d). *Studies on Hysteria. S. E.,* 2. London: Hogarth.

Freud, S. (1900a). *The Interpretation of Dreams. S. E., 4–5*. London: Hogarth.

Freud, S. (1901b). *The Psychopathology of Everyday Life: Forgetting, Slips of the Tongue, Bungled Actions, Superstitions and Errors. S. E., 6*: vii–296. London: Hogarth.

Freud, S. (1905a). On psychotherapy. *S. E., 7*: 257–268. London: Hogarth.

Freud, S. (1905b). *Jokes and Their Relation to the Unconscious. S. E., 8*: 1–247. London: Hogarth.

Freud, S. (1910a). Five lectures on psycho-analysis. *S. E., 11*: 1–56. London: Hogarth.

Freud, S. (1911b). Formulations on the two principles of mental functioning. *S. E., 12*: 213–226. London: Hogarth.

Freud, S. (1911c). Psycho-analytic notes on an autobiographical account of a case of paranoia (dementia paranoides). *S. E., 12*: 3–82. London: Hogarth.

Freud, S. (1912–13). *Totem and Taboo: Some Points of Agreement between the Mental Lives of Savages and Neurotics. S. E., 13*: vii–162. London: Hogarth.

Freud, S. (1914c). On narcissism: an introduction. *S. E., 14*: 67–102. London: Hogarth.

Freud, S. (1914d). On the history of the psycho-analytic movement. *S. E., 14*: 1–66. London: Hogarth.

Freud, S. (1914g). Remembering, repeating and working-through (further recommendations on the technique of psycho-analysis, II). *S. E., 12*: 145–156. London: Hogarth.

Freud, S. (1915e). The unconscious. *S. E., 14*: 159–215. London: Hogarth.

Freud, S. (1916–17). *Introductory Lectures on Psycho-Analysis. S. E., 15–16*: 1–240. London: Hogarth.

Freud, S. (1917e). Mourning and melancholia. *S. E., 14*: 237–258. London: Hogarth.

Freud, S. (1921c). *Group Psychology and the Analysis of the Ego. S. E., 18*: 65–144. London: Hogarth.

Freud, S. (1925h). Negation. *S. E., 19*: 233–240. London: Hogarth.

Freud, S. (1926d). *Inhibitions, Symptoms and Anxiety. S. E., 20*: 77–175. London: Hogarth.

Freud, S. (1927d). Humour. *S. E., 21*: 159–166. London: Hogarth.

Freud, S. (1927e). Fetishism. *S. E., 21*: 147–158. London: Hogarth.

Freud, S. (1937c). Analysis terminable and interminable. *S. E., 23*: 209–254. London: Hogarth.

Freud, S. (1940e). Splitting of the ego in the process of defence. *S. E., 23*: 271–278. London: Hogarth.

Freud, S. (1950a). A project for a scientific psychology. *S. E., 1*: 281–388. London: Hogarth.

Fromm, E. (1964). Humanism and psychoanalysis. *Contemporary Psychoanalysis, 1*: 69–79.

Frosh, S. (2009). *Hate and the Jewish Science. Anti-Semitism, Nazism and Psychoanalysis. Revised Edition*. London: Palgrave Macmillan.

Gadamer, G. (1975). *Truth and Method*. London: Continuum.

Gaddini, E. (1969). On imitation. *International Journal of Psychoanalysis, 50*: 475–484.

Giustiniani, V. R. (1985). Homo, humanus, and the meanings of "humanism". *Journal of the History of Ideas, 46*(2): 167–195.

Glasser, M. (1979). Some aspects of the role of aggression in the perversions. In: I. Rosen (Ed.), *Sexual Deviation*. Oxford: Oxford University Press.

Goetschel, W. (1994). *Constituting Critique. Kant's Writing as Critical Praxis*. Durham, NC: Duke University Press.

Govrin, A. (2016). *Conservative and Radical Perspectives on Psychoanalytic Knowledge: The Fascinated and the Disenchanted*. London: Routledge.

Gray, P. (1994). *The Ego and Analysis of Defense*. Northvale, NJ: Jason Aronson.

Green, A. (1975). The analyst, symbolization and absence in the analytic setting (on changes in analytic practice and analytic experience)—in memory of D. W. Winnicott. *International Journal of Psychoanalysis, 56*: 1–22.

Green, A. (2002). *Time in Psychoanalysis*. London: Free Association.

Grinberg, L. (1962). On a specific aspect of countertransference due to the patient's projective identification. *International Journal of Psychoanalysis, 43*: 436–440.

Grossman, W. I. (1992). Hierarchies, boundaries, and representation in a Freudian model of mental organization. *Journal of the American Psychoanalytic Association, 40*: 27–62.

Grotstein, J. S. (1990). The "black hole" as the basic psychotic experience: some newer psychoanalytic and neuroscience perspectives on psychosis. *Journal of the American Academy of Psychoanalysis, 18*: 29–46.

Grotstein, J. S. (2009). *"... But at the Same Time and on Another Level ...": Psychoanalytic Theory and Technique in the Kleinian/Bionian Mode, Vol. 1*. London: Karnac.

Hadas, M. (1958). *The Stoic Philosophy of Seneca*. New York: W. W. Norton.

Hanaghan, J. (1966). *Freud + Jesus*. Monkstown, Dublin: Runa Press.

Hartmann, H. (1939). *Ego Psychology and the Problem of Adaptation*. D. Rapaport (Trans.). New York: International Universities Press, 1958.

Heine, H. (1826). *Travel Pictures*. Brooklyn, NY: Archipelago, 2008.

Heine, H. (1840). *Ludwig Borne: A Memorial* (J. L. Sammons, translator and editor, 2006) Rochester New York: Camden House.

Hopper, E. (1995). A psychoanalytic theory of drug addiction: unconscious fantasies of homosexuality, compulsions and masturbation within the context of traumatogenic process. *International Journal of Psychoanalysis, 76*: 1121–1142.

Horney, K. (1991). The goals of analytic therapy. *American Journal of Psychoanalysis, 51*: 219–226.

Howell, E., & Blizzard, R. (2009). Chronic relational trauma disorder: A new diagnostic scheme for borderline personality and the spectrum of dissociative disorders. In: P. Dell & J. O'Neill (Eds.), *Dissociation and the Dissociative Disorder*. New York: Routledge.

James, W. (1890). *The Principles of Psychology, Volumes 1–2*. Cambridge, MA: Harvard University Press, 1981.

Jaques, E. (1965). Death and the mid-life crisis. *International Journal of Psychoanalysis, 46*: 502–514.

Jones, E. (1916a). The theory of symbolism. *British Journal of Psychology, 9*: 181–229.

Jones, E. (1916b). The theory of symbolism. In: *Papers on Psychoanalysis* (pp. 87–144). London: Maresfield Reprints, 1948.

Jones, E. (1951). The psychology of the Jewish question. In: *Essays in Applied Psychoanalysis, Vol. 1* (pp. 284–300). London: Hogarth.

Joseph, B. (1982). Addiction to near-death. *International Journal of Psychoanalysis, 63*: 449–456.

Joseph, B. (1985). Transference: The total situation. *International Journal of Psychoanalysis, 66*: 447–454.

Jung, C. G. (1936). Wotan. In: *Essays on Contemporary Events. The Psychology of Nazism* (pp. 10–24). Princeton, NJ: Bollingen.

Kapur, R., & Campbell, J. (2004). *The Troubled Mind of Northern Ireland*. London: Karnac.

Katan, M. (1949). Schreber's delusion of the end of the world. *Psychoanalytic Quarterly, 18*: 60–66.

Katan, M. (1950a). Schreber's hallucinations about the "Little Men". *International Journal of Psychoanalysis, 31*: 32–35.

Katan, M. (1950b). Structural aspects of a case of schizophrenia. *Psychoanalytic Study of the Child, 5*: 175–211.

Katan, M. (1954). The importance of the non-psychotic part of the personality in schizophrenia. *International Journal of Psychoanalysis, 35*: 119–128.

Kernberg, O. F. (1992). *Aggression in Personality Disorders and Perversions*. New Haven, CT: Yale University Press.

Khan, M. M. R. (1963). The concept of cumulative trauma. *Psychoanalytic Study of the Child, 18*: 286–306.

King, P., & Steiner, R. (1992). *The Freud-Klein Controversies, 1941–1945*. London: Routledge.

Klein, G. (2009). *Streetlights and Shadows. Searching for Keys to Adaptive Decision Making*. Cambridge, MA: MIT Press.

Klein, M. (1923). Early analysis. In: *The Writings of Melanie Klein, Vol. 1* (pp. 77–105). London: Hogarth.

Klein, M. (1929). Personification in the play of children. In: *The Writings of Melanie Klein, Vol. 1* (pp. 199–209). London: Hogarth.

Klein, M. (1930). The importance of symbol formation in the development of the ego. In: *The Writings of Melanie Klein, Vol. 1* (pp. 219–232). London: Hogarth.

Klein, M. (1931). A contribution to the theory of intellectual inhibition. In: *The Writings of Melanie Klein, Vol. 1* (pp. 236–247). London: Hogarth.

Klein, M. (1932). *The Psychoanalysis of Children: The Writings of Melanie Klein, Vol. 2*. London: Hogarth.

Klein, M. (1935). A contribution to the psycho-genesis of manic depressive states. In: *The Writings of Melanie Klein, Vol. 1* (pp. 262–289). London: Hogarth.

Klein, M. (1946). Notes on some schizoid mechanisms. *International Journal of Psychoanalysis, 27*: 99–110.

Klein, M. (1957). *Envy and Gratitude*. In: *The Writings of Melanie Klein, Vol. 3* (pp. 176–235). London: Hogarth.

Kohon, G. (1999). The greening of psychoanalysis: André Green in dialogues with Gregorio Kohon. In: G. Kohon (Ed.), *The Dead Mother. The Work of André Green*. London: Routledge.

Kohut, H. (1971). *The Analysis of the Self*. New York: International Universities Press.

Kuriloff, E. (2014). *Contemporary Psychoanalysis and the Legacy of the Third Reich. History, Memory, Tradition*. New York: Routledge.

Lacan, J. (1953). The function and field of speech and language in psychoanalysis. In: B. Fink (Ed.), *Ecrits* (pp. 197–268). New York: W. W. Norton.

Lacan, J. (1957–58). Lecture 5. http://esource.dbs.ie/bitstream/handle/10788/156/Book-05-the-formations-of-the-unconscious.pdf?sequence=1.

Landauer, K. (1924). "Passive" Technik: Zur Analyse narzißtischer Erkrankungen. *Internationale Zeitschrift für Psychoanalyse, 10*: 415–422.

Levenson, E. A. (1991). *The Purloined Self*. New York: Contemporary Psychoanalysis Books.

Levenson, E. A. (1992). Harry Stack Sullivan: From interpersonal psychiatry to interpersonal psychoanalysis. *Contemporary Psychoanalysis, 28*: 450–466.

Lévi-Strauss, C. (1952). Father Christmas executed. http://varenne.tc.columbia.edu/texts/levstcld093fathchri.pdf.

Loewald, H. (1960). On the therapeutic action of psychoanalysis. *International Journal of Psychoanalysis, 41*: 16–33.

Loewald, H. (1978). *Psychoanalysis and the History of the Individual*: New Haven Ct: Yale University Press.

Macfarlane, R. (2015). *Landmarks*. London: Hamish Hamilton.

Makari, G. (2008). *Revolution in Mind*. New York: HarperCollins.

Mead, G. H. (1904). The relations of psychology and philology. *Psychological Bulletin, 1*: 375–391.

Mead, G. H. (1934). *Mind, Self, and Society: From the Standpoint of a Social Behaviorist*. Chicago, IL: University of Chicago Press.

Meltzer, D. (1968). Terror, persecution, dread. *International Journal of Psychoanalysis, 49*: 396–400.

Meltzer, D. (1975). Adhesive identification. *Contemporary Psychoanalysis, 11*: 289–310.

Meltzer, D. (1992). *The Claustrum: An Investigation of Claustraphobic Phenomena*. London: Karnac.

Miller, I. (1987). William James and the psychology of consciousness—beginnings of the American school. *Contemporary Psychoanalysis, 23*: 299–313.

Miller, I. (1991). Experiential psychoanalysis and the emergence of selves. *Journal of the American Acadamy of Psychoanalysis, 19*(1): 67–83.

Miller, I. (1993). Ferenczi, RN, and the struggle for equal ground. *Journal of the American Acadamy of Psychoanalysis, 21*: 291–302.

Miller, I. (2000). Benjamin Wolstein, the last social pragmatist. *Contemporary Psychoanalysis, 36*: 343–359.

Miller, I. (2015). *On Minding and Being Minded*. London: Karnac.

Miller, I. (2016a). *Defining Psychoanalysis: Achieving a Vernacular Expression*. London: Karnac.

Miller, I. (2016b). "No Tears as Her Children Cry": Terror in literary depiction and psychoanalytic process. Presentation at the XIX International Federation of Psychoanalytic Societies Meeting, New York City.

Miller, I. (2017). Reading Beckett in the context of psychoanalysis: a literary bridge between one person and two person psychology. *British Journal of Psychotherapy, 33*: 456–469.

Miller, I., & Souter, K. (2013). *Beckett and Bion: The (Im)Patient Voice in Psychotherapy and Literature*. London: Karnac.

Miller, I., & Sweet, A. D. (2017). Psychic rigidity, therapeutic response and time: Black holes, white holes, "D" and "d". *International Forum of Psychoanalysis, 26*: 97–104.

Minkowski, E. (1999). To reverberate. D. Bouchette (Trans.) as "Retenir (l'auditif)" in *Vers un cosmologie: Fragments philosophique* (Ch. 9, pp. 101–110). Paris: Editions Payot et Rivages, 2015.

Mitchell, S. A., & Aron, L. (1999). Editors' preface in S. A. Mitchell & L. Aron (Eds.), *Relational Psychoanalysis: The Emergence of a Tradition* (pp. ix–xx). Hillsdale, NJ: Analytic Press.

Modiano, P. (2015). *The Occupation Trilogy: Place D'Etoile, The Night Watch, Ring Roads*. London: Bloomsbury.

Money-Kyrle, R. (1965). Success and failure in mental maturations. In: *The Collected Papers of Roger Money-Kyrle* (pp. 397–406). Strathtay, UK: Clunie Press, 1978.

Money-Kyrle, R. (1968). On cognitive development. *International Journal of Psychoanalysis, 49*: 691–698.

Moore, T. V. (1921). The parataxes: A study and analysis of certain borderline mental states. *Psychoanalytic Review, 8*: 252–283.

Moore, T. V. (1945). A century of psychology in its relationship to American psychiatry. In: J. K. Hall, G. Zilboorg, & H. A. Bunker (Eds.), *One Hundred Years of American Psychiatry* (pp. 443–478). New York: Columbia University Press.

Morton, J., & Frith, U. (1995). Causal modeling: a structural approach to developmental psychology. In: D. Cicchetti & D. J. Cohen (Eds.), *Developmental Psychopathology, Vol. 1: Theory and Methods* (pp. 357–390). New York: Wiley.

Nahum, J. P. (2002). Explicating the implicit. *International Journal of Psychoanalysis, 83*(5): 1051–1062.

Nirenberg, D. (2013). *Anti-Judaism. The History of a Way of Thinking*. New York: W. W. Norton.

Ogden, T. (1992). *The Primitive Edge of Experience*. New York: Jason Aronson.

Ogden, T. (1994). The analytic third: Working with inter-subjective clinical facts. *International Journal of Psychoanalysis, 75*: 3–19.

Ogden, T. (2012). *Creative Readings*. London: Routledge.

O'Shaughnessy, E. (1981). A clinical study of a defensive organization. *International Journal of Psychoanalysis, 62*: 359–369.

O'Shaughnessy, E. (1992). Enclaves and excursions. *International Journal of Psychoanalysis, 73*(4): 603–614.

O'Shaughnessy, E. (1999). Relating to the super-ego. *International Journal of Psychoanalysis, 80*: 861–870.

Ramis, H. (1993). *Groundhog Day*. Culver City, CA: Columbia Tristar Home Video.

Rapaport, D. (1950). On the psycho-analytic theory of thinking. *International Journal of Psychoanalysis, 31*: 161–170.

Reich, W. (1972). *Character Analysis (Third Edition)*. New York: Farrar, Straus and Giroux.

Reik, T. (1937). *Surprise and the Psychoanalyst*. New York: E. P. Dutton.

Reik, T. (1948). *Listening with the Third Ear*. New York: Noonday Press, 1998.

Rickman, J. (1951). Number and the human science. In: P. King (Ed.), *No Ordinary Psychoanalyst—the Exceptional Contributions of John Rickman*. London: Karnac, 2003.

Riesenberg-Malcolm, R. (1999). *On Bearing Unbearable States of Mind*. London: Routledge.

Riviere, J. (1936). On the genesis of psychical conflict in earliest infancy. *International Journal of Psychoanalysis, 17*: 395–422.

Rosenfeld, H. (1964). The psychopathology of drug addiction and alcoholism: A critical review of the psycho-analytic literature. In: *Psychotic States: a Psychoanalytical Approach* (pp. 217–242). London: Karnac, 1982.

Rosenfeld, H. (1965). *Psychotic States: a Psychoanalytical Approach*. London: Hogarth.

Rosenfeld, H. (1971). A clinical approach to the psycho-analytical theory of the life and death instincts: an investigation of the aggressive aspects of narcissism. *International Journal of Psychoanalysis, 52*: 169–178.

Rosenfeld, H. (1987). *Impasse and Interpretation*. London: Routledge.

Sandler, J., & Dreher, A. U. (1996). *What Do Psychoanalysts Want?* London: Routledge.

Schachtel, E. (1959). *Metamorphosis. On the Development of Affect, Perception, Attention, and Memory*. New York: Basic Books.

Schafer, R. (1960). The loving and beloved superego in Freud's structural theory. *Psychoanalytic Study of the Child, 15*: 163–188.

Schafer, R. (1997). *Contemporary Kleinians of London*. Madison, CT: International Universities Press.

Searles, H. F. (1965). *Collected Papers on Schizophrenia and Related Subjects*. New York: International Universities Press.

Segal, H. (1957). Notes on symbol formation. *International Journal of Psychoanalysis, 38*: 391–397.

Segal, H. (1972). A delusional system as a defence against re-emergence of a catastrophic situation. *International Journal of Psychoanalysis, 53*: 393–403.

Segal, H. (1979). Postscript to "Notes on symbolization". In: *The Work of Hanna Segal* (pp. 60–65). New York: Jason Aronson.

Segal, H. (1986). *The Work of Hanna Segal: A Kleinian Approach to Clinical Practice*. London: Free Association.

Shakespeare, W. (c. 1596–99). *The Merchant of Venice*. In: *Complete Works of William Shakespeare*. Oxford: Oxford University Press, 1993. http://shakespeare.mit.edu/merchant/full.html.

Skelton, R. M. (2006). Ireland. In: R. M. Skelton, B. Burgoyne, J. Grotstein, M. Stein, & C. van Velsen (Eds.), *The Edinburgh International Encyclopaedia of Psychoanalysis* (p. 255). Edinburgh, UK: Edinburgh University Press.

Skogstad, W. (2013). Impervious and intrusive: The impenetrable object in transference and countertransference. *International Journal of Psychoanalysis, 94*: 221–238.

Sohn, L. (1985). Narcissistic organization, projective identification and the formation of the identificate. *International Journal of Psychoanalysis, 66*: 201–213.

Somer, E. (2009). Opioid use disorder and dissociation. In: P. F. Dell, & J. A. O'Neil (Eds.), *Dissociation and the Dissociative Disorders: DSM-V and Beyond* (pp. 511–518). New York: Routledge.

Spillius, E. B., Milton, J., Garvey, P., Couve, C., & Steiner, D. (Eds.) (2011). *The New Dictionary of Kleinian Thought*. London: Routledge.

Spinoza, B. (1677). *Ethics*. London: Penguin, 1996.

Steiner, J. (1993). *Psychic Retreats: Pathological Organizations in Psychotic, Neurotic and Borderline Patients*. London: Routledge.

Steiner, J. (2011). *Seeing and Being Seen: Emerging from a Psychic Retreat*. London: Routledge.

Stern, D. B. (1987). Unformulated experience and transference. *Contemporary Psychoanalysis, 23*: 484–490.

Stern, D. B. (1990). Courting surprise—unbidden perceptions in clinical practice. *Contemporary Psychoanalysis, 26*: 452–478.

Stern, D. B. (2009). Dissociation and unformulated experience: a psychoanalytic model of mind. In: P. F. Dell, & J. A. O'Neil, *Dissociation and the Dissociative Disorders: DSM-V and Beyond* (pp. 635–662). New York: Routledge.

Stern, D. N., Sander, L. W., Nahum, J. P., Harrison, A. M., Lyons-Ruth, K., Morgan, A. C., Bruschweiler-Stern, N., & Tronick, E. Z. (1998). Non-interpretive mechanisms in psychoanalytic therapy: The "something more" than interpretation. *International Journal of Psychoanalysis, 79*: 903–921.

Strachey, J. (1934). The nature of the therapeutic action of psychoanalysis. *International Journal of Psychoanalysis, 15*: 127–159.

Sullivan, H. S. (1954). *The Psychiatric Interview*. London: Tavistock.

Sullivan, H. S. (1955). *The Interpersonal Theory of Psychiatry*. London: Tavistock.

Sutherland, J. D. (1989). *Fairbairn's Journey into the Interior*. London: Free Association.

Sweet, A. D. (2010). Automata states and their relation to primitive mechanisms of defence. *Psychoanalytic Psychotherapy, 24*(2): 101–114.

Sweet, A. D. (2011). The automaton self: defensive organisation, psychodynamics and treatment approaches. *Psychodynamic Practice, 17*(4): 387–402.

Sweet, A. D. (2012). Black holes: some notes on time, symbolization and perversion in the psychodynamics of addiction. *International Forum of Psychoanalysis, 21*(2): 94–105.

Sweet, A. D. (2013). Thoughts without a thinker, mimetic fusing and the anti-container considered as primitive defensive mechanisms in the addictions. *Psychoanalytic Psychotherapy, 27*(2): 140–153.

Sweet, A. D., & Miller, I. S. (2016). Bingeing on sobriety: White holes, black holes and time's arrow in the intra-psychic worlds of addicted and substance abusing patients. *British Journal of Psychotherapy, 32*(2): 159–174.

Symington, N. (1986). *The Analytic Experience*. London: Free Association.

Szalita, A. (1984). On becoming a psychoanalyst. *Scandinavian Psychoanalytic Review, 7*: 3–12.

Tausk, V. (1934). Ibsen the druggist. *Psychoanalytic Quarterly, 3*: 137–141.

Tuckett, D., Basil, R., Birksted-Breen, D., Bohm, T., Denis, P., Ferro, A., Hinz, H., Jemstedt, A., Mariotti, P., & Schubert, J. (2008). *Psychoanalysis Comparable & Incomparable*. London: Routledge.

Tustin, F. (1972). *Autism and Childhood Psychosis*. London: Hogarth.

Waelder, R. (1924). The psychoses. Their mechanisms and accessibility to influence. *International Journal of Psychoanalysis, 10*: 393–414.

Waelder, R. (1936). The principle of multiple function: Observations on over-determination. *Psychoanalytic Quarterly* (2007), *76*: 75–92.

Waelder, R. (1937). The problem of the genesis of psychic conflict in earliest infancy. *International Journal of Psychoanalysis, 18*: 406–473.

Waelder, R. (1951). The structure of paranoid ideas—a critical survey of various theories. *International Journal of Psychoanalysis, 32*: 167–177.

Williams, P. (2010). *Invasive Objects: Minds under Siege*. London: Routledge.

Winnicott, D. W. (1949). Hate in the counter-transference. *International Journal of Psychoanalysis, 30*: 69–74.

Winnicott, D. W. (1953). Transitional objects and transitional phenomena—a study of the first not-me possession. *International Journal of Psychoanalysis, 34*: 89–97.

Winnicott, D. W. (1958). *Collected Papers: Through Paediatrics to Psychoanalysis*. London: Hogarth.

Wisse, R. (2013). *No Joke. Making Jewish Humor*. Princeton, NJ: Princeton University Press.

Yerushalmi, Y. H. (1991). *Freud's Moses. Judaism Terminable and Interminable*. New Haven, CT: Yale University Press.

INDEX

For Product Safety Concerns and Information please contact our EU representative GPSR@taylorandfrancis.com
Taylor & Francis Verlag GmbH, Kaufingerstraße 24, 80331 München, Germany

www.ingramcontent.com/pod-product-compliance
Ingram Content Group UK Ltd.
Pitfield, Milton Keynes, MK11 3LW, UK
UKHW022017180926
475701UK00005B/892
* 9 7 8 1 7 8 2 2 0 5 6 4 7 *